anglistik & englischunterricht

Teaching Contemporary British Fiction

# Teaching Contemporary British Fiction

Verantwortliche Herausgeberin
für den thematischen Teil des Bandes:
Merle Tönnies

UNIVERSITÄTSVERLAG WINTER
HEIDELBERG

Gabriele Linke · Erwin Otto · Holger Rossow
Gerd Stratmann · Merle Tönnies (Hg.)

# anglistik & englischunterricht

## Band 69

## Teaching Contemporary British Fiction

UNIVERSITÄTSVERLAG WINTER
HEIDELBERG

Bibliografische Information der Deutschen Nationalbibliothek
Die Deutsche Nationalbibliothek verzeichnet diese Publikation in der Deutschen Nationalbibliografie; detaillierte bibliografische Daten sind im Internet über *http://dnb.d-nb.de* abrufbar.



ISBN 978-3-8253-5288-2
ISBN 3-8253-5288-9
ISSN 0344-8266

Anschrift der Redaktion:
Universität Rostock, Institut für Anglistik und Amerikanistik
18051 Rostock


Imprimé en Allemagne · Printed in Germany
Druck: Memminger MedienCentrum AG, 87700 Memmingen
Gedruckt auf umweltfreundlichem, chlorfrei gebleichtem und alterungsbeständigem Papier
Den Verlag erreichen Sie im Internet unter: www.winter-verlag-hd.de

*Contents*

*Steven Barfield (London), Anja Müller-Wood (Mainz), Philip Tew (West London) and Leigh Wilson (London)*

# *Introduction*

## *1. Teaching Contemporary British Fiction Conference, 29 May 2004*

Within English Studies over the past decade undoubtedly there has been growing attention paid to contemporary British fiction, and this represents naturally enough a research area of great interest to many members of the UK Network for Modern Fiction Studies (UKNMFS). Increasingly many academics followed this emergent trend and were actively engaged not only in scholarship, but in teaching in this field. As a plethora of courses developed in an apparently ad hoc fashion, the UKNMFS felt two general issues might be usefully addressed: first, the pedagogic practice and its relationship to issues of canonicity, historiography, and cultural contexts; second, it might be time to reconsider the innate essentialism implicit in courses that focus simply on themes of postmodernism, ethnicity or gender. These matters needed to be considered not simply in a theoretical context (and such debates are so often finally a *regressus ad absurdum* toward points of conceptual difference and disagreement), but with regard to pedagogic practice itself and practical needs and requirements of the contemporary academy. This was the initial thinking that lay behind the idea for the international UKNMFS conference "Teaching Contemporary British Fiction", held at the University of Westminster in association with the British Council in 2004, on which this collection of essays is based. Teaching the contemporary tends to be lumped into a larger pedagogic context, one beset by all sorts of misconceptions and assumptions.

One accusation potentially levelled against the arts and humanities in Higher Education in general, and at literary studies in particular, is that its practitioners are at best deeply conservative and crustily old-fashioned in their attitude towards both teaching and pedagogy, and notions of literary value and worth. At worst, according to such accounts, the practitioners in these areas are wholly oblivious to any pedagogic approach that does not revolve around the traditional issue of which texts they as academics choose to research and teach within a course. Literature teachers, after all, according to the accounts purveyed by their academic peers, are supposedly still addicted to the 'trusted' essay format as their main mode of assessment, despite the plethora of alternatives used in the sciences and social sciences to offer new opportunities for learning. Furthermore, they are often thought (one would hope inaccurately) to see their essential pedagogic role as the dissemination of knowledge in an active teacher directed mode to passive, absorptive students. 'Student-centred education', 'reflective practice', 'lifelong learning', and their accompanying well-established theories and practices are often thought to be factors that do not affect what goes on at 'the chalk-face' of teaching literature in the University. Although such myths seem to derive from an anachronistic vision of a Leavisite past and its residues in current practice, nevertheless the underlying sense that many English scholars are variously resistant to the periodisation of the contemporary field, suspicious of that field's overall relevance unless filleted by the essentialism of identity politics and moreover they object to any other theoretical readings apart from those informed a very narrow range of continental 'high theorists', when taken together suggests a neo-conservatism of the aging radicals of the 1980s and their acolytes, who define the subject according to deconstructive readings and their own forms of canonicity.

A key incipient challenge therefore that was implicit in the subtext of the proposed event, which was to consider such a range myths, and hopefully prove them either misguided or even wrong in terms of the practice of teaching contemporary British fiction, a field that it appeared from anecdotal evidence are beginning to offer new forms of progressive thinking and radicalism perhaps unusual for literary studies. The gauntlet was thrown down for professional literature teachers to think seriously about their own teaching and their students' learning in conjunction with a body of fiction where there were few fixed boundaries, very limited established principles of critical engagement, and no clear and well-defined existing canon of texts. In addition, the contemporary nature of this literature offers unusual opportunities, as well as potential pitfalls, for mutual interactions between diverse students and academics, as they both share a recent, common history which these texts address and speak to. The essays in this collection demonstrate just how well and how intelligently literature teachers rose to this series of challenges.

On the day itself, the sessions served to respond to clusters of practice and interest: from the use of theory, the issue of canonicity, including links to creative writing within the curriculum and overseas perspectives on British texts, to student classroom and learning experience. Other areas were covered by the papers included genre, marginality and difficulty and to conclude a final round table linked issues within the academy to the other institutions of literary culture, publishing, reviewing and writing. The members of the panel were Josh Lacey, Reviews Editor of the Guardian, novelist and short story writer Toby Litt, included in the Granta Best Young British Novelists of 2003, and leading academics involved in the field, Philip Tew and Leigh Wilson.

The first session on the use of theory covered first questions around the use of cultural materialist frameworks in the teaching of contemporary fiction, comparing its effects, conceptual, political and in terms of classroom experience, with the critiques of cultural Marxism, then the pedagogical uses of psychoanalysis, and how a study of canonicity raised questions about the choice of theories used in the teaching of contemporary novels – specifically the centrality of postcolonialism, postmodernism and general theories of marginality. Canonicity was also addressed in the student-centred practice session, in a paper that considered the crisis of legitimacy in English studies engendered by the theory wars, and its possible resolution through the close reading of contemporary texts and their irrepressible popularity for students. Also this session considered ways of using contemporary writing to provoke a lively interest in literature in students who may otherwise feel alienated by it. A further paper drew upon popular cultural forms – rock and pop music – in considering an innovative approach to classroom practice. A session in the afternoon considered the perspectives of American, German and Greek students, considering their particular cultural engagement with contemporary British texts and the demands this may make on the classroom environment. The final academic session considered genre fiction, the postcolonial and questions of difficulty (or obscurity) as challenges to pedagogic practice.

The round table was an excellent reminder that we are part of a wider cultural industry, and in particular that issues of canonicity are not just about conceptual academic debate, but are also grounded in the decisions – aesthetic and commercial – of publishing and journalism, and indeed in readerly demands. In the round table, and participants' further reflections after the event, it was felt that the day was successful in combining textual exegesis, the cultural politics of pedagogy and a thoroughly grounded sense of the academic's role in teaching real groups of students in real time. This sense of current practice offered a way of synthesising a whole range of different perspectives from different areas of the globe, and is we hope is reflected in the revised papers that make up this volume, and moreover we anticipate that together as a whole they may well offer an intriguing perspective on the contemporary scene.

## *2. From the Outside Looking In ...*

Many of the contributions to this collection address the issue of difficulty, whether they identify difficulty as an inherent quality of a text or as something experienced in the effort of teaching it. Whichever may be the case, the struggles which often emerge in teaching contemporary fiction question the critical prejudice that it is unworthy of academic attention. But not only intellectually challenging texts are difficult to teach: the category 'difficult' is in itself unstable, a question of perspective. What one person deems complex may appear straightforward to another – depending on one's knowledge, reading experience and cultural background. This last problem can be particularly thorny even for those united (or divided) by a common language, as is demonstrated here by articles dealing with the teaching of contemporary British fiction in Anglophone cultures outside of the UK.

One obvious way of tackling the problem of cultural literacy is to contextualise. Doryjane Birrer and Mike Doherty have both taught courses in contemporary British fiction in the USA, where many of their students have either no knowledge of contemporary Britain or what they do know is tainted by hackneyed myths and clichés. While they identify a common problem, the texts they teach invite different forms of contextualisation. Whereas Birrer proposes to teach contemporary fiction by illuminating the academic and theoretical milieu out of which her set texts emerged, Doherty assists students by explaining the dense network of popular cultural references in contemporary fiction.

Recounting the battles amongst critical schools in the 1980s or explaining the intricacies of prog rock, as these articles do, may suggest that their perspectives are worlds apart. However, in different ways both point to contemporary literature's troubled infatuation with history. In line with a broader trend in contemporary literature, most contributions discuss texts that are not actually set in the present. Student readers' distance to even the recent past creates its own sort of stumbling block: historical knowledge – or life experience – that we take for granted may blind us to how alien the worlds of these texts may be for our students. Rather than calling up personal recollections and emotions (the famous question "Where were you?"), references to a political figure such as Margaret Thatcher or an event such as Chernobyl are more likely, at best, to drive students to the internet or, at worst, to leave them confused. If even the recent past is a blank space requiring annotation, then how are we to teach texts about more distant historical periods? If students know little about history, how can we teach books which seek to rewrite established historical narratives? The premise of historiographic metafiction – that history can be retold from the perspective of the underdog or the excluded – only has force (or, arguably, any point at all) if the reader is aware of the grand narrative that is being rewritten. Before the stories of the past can be deconstructed, they must be told. This does of course raise the risk that students may be attracted not to the subversive reinterpretation but the more comforting original version – a risk that may have to be taken.

Paradoxically, then, solving the difficulty of comprehension through contextualisation may only create a new set of problems. This approach may reduce literary analysis (which already comes up short in academic education) to the mere identification and enumeration of historical data and cultural anecdotes. It may provide students with factual knowledge, but not with the tools to decipher and understand literature's textual strategies. While contextual information is important, it should be supplemented by rigorous engagement with the text as a meaning-producing structure. The importance of close reading, even in the case of historical fiction, is discussed by Anja Müller-Wood in her article on Ian McEwan's *Atonement.* Although the novel could easily be contextualised, this task is rendered difficult by its critical stance on the uses and misuses of historical conventions in both collective and personal mythologies. To simply contextualise such myth making would likely affirm it rather than fostering students' critical abilities to analyse and if necessary resist the text.

Like Müller-Wood, Sarah Crangle puts the text rather than context at the centre of her analysis of Christine Brooke-Rose's *Such.* Explicitly setting out to tackle a famously difficult novel, Crangle not only makes an argument for close literary investigation in teaching, she also suggests that such a refocusing of critical attention might help rethink literary scholarship in ways suggested already by Susan Sontag in her famous call for an "erotics of art".

Along with the difficulties of context and text, there is another, both more basic and more elusive dimension in teaching contemporary British literature: the English language. And though it may seem counterintuitive, it is precisely on this point that British teachers of contemporary fiction have the most to learn from their non-Anglophone colleagues in many countries. Precisely because they teach literature to non-native speakers, they must attend more carefully to the linguistic ambiguities and unspoken cultural assumptions of literary texts. Far from being irrelevant to the very different needs of Anglophone university teachers, this outside perspective may draw attention to more universal challenges faced by teachers and students of literature which are not unique to "foreign" contexts. Furthermore, dealing with these added difficulties may open up new views of literature that can feed into a broader reconsideration of what is the task of literary criticism. Whether speaking from the inside or the outside: in addressing essential question regarding the teaching of contemporary British fiction, these essays also remind us of why literature remains a relevant field of study and should continue to be taught.

### *3. Reflective Practice*

There is significant evidence in this collection that shows these representatives of the profession are critical, 'reflective practitioners', to use the well-known formulation of Donald Schön.[1] In the classroom, there is even evidence (supported by presentations) that the practice of certain lecturers is by and large, performative, 'reflection-in-action' based upon what they see happening in their classes and their reflections upon this. Clearly many academics in the field engage with students in their concrete actuality as diverse groups of people with their own complex cultural and social identities and, on the whole, are much more facilitators of intellectual growth and independent thinking, than simple 'narrowcasters' of unequivocal knowledge.[2] Moreover, there is significant evidence here of 'good practice' that is suggestive of Kolb's celebrated 'cycle of experiential learning' (where critical reflection serves as a main way we make meaning out of experience)[3], for both teacher and students. This stands out in practice, together with an implied active and collaborative view of learning that does not shy away from exploring and questioning the hidden assumptions of an implied curriculum. These essays demonstrate why and how strategies for teaching contemporary British fiction must needs be continually innovative to serve the needs of our continually changing political, social and intellectual contexts.

The period between the initial call for papers for the conference and the putting together of this collection saw huge growth in courses and research activity in the field of contemporary writing, and this has been reflected in the growing numbers of series, books and articles concerned with such fiction published over the last few years. Although, clearly, the field shares much with the analysis of fiction articulating ideas of sexual orientation, feminism, postcolonialism and postmodernism, increasingly as many academics are beginning to recognise contemporary British fiction has emerged as a relatively autonomous, and extremely popular, field of both study and research. As such, many argue that this field's emergence is in significant part a response to student demands. Moreover, its dynamics are seemingly somewhat different to those that shaped gender studies, feminism, postcolonialism and postmodernism.

Increasingly, the contemporaneous gaze seems bewitched by the utterly contemporary, so much so that by the time of writing this introduction, courses are already emerging on post-millennial fiction, focused largely on literary aesthetics since 9/11. The conference seems increasingly to have been a response to a nascent cultural force that has yet to run its course. As Pierre Bourdieu points out in *The Field of Cultural Production*, writers (and logically critics) seem obliged to explore generational difference in some way, resulting in 'different position-takings, or even opposing ones (which will tend to cancel each other out)'.[4] The effect on the contemporary of such anteriority and cyclical emergence are among the other shaping forces considered in the following papers.

*Notes*

1 Donald Schön: *The Reflective Practitioner: How Professionals Think in Action*, New York, 1983.
2 Paul Ramsden: *Learning to Teach in Higher Education*, 2nd Edition, London, 2002.
3 David A. Kolb: Experiential *Learning: Experience as a source of Learning and Development*, Englewood Cliffs, NJ, 1984.
4 Pierre Bourdieu: The Field of Cultural Production: Essays on Art and Literature, Cambridge, 1993, p. 65.

*Leigh Wilson (Westminster)*

# Teaching Contemporary British Fiction: Some Preliminary Considerations

The articles in this collection all address in various and provocative ways the challenge of teaching contemporary British fiction, across differing student expectations, across genres and indeed across continents. What echoes through them all, though, sometimes implicitly and sometimes explicitly, is the extent to which a consideration of the pedagogic implications of this area of writing exposes certain aspects of the academy *per se* (in particular in the articles by Doryjane Birrer, Nick Bentley, Robert Bond and Anja Müller-Wood). Even the title – contemporary British fiction – historicises and makes visible those assumptions and determinants which constitute academic critical practice. As James English points out, until fairly recently the contemporary in university English departments meant 'fiction of the entire postwar period'. He locates the shift in usage as occurring in the mid-1980s, when a number of writers "pointed to the 1970s as the fulcrum point of a decisive historical shift".[1] Of course, too, the use of 'British' and 'fiction' raise questions and problems related to nation, and to the whole notion of 'English literature' and its expansive sense of its subject in the last few decades. The challenges implicit in each of these terms have been picked up to varying degrees by most of the recent commentators on contemporary British fiction. However, in most, the determinants of current usage and the challenges to these terms have been seen as attributes of the fiction itself. So, for example, the first part of Jago Morrison's *Contemporary Fiction* gives four "contextual frameworks" through which to read contemporary fiction – history, narrative, gender and 'race' – with the implicit suggestion that the privileging of these four areas is demanded by the novels themselves.[2]

What I want to suggest in this article, as a way of framing and introducing the debates addressed in the following articles, is that what the teaching of contemporary fiction crucially demands is scrutiny, not just of the novels, but of our own orthodoxies as teachers, academics and critics. As teachers, academics and critics, we try to teach our students not to make assertions and claims without substantiating them, without showing an awareness of the critical debate around any topic, and to properly locate their own arguments within it. This is, of course, how we are trained as academics and what we practise in our own work.

However, when approaching the contemporary, a number of problems immediately arise for both ourselves and our students. The contemporary has become an incredibly popular area of interest for academics and, in particular, for students.[3] Indeed, the difficulty in engaging students with earlier literary periods is well documented in this issue (see the articles by Mike Doherty and Richard Hudson), and a number of lively contemporary fiction courses on a degree has become an important draw for students. Against this intense interest, though, the pedagogic apparatus of the subject is problematic. The further reading lists we write for our students are dominated by 'survey works', and often more specific essays and articles tend to be journalistic, or by writers themselves, and these demand a very different kind of critical usage. When considering the teaching of contemporary fiction, though, the problems related to the practices of teachers and academics go beyond reading lists, and have potentially more damaging effects in terms of the critical abilities we foster in our students. Devising a syllabus, putting together a further reading list, advising and teaching our students all depend upon the academic's own critical sense, a sense trained to depend on existing critical positions and paradigms. It is often the case, of course, that these are engaged with in order to challenge or overturn them, but nevertheless they are a vital starting point. In writing about and teaching contemporary fiction, these paradigms are in the process of becoming, are "still in formation" to use Ruth McElroy's phrase in her article. A number of contributors to the issue rightly point out that this offers rich pedagogic possibilities, in particular in engaging students from backgrounds not traditionally represented in the academy (see Bentley and McElroy's articles). However, at the same time, because they don't yet exist as a 'canon', that seeming institutional necessity, the danger is that the partial vacuum is now in the process of being filled with improperly examined orthodoxies; that the area is becoming set in a way that damages not only the critical work but the way we educate our students.

Since 2000, the number of critical works published which address contemporary British fiction has increased enormously.[4] Whether single-authored or edited collections, what is noticeable about many of these is that they are primarily directed toward undergraduate students, and that consequently even chapters on specific writers or novels have a 'survey' quality to them. In attempting to map the terrain, writers and editors draw again and again on the broad frameworks used in Morrison's book cited above: history, narratives and the various constituents of identity (sexuality, gender, ethnicity, nationality). What is never really addressed is the extent to which these frameworks are the demand of the fiction or the demand of the critics. More particularly, what is rarely addressed is the extent to which the canonising of certain writers and works – those indeed which most clearly seem to demand such a reading – in fact serves the unspoken interests of the academy. In the rigorous and theoretically engaged environment of the contemporary academy, why should this be?

In attempting to suggest the beginning of an answer to this question, James English's recent collection for Blackwell is a provocative starting point. While it too includes sections and chapters on nationality, ethnicity, gender, history, and so on, its first section has as its broad title "The institutions of commerce". Indeed, in English's introduction he suggests that the collection as a whole focuses on those institutions which create fictional spaces – publishing, bookselling, literary journalism, the academy – and on the necessary and complex intersection of the literary with the commercial.[5] In a chapter in this first section, English and John Frow argue for a more complex analysis of the growth of literary celebrity in the UK. The contemporary literary scene is, they argue, created through the interaction of a number of institutions which together they call the 'literary-value industry'.[6] These institutions – publishing, bookselling, journalism, literary prizes and festivals, the academy – are concerned not simply with making money, but with the complexities of canon formation. They are concerned with the creation of certain notions of value.[7] As an example, the authors cite Granta's list of "Best of the Young British Novelists", created in its first year through the magazine's collaboration with the Book Marketing Council. This is a compelling argument, and is certainly a welcome rethinking of the link between value and commerce in contemporary British culture. However, English and Frow's inclusion of the academy within their 'literary-value industry', while legitimate, throws up some interesting questions not addressed in their chapter.

The academy does indeed engage in canon formation in the area of contemporary British fiction – through syllabus choices, the selection of research and publication topics, through conferences. This can be seen in the authors and works covered by all those books and series published since 2000. McEwan, Ishiguro, Byatt, Barker, Carter, Rushdie, Kureishi, A.L. Kennedy, Winterson, occasionally Ballard, Sinclair, Crace; these names appear over and over again in the contents pages and in publisher's catalogues. Of course, these are the names promoted and valued by the rest of the 'literary-value industry' – publishers, reviewers, the judges of literary prizes – and academics are certainly dependent to an extent on the decisions of the first of these. However, it is clear too that these selections are repeated again and again in curricular choices (see Nick Bentley's article). What is not acknowledged, however, is the extent to which such canonisation in practice is at odds with the theoretical orthodoxies of the subject over the last few decades. English and Frow's demarcation of the 1980s as the decade when the contemporary became contemporary coincides with the 'theory wars' in the British academy, and the victor's fundamental challenge to ideas of literary value till then embedded in the institutions of the subject. While a few in the academy and most of those outside it, or on its margins, see this as its greatest problem,[8] certainly from the point of view of teaching, the academy itself has fairly wholesale rejected pedagogic techniques which focus on the revelation of value. Practical criticism and the idea of a 'great tradition' appear to play little part in our practices today. Close reading ferrets out not value, but *différance*, gaps, silences, the operations of power (patriarchal, colonial, heterosexual), the constructions of identity. However, the problem arises then: if we cannot speak of value, how do we convince our students that certain works are worth reading, let alone studying? If the academy takes part in the construction of value, in the creation of a canon, yet cannot speak of value, it engages in just such an obfuscation, just such a veiling of institutional power, that we daily ask our students to notice in literary texts.

As Clive Bloom has argued, contemporary critical and pedagogic practice in the discipline is in part the result of two things, both of which severely undermine the legitimacies of these practices. Paradoxically, the effects of post-structuralist theories combine with the onslaught of contemporary economic and political orthodoxies, as dominant of course in the university as elsewhere, to shake the foundations of the subject.[9] These may not be a bad thing, of course, and the shaking of foundations, or rather their unmasking as ideological, is central to post-structuralist theory. However, while anxiety over the legitimacy of the subject is very real, institutionally and most often in practice is it denied. The anxiety creates symptoms rather than rigorous critical practices. While this is a determining factor across the curriculum and across specialities, in the area of contemporary fiction it is particularly powerful, for reasons I have suggested above.

As a result of these unaddressed problems, the curricula choices and critical frameworks in courses on contemporary British fiction have become fixed and 'canonical' incredibly quickly in order to provide justification for the subject. Most obviously, novels are chosen which seem to speak to us as academics in a language we recognise, which seem themselves structured around the subsections of current academic interest and therefore of the curricula – the postcolonial, the queer, the feminist, and so on. Novels are chosen which seem to reflect back to us our own concerns, which justify them and make them seem self-evident. Our orthodoxies remain unchallenged, and are passed on to students as such via the very novels we ask them to read.

In this regard, the recent widespread 'canonisation' of one novel in particular is exemplary. Nick Bentley in this issue suggests that Zadie Smith's novel *White Teeth* (2000) is one of the twelve most taught titles on university courses in contemporary fiction, and certainly the novel is unique among novels by young writers (under 40, say) in its already achieved status in terms of curriculum presence and critical attention.[10] As acknowledged by Peter Childs, justifying the inclusion of Smith in his survey of the field, the novel "has become the most likely British novel of the new millennium to be studied at University".[11] It is also, as Childs implicitly attests, one of the most likely books to appear in recent critical works. It is included in all of the books cited in note 5, with the exception of Jago Morrison's, which doesn't just focus on the British scene, but looks at US fiction too. Without exception, these critical works take up *White Teeth* as a useful and credible representation of the issues of multiculturalism and national identity in contemporary Britain, and by implication as a novel which demonstrates certain critical positions. Dominic Head, for example, sees the novel as "artfully constructed as the definitive representation of twentieth-century British multiculturalism".[12] In his introduction to his edited collection, Nick Bentley rightly suggests that in some ways "[n]ovelists often occupy the middle ground between literary theory and popular culture".[13] However, one result of this may be that novels simply become bridges between the academy and our students, the means by which we teach our theories, rather than works which themselves are seen as critiquing and challenging critical orthodoxies, or which we can critique.

Undoubtedly *White Teeth* is an attempt to represent something about the experience of those outside of the dominant 'white British' culture, and to explore ideas of hybridity, and Smith's educational background makes it likely that various theoretical positions have influenced her novel.[14] However, this is not the issue. The issue is the extent to which the assimilation of the novel by the academy attests to an obfuscation of the discipline's own blind spots, and its subsequent complicity with forces it purports to challenge. One of the questions rarely addressed by work on Smith is why the novel was/is so popular, aside from analysing marketing and packaging techniques, of both the novel and its author.[15] The novel has been a huge bestseller. In his chapter on the novel, Fred Botting considers it not just in terms of multiculturalism, but in terms of the assimilation of different identity positions by the corporate and consumerist in contemporary culture. However, he focuses on the novel's seeming resolution of these anxieties, rather than in its problematic treatment of the issues and its own publishing history as being symptomatic of them (as is persuasively argued in Robert Bond's article).[16] If the success of the novel is dependent to some degree on its own repackaging of multiculturalism in a way that suits the tastes of so many readers, and indeed so many white readers, its 'canonisation' occludes these problems, and postcolonialism as taught through this novel remains a straightforwardly liberatory affair.[17] Also, what is infrequently remarked on in the critical work on *White Teeth* is that it is a comic novel, and that Smith has quite self-consciously placed her work within a very particular comic tradition, one that she associates with E.M. Forster, one that she sees as humane, liberal, and committed to the novel as a tool for teaching ethical living.[18] Of course, Smith's works should not prescribe the way the novel is read, but they are an indication of an aspect of the novel and her work generally so far completely ignored by academic critics.[19]

In his review of Randall Stevenson's 1960-2000 volume in *The Oxford Literary History*, the critic James Wood, while claiming much that is dubious, does pick up on the relation between the occluded problem of literary value and the orthodoxies of the academy.[20] Stevenson, he suggests, constructs his survey around those social trends which have become central to the discipline – feminism, postcolonialism, and so on – but in doing so leaves out many writers of importance simply because they don't fit into such a scheme. For Wood, the most "egregious" example of this is the scant treatment of Penelope Fitzgerald in the Oxford volume.[21] My own example would be another writer whose recent death, like Fitzgerald's, has separated her from the contemporary, but whose work has always been something of a riposte to academic orthodoxies, and whose critical treatment is useful in beginning to suggest the blindspots of the academy.

In Stevenson's book, and in contemporary academic criticism and curricula choices more generally, Muriel Spark's work has been treated with some strangeness. Indeed, Spark's work has suffered at the hands of most of its critics. It has been misread not just by older liberal humanist critics such as David Lodge and Malcolm Bradbury, who wish to see in Spark tidy aesthetic resolution as an analogy for moral commitment; indeed who wish to see her as a liberal humanist.[22] In the last few years a number of critics pointedly not liberal humanists have taken up Spark's work, and also misread her, reading her "deliberate cunning"[23] as "transgression", as the playfulness of *differance* or the queering of relations. In a comparative essay on Charlotte Brontë's *Villette* and Spark's most well known novel, *The Prime of Miss Jean Brodie* (1961), Patricia Duncker reads both as presenting women beyond the limits of patriarchal conventions. Of Lucy Snowe and Jean Brodie she writes:

> Both women are travellers, adventurers. They are women on the loose, free and independent women. And therefore dangerous[...]. Both *Villette* and

*The Prime of Miss Jean Brodie* are texts about women breaking the rules, knowingly, deliberately and without fear.[24]

According to Duncker, the 'danger' embodied in these characters is crucially not just about women's desire for power, but women's desire for each other. Brodie's defeat at the end of the novel is therefore read as Spark's partial compromise with already existing patriarchal "fixed plots' which determine the fate of 'ambitious, powerful women".[25] The destructive thing which the novel reveals, then, is patriarchy; its others – female desire and queerness – before they are finally defeated are liberatory, positively destabilising and transgressive.

As a reading of Spark's novel, this is deeply problematic, not because the novel doesn't contain these elements, but because it misses the central conflict of the novel, and it is this conflict which most challenges the orthodoxies of critical practice. *The Prime of Miss Jean Brodie* is about the relation of truth to lies, of good and evil, to a particular economy of storytelling. Miss Brodie has power over her girls because she is economical with the truth. But being economical with the truth is not simply for Spark a euphemism for lying – it is a necessary quality for successful art. Spark's novel, and indeed all of her work, acts out the maxim that "where there was a choice of various courses, the most economical was the best".[26] Her work is clipped, elliptical and short. Her narrative voices are secretive, withholding details of motivation, psychology and moral status. Within Miss Jean Brodie, this principle of economy is responsible for manipulation, betrayal, indeed the consequences of fascism both within the classroom and in 1930s Europe. Yet the girls' pleasure as 'readers' of Miss Brodie are utterly dependent on this economy, as is the pleasure too of any reader of Spark's novel. Miss Brodie is indeed a powerful woman, but the ambiguity around her as storyteller is not about reading this as liberatory transgression. It does not make positive her dangerousness, rather it works to increase our own, for Spark's narrative implicates the practice of reading, and the reader, in this dangerous economy. In her lecture from 1970, "The Desegregation of Art", Spark challenges the "art and literature of sentiment and emotion" because it does not tell the truth. She says:

> The cult of the victim is the cult of pathos, not tragedy. The art of pathos is pathetic, simply; it has reached a point of exhaustion, a point where not the subject matter but the art form itself is crying to heaven for vengeance [...]. We should know ourselves better by now than to be under the illusion that we are all essentially aspiring, affectionate, and loving creatures. We do have these qualities, but we are aggressive too.[27]

What Spark doesn't say in this lecture, but what is crucial to her importance, is that her work suggests that novels and novel reading are not just about this aggression, but are it. Seeing the novel and its readers, in particular its professional readers, as part of this makes these activities far more dangerous, but it does begin to make possible questions about the practice of reading, literary value, and the construction of a canon.

In his review of Randall Stevenson's book, Wood's riposte is to argue for the return of serious consideration of authorial intention and autonomous aesthetic value – only through these, he says, can the critic gain any sense of which are the 'best' works.[28] This, as we know, would create more problems than it would solve for the conceptual framework of the discipline. Rather, the teaching of and research into contemporary fiction needs to be a place for far more self-conscious criticism of our own dogmas. In our curricula selection, our teaching and our own critical writing, we need to interrogate more fully the area of 'contemporary British fiction' as it comes into being. The articles in this collection, in their scrutiny of the relation between teaching contemporary fiction and the discipline's bases and assumptions, begin this process.

## *Notes*

1 English (2006: 1).
2 Morrison (2003: 7).
3 English and Frow (2006: 46).
4 See: Jago Morrison (2003); Lane, Megham & Tew (2003); Tew (2004); Bentley (2005); Childs (2005); Acheson and Ross (2005); English (2006). There are also *Palgrave's Reader's Guides in Essential Criticism* – on McEwan, Kureishi, Winterson and Barnes – and Manchester University Press's series, *Contemporary British Novelists*, with titles on Winterson, Barker, Swift, Ballard and Welsh.
5 English (2006: 3, 6-8).
6 English and Frow (2006: 46).

7 *Ibid.*, 47.
8 For example, Bloom (1994) and (2001). For critics outside the academy, see James Wood (2004), where he bemoans in particular the loss of the privileged place for intention and value. See also the debate in the pages of the *Guardian* between journalist Geoffrey Wheatcroft (2002) and Jonathan Dollimore (2002).
9 Clive Bloom (2001: 136-139, 87-89).
10 It is noticeable that, among those novelists chosen by Granta as the "Best Young British Novelists" in 2003, only Smith, A.L. Kennedy and Alan Warner have much of presence on curricula and critically. A.L. Kennedy appeared on the 1993 list also, and both she and Warner are seen within the academy as part of recent 'Scottish' writing that raises questions regarding national identity and the centrality of 'Englishness'.
11 Childs (2005: 19).
12 Head (2003: 106).
13 Bentley (2005: 5).
14 See, for example the consideration of the novel's relationship with recent work by Donna Haraway in Head (2003: 117) and Botting (2006: 39).
15 See Head (2003: 106-107).
16 Botting (2006: 28).
17 Huggan (2001) is a welcome exception to this, but was too early to include consideration of the *White Teeth* phenomenon.
18 Smith (2003).
19 Moore-Gilbert (2005:109) does acknowledge this aspect of *White Teeth* and of Smith's work generally, but reads it as one aspect of her representation of 'intercultural relations'.
20 James Wood was one of the few critics whose initial response to *White Teeth* was less than celebratory. See Wood (2000).
21 Wood (2004).
22 Quoted in McQuillan (2002: 1ff).
23 Spark (1971-2: 25).
24 Duncker (2002: 68, 74).
25 *Ibid.*, 73.
26 Spark (1965: 102).
27 Spark (1971-2: 26).
28 Wood (2004).

## *Bibliography*

Acheson, James and Sarah C.E. Ross (Eds.): *The Contemporary British Novel*, Edinburgh, 2005.

Bentley, Nick (Ed.): *British Fiction of the 1990s*, London, 2005.

Botting, Fred: "From excess to the new world order". – In Nick Bentley (Ed.): *British Fiction of the 1990s*, London, 2005.

Bloom, Clive: *Literature, Politics and Intellectual Crisis in Britain Today*, Basingstoke, 2001.

Bloom, Harold: *The Western Canon*, New York, 1994.

---: *How to Read and Why*, London, 2001.

Childs, Peter: *Contemporary Novelists: British Fiction Since 1970*, Basingstoke, 2005.

Dollimore, Jonathan: "Clash of Culture", *Guardian*, 2002 [http://education.guardian.co.uk/print/0,,4447176-48826,00.html] (28 June 2006).

Duncker, Patricia: "The Suggestive Spectacle: Queer Passions in Bronte's *Villette* and *The Prime of Miss Jean Brodie*". – In Martin McQuillan (Ed.): *Theorizing Muriel Spark: Gender, Race, Deconstruction*, London, 2002.

English, James F.: "Introduction: British Fiction in a Global Frame". – In James F. English (Ed.): *Concise Companion to Contemporary British Fiction*, Oxford, 2006.

English, James F. & John Frow: "Literary Authorship and Celebrity Culture". – In James F. English (Ed.): *Concise Companion to Contemporary British Fiction*, Oxford, 2006.

Head, Dominic: "Zadie Smith's *White Teeth*; Multiculturalism for the Millennium". – In Richard Lane, Richard J., Rod Mengham & Philip Tew (Eds.): *Contemporary British Fiction*, Cambridge, 2003.

Huggan, Graham: *The Post-Colonial Exotic: Marketing the Margins*, London, 2001.

Lane, Rod Mengham and Philip Tew (Eds.): *Contemporary British Fiction*, Cambridge, 2003.

McQuillan, Martin (Ed.): *Theorizing Muriel Spark: Gender, Race, Deconstruction*, London, 2002.

Moore-Gilbert, Bart: "Postcolonialism and 'The Figure of the Jew': Caryl Phillips and Zadie Smith". – In James Acheson and Sarah C. E. Ross (Eds.) *The Contemporary British Novel*, Edinburgh, 2005.

Morrison, Jago: *Contemporary Fiction*, London, 2003.

Smith, Zadie: "Love, Actually". *Guardian*, 1 November 2003 [http://books.guardian.co.uk/review/story/0,12084,1074217,00.html] (28 June 2006). The article is based on Smith's 2003 Orange Word Lecture, "E.M. Forster's Ethical Style: Love, Failure and the Good in Fiction", 22 October 2003, London.

Spark, Muriel: *The Prime of Miss Jean Brodie*, London, [1961] 1965.

---: "The Desegregation of Art", *American Academy of Arts and Letters Proceedings*, Series 2, 21/22, 1971-2.

Tew, Philip: *The Contemporary British Novel*, London, 2004.

Wheatcroft, Geoffrey: "Policing Academe", *Guardian*, 25 June 2002, [http://education.guardian.co.uk/print/0,,4447460-48826,00.html] (28 June 2006).

Wood, James: "The Smallness of the 'Big' Novel: Human, All Too Human", *New Republic*, 24 July 2000; reprinted in Wood, *The Irresponsible Self: On Laughter and the Novel* (2004) London.

---: "The Smallest Sardine", *London Review of Books*, 26:10, 20 May 2004, review of Randall Stevenson, *The Oxford English Literary History, Vol XII: 1960-2000. The Last of England*, Oxford, 2004 [http://www.lrb.co.uk/v26/n10/wood02_.html] (28 June 2006).

*Nick Bentley (Keele)*

# Developing the Canon: Teaching Contemporary British Fiction

## *1. Introduction*

Contemporary British fiction is an area of literary studies that has been developing steadily over the last twenty years or so and most universities now run courses covering the period. And yet it is an area that has its own peculiarities and issues. The very nature of the contemporary means that the range of authors and texts being taught is more fluid than more established areas of literary study and the potential list is continually being added to. Is it possible therefore to speak of a canon of contemporary British fiction, and if so, who would be included in such a canon and what are the themes and theories driving the selection of texts and writers?

This article attempts to answer some of these questions. It begins by re-assessing the canon debate of the 1980s and early 1990s and identifying some of the positions and limitations of that debate. One of the factors involved in the identification of a contemporary canon is knowledge of the range of texts and authors currently being taught on university English courses. This was the thinking behind the compilation of a database that attempted to give an accurate, if limited, indication of such a list. The Contemporary Canons Database was conceived as a way of discovering and collating this information and making it available for relevant future research. The data collected allows for the possibility of identifying the development of a canon of British authors and texts from the period. By analysing the data it is possible to consider the common cultural themes and literary forms that are currently important. After identifying the main texts and themes, this article explores the theoretical perspectives that are informing the choice of texts being taught, such as postmodernism, postcolonialism, (post-)feminism, and New Historicism. The aim of the article, therefore, is to investigate the complex interaction of texts, themes and theories informing the selection of contemporary British novels on university courses. It must be emphasised that the Contemporary Canons Database is an ongoing project and is not yet complete. This article, therefore, represents partly a progress report and partly an indication of preliminary findings.

## *2. The Canon Debate*

In a paper given as a lecture in Cambridge in 1987, Marilyn Butler identified the crisis facing the traditional British canon in the face, firstly, of the rise of the United States as the dominant economic and cultural influence in the world, and secondly, the move by those areas of the world that have been influenced by British imperial power to shake off the cultural models and canons imposed upon them after decolonisation. She writes: "The loss of British national prestige must entail a threat to the so-called authority of English literary classics."[1] Butler's comments are an intervention in the canon debate that was taking place during the eighties and into the early part of the 1990s on both sides of the Atlantic. After identifying the "new Modernist-Romantic" canon developed at Columbia, Yale and Cornell by the last generation, she suggests: "It would be premature to offer rival international or British inner-city canons: those have to emerge with time, and with the raising of the consciousness of those currently marginalised."[2] She suggests that a new corpus of such works emerging from writers from marginalised communities was still wanting in the late eighties, but that it was perhaps imminent. Nearly twenty years have elapsed since Butler's comments and it would be reasonable to suggest that such a canon (or group of canons) now exists. However, if this canon has now emerged it has been affected by several issues that problematise the whole notion of what constitutes a 'canon', as well as the processes involved in its formation, evolution and survival.

Trying to identify the emergence of a contemporary canon has distinctly different contexts than the maintenance and revision of an established canon of past literary works. Firstly, in identifying a contemporary canon you are essentially starting from scratch; there is no already fixed list of canonical texts with which you can engage or contest. And, of course, the formation of a canon of contemporary or post-war literature is itself affected by the canon debate of the eighties and nineties. The debate was often polemical – more so in the United States than in Britain – and revealed a distinct opposition between the conservatives and the revisionists. The conservative position, led in the US by Allan Bloom in an educational context and Harold Bloom in a literary one, represented a range of anxieties concerning the perceived lessening of critical evaluation with regard to the inclusion on literature courses of previously overlooked works, especially by women, working class authors, and writers from marginalised ethnic backgrounds. For Harold Bloom, the threat within the institution of literature came from what he perceived as a wholesale move towards ideological criteria for literary evaluation as opposed to strictly aesthetic concerns. Bloom's intervention in the debate called for a resistance to this perceived trend. In his influential book, *The Western Canon*, he writes:

> We need to teach more selectively, searching for the few who have the capacity to become highly individual readers and writers. The others, who are amenable to a politicised curriculum, can be abandoned to it.[3]

Bloom was suspicious of academics rather than "readers and writers" determining the canon. He viewed those with a political agenda (tellingly described as "others") as too likely to be over-responsive to literary and ideological fashions and to the demands of political correctness. For Bloom, this could only produce a historically transient list of 'great works', undermining the very notions of permanency and essentialism embedded in the ideas of a canon – a body of works that should be preserved and handed on to future generations of readers. In response to this threat, he identified a more permanent process of canon formation driven by authors themselves. His model of the canon is based on writers making Oedipal responses to literary fathers, combined with a re-working of T.S. Eliot's idea of new works engaging with those of the past as set out in "Tradition and the Individual Talent" (1920). For Bloom, the emerging 'great' writers of any contemporary literary culture need to enter into a dialogue with the past, thus producing an organic process of canon evolution based on the aesthetic judgements of both writers and critics.

Bloom's opposition between what he identified as aesthetic judgement and political criteria represents the basis for the canon debate, and Bloom set himself against the so-called revisionists, a group identified in the seventies and eighties as being influenced by Marxist, feminist and ethnic minority-motivated theories and discourses.

In Britain, the debate was less polemical, but the politics of the canon was still to the fore in two of the most important commentators on the subject: Terry Eagleton and Frank Kermode. In *Literary Theory: An Introduction*, Eagleton offers a Marxist re-analysis of the concept of literature, and thereby the canon, by stressing the arbitrary and ideological nature of the historical definition of certain works as 'literature' as opposed to the non-literary. Eagleton's position offers a radical challenge to the notion of the canon, as it suggests that the structural and philosophical framework on which it relies is itself suspect. As he writes:

> It will not do to see literature as an 'objective', descriptive category, neither will it do to say that literature is just what people whimsically choose to call literature [...] literature does not exist in the sense that insects do, and the value-judgements by which it is constituted are historically variable [...] They refer in the end not simply to private taste, but to the assumptions by which certain social groups exercise and maintain power over others.[4]

For Eagleton, the process of forming a canon is artificial, historically contingent and based, in the last instance, on the prevailing frameworks of power within a society. The whole idea of a timeless canon of great works, therefore, becomes suspect.

Frank Kermode attempted to shift the thinking about the canon away from the standoff between the ideological and the aesthetic to concentrate on the practical benefits of having a list of 'great' works to which people could refer. In a piece entitled "Canon and Period" published in 1988, Kermode identifies the challenge to the traditional canon in the late eighties in the US posed by what he calls the "cunning alliance of three forces [...]: Feminism, Afro-Americanism and Deconstruction".[5] He stresses, however, that these movements are not necessarily a challenge to the *concept* of the canon, as Eagleton argues, but rather that they are involved in reshaping the canon, whilst at the same time keeping the structural logic of canons as a whole. For Kermode, the new forces in literary and cultural criticism represent "not a plan to abolish the canon but one to capture it".[6]

Kermode accepts Eagleton's point that canons are part of the wider frameworks of power and ideology that extend beyond literature, but he also recognises their value; not by reference to the traditional liberal humanist value system as advocated by Bloom, but as a useful way of arranging information and knowledge: "So canons are complicit with power; and canons are useful in that they enable us to handle otherwise unmanageable historical deposits."[7] Kermode replaces an ethical and aesthetic evaluation system with an epistemological one, although, in doing so, he is ambivalent towards the question of how this epistemological judgement is necessarily partial, as it is dependent on the value systems that inform the selection of texts and authors.

This leads us on to, in my view, the most important work on the literary canon emerging from this period: John Guillory's *Cultural Capital: The Problem of Literary Canon Formation*, published in 1993. Guillory provides an analysis of the educational structures that determine the nature of the canon as it appears in actual school and university syllabuses. Drawing on the theories of Pierre Bourdieu, Paul de Man, Etienne Balibar and Pierre Macherey he develops an analysis of the canon as a culturally and historically contingent concept that negotiates the logic of cultural capital. He writes:

> Where the debate speaks of the literary canon, its inclusions and exclusions, I will speak of the school, and the institutional forms of syllabus and curriculum [...] how works are preserved, reproduced, and disseminated over successive generations and centuries. Similarly, where the debate speaks about the canon as representing or failing to represent particular social groups, I will speak of the school's historical function of distributing, or regulating access to, the forms of cultural capital.[8]

For Guillory, canon formation is an ideological process, but one that should respond to the specific 'consumers' of 'cultural capital'. Canon formation, therefore, should be based on the specific contexts for which it functions, for the school or university itself: "While the debate over the canon concerns what texts should be taught in the schools, what remains invisible in this debate – too large to be seen at all – is the school itself."[9] Guillory scrutinises many of the assumptions that are shared by both sides in the canon debate. In particular, he investigates the relationship between canonical and noncanonical works with respect to the social identity of authors. He sees canon formation as intrinsically bound up with social forces and yet is suspicious of the assumption that authors from minority backgrounds necessarily represent those minority cultures in a simple line of transference. He goes on to question the value of designating works as canonical and noncanonical and the effects that has in pedagogical institutions.

To pursue Guillory's ideas further, a model that inverts the hierarchical structure of the canon – to suggest that it should be formed from below, not imposed from above – seems to be potentially liberating. This could be called a postmodern model of canon formation, one which rejects the idea of a single monolithic body of great works, as suggested by Bloom, but is rather a series of partial, plural and distinctly multicultural canons that are responsive to the particular situation in which each separate institution operates. In this context, for example, it might be inappropriate to make a class in multicultural London or Birmingham read a range of works by dead, white, male authors, irrespective of the aesthetic quality of their work and their centrality to a certain tradition. The teacher should have the power to form an alternative canon that is sensitive to the specific needs, interests and aspirations of the class s/he has to teach. The texts and authors included on such a syllabus should not be seen as 'noncanonical' but rather as an alternative canon, but one that does not necessarily reproduce hegemonic values. This might seem idealistic and impractical given that the individual teacher is often subject to a range of institutional restrictions. However, to aid this possibility and allow the individual teacher to make an informed choice of texts to include on a course reading list it would be useful to have a sense of what texts and authors are currently being taught in university English departments.

## *3. The Contemporary Canons Database*

This was one of the motivations behind the development of a project called the Contemporary Canons Database. Two things struck me about the canon debate in the eighties and nineties. Firstly, how far the debate assumed what was being included on university syllabuses without offering too much concrete evidence. The debate often relied on the comments of others, anecdotal evidence and general fears and anxieties. Secondly, the canon debate was centred on past literary periods and genres; there had been hardly any work done to identify a canon of contemporary literature, although Bloom offered a tentative and speculative list of authors he anticipated would become canonical.[10]

The Contemporary Canons Database aims to fill this lack of information. It is a resource that attempts to provide accurate and empirical data regarding the range and number of contemporary British texts and authors being taught in UK universities at the beginning of the twenty first century. At the time of writing (August 2005) the data is still being collated, so this article represents a progress report and preliminary findings, but eventually the information will be published in the form of an online database.[11]

I have been putting the database together over the past two years and I am grateful to those people who have provided me with the relevant information.[12] So far, I have collated information from courses run in nineteen university English departments. Before looking at some of the preliminary findings, however, I must make a few comments on the parameters and limitations of the research:

1. The research was gathered through a mixture of direct contact with people running contemporary literature courses, and by gaining information from English department websites. There is, therefore, a divergence in terms of the way the information was gathered. With respect to departmental websites, it must be assumed that, although the information may sometimes be out of date, the texts included on reading lists have been studied at some time over the last two or three years.
2. The data was gathered over a period of two years, referring to courses running between September 2002 and June 2004. Given the rapid change around of staff and modules in today's English departments it is not guaranteed that these courses are still running, or that the same texts are still being taught at the institutions stated.
3. The data is essentially quantitative rather than qualitative and cannot show the emphasis placed on individual texts and authors within a module or course structure. Nor can it show which elements or themes of the text were emphasised and how they

were connected to other texts on the module. In addition, I decided not to discriminate between where the texts appeared in terms of levels in a degree programme, although there is an indication made between undergraduate and postgraduate courses.

4. The project as a whole can in no sense be seen as providing a complete picture, as it only deals with a selection of British university English departments. It does not take into account texts taught in higher education institutions outside of the UK. There is, therefore, a natural bias towards British fiction and/or those texts by non-British writers that have an international reputation. I decided to include all authors, irrespective of nationality, if they appeared on courses that covered contemporary fiction. Toni Morrison and Margaret Atwood, therefore, appear in the list below despite them not being part of a 'British' canon.
5. It may also be argued that certain university departments are more influential than others. This is a contentious issue that my quantitative approach fortunately, for me, avoids.
6. Finally, it must be stressed that university syllabuses are only part of the process of canon formation (although a very important part) and the data does not take account of the influence of other factors in the content of a canon such as school syllabuses (and governmental influence in the production of these), literary journalism, literary prize culture, and the importance of film, TV and radio adaptations. What I hope will be useful to future researchers is the possibility to compare these other areas with what texts are being taught in higher education.

The information gathered by the research is collated under several headings. These are: Author; Title; Nationality; Gender; Module; University; Region.[13] The appendix at the end of this article shows an indication of how the database will look once completed. The beauty of having this information in an electronic database form is that it is possible to rearrange the criteria to show different emphases; for example, it is possible to arrange the data in terms of author, nationality, gender or any of the other headings, depending upon the nature of the information required.

Overall, then, the database will provide a sketch, rather than a complete picture. However, it does give us an insight into which texts are currently being taught or have been taught over the past two or three years. From this information it is possible to reach a few tentative conclusions about the formation of a canon, or canons of contemporary fiction.

## *4. Preliminary Findings*

### *4.1. Texts*

What has emerged from the preliminary data is that the following twelve authors represent those most often taught on contemporary and post-war literature courses in British university English departments, with an indication of which of their works were most often used (the authors are arranged in alphabetical, not quantitative order):

| | |
|---|---|
| Martin Amis | *London Fields* |
| Margaret Atwood | *Alias Grace*<br>*Surfacing* |
| Pat Barker | *Regeneration* |
| Julian Barnes | *England, England*<br>*Flaubert's Parrot*<br>*A History of the World in 10½ Chapters* |
| Angela Carter | *The Passion of New Eve*<br>*The Bloody Chamber* |
| Doris Lessing | *The Golden Notebook*<br>*The Grass is Singing*<br>*Briefing for a Descent into Hell* |
| Ian McEwan | *Atonement* |
| Toni Morrison | *Beloved* |

| | |
|---|---|
| Salman Rushdie | *Midnight's Children*<br>*Shame*<br>*The Satanic Verses* |
| Zadie Smith | *White Teeth* |
| Graham Swift | *Waterland*<br>*Last Orders* |
| Jeanette Winterson | *Oranges Are Not the Only Fruit*<br>*Sexing the Cherry* |

### *4.2. Themes*

From this list of authors and texts it is possible to draw some conclusions regarding the thematic, ideological and aesthetic influences informing the current teaching of contemporary fiction. There are five main areas to be identified, some of which reflect formal concerns, others thematic, although, it should be stressed that the form and content of the texts should not be seen as separate categories with respect to individual texts.

The first identifiable theme is the emphasis on texts that in some way foreground the act of writing itself. Many of the texts represent self-reflexive writing: a mode of fiction that alerts the reader to its own fictional status and questions the nature of communication through language. Varieties of this might include metafiction, genre writing, parody and pastiche. Each of the authors and texts identified in the list, to lesser or greater extent, reflect this kind of self-consciousness towards the textuality of writing. A particular example is Martin Amis's *London Fields,* a novel that plays with the reader's experience of fiction by including an author that is ostensibly writing down events as they happen to him, but framed within a pastiche of a hardboiled detective novel of the mid twentieth century.

The second characteristic relates to a tendency to include novels that in some way blur the distinctions between high and popular culture. Again, this can be achieved through self-conscious parodies of popular fictional forms with an intellectual awareness of the hidden assumptions and ideologies of these popular genres. The novels in the list by Martin Amis, Julian Barnes, Angela Carter, and Salman Rushdie are of particular relevance here. Angela Carter's *The Bloody Chamber*, for example, interrogates the ideological meanings hidden in children's fairy tales by offering alternative versions that tend to subvert the patriarchal narratives that are embedded in the original stories.

Both of the first two characteristics clearly relate to a broad theme in contemporary literature: postmodernism. This is also the case with the third area: the number of historical novels on the list, and in particular, historical novels that explore the relationship between history and fiction, and/or are interested in problematising an understanding of history as a linear, monolithic account of the events of the past. Many of the novels identified are concerned to offer multiple and unofficial representations of the past to challenge the way in which prevailing historical accounts have obscured minority and marginalised experiences. Specific examples from the list include the works by Pat Barker, Julian Barnes, Angela Carter, Ian McEwan, Salman Rushdie, Graham Swift and Jeanette Winterson. Swift's *Waterland* is a good example. This novel interweaves official historical events with a family's genealogy, with personal memories from the main characters. All of this is presented in a contemporary framework in which history as a cultural interest, and as an academic subject, is seen to be under threat.

The fourth area relates to the popularity of novels that deal with ethnic and cultural experiences that lie outside of the UK, or include characters from marginalised or excluded ethnic backgrounds. This would include writers such as Margaret Atwood, Doris Lessing, Toni Morrison, Salman Rushdie and Zadie Smith. Many of the writers that are not identified in the top twelve also fell into this category suggesting that it is a much wider theme.

The final category is the number of female writers included on the list (Atwood, Barker, Carter, Lessing, Morrison, Smith, and Winterson). In fact seven of the twelve are women writers. This is not to say that they are all necessarily interested in feminist or gender issues (although many are). It is a particular characteristic of contemporary fiction that the gender balance could be said to be more or less even, a fact that probably could not be said of the canonical lists of any other literary period or genre (with the possible exception of the Victorian novel).

*4.3. Theories*

Now it isn't difficult to see the relationship here between the theoretical preoccupations of contemporary literary studies and the selection of texts currently being taught in universities. In particular, we can identify four main areas. Firstly, as already suggested, there is the influence of the theories of postmodernism and poststructuralism; theories that combine an interest in the problematisation of the representational function of language with stylised techniques such as metafiction, parody and pastiche. Also the importance of Jean-Francois Lyotard's "suspicion towards metanarratives", an influential idea in postmodern theory, can be seen to be integral in the questioning of past philosophies and ideologies in terms of ethnicity, gender and sexuality.[14]

The second major influence in literary and cultural theory over the last twenty years or so is postcolonialism. This focus covers a wide range of specific ethnicities and collective marginalised experiences, and can be identified as influencing many of the texts on the list. In particular, theories around the decolonization of literature, the emergence of new ethnicities, diaspora, hybridity, otherness, racism and the narratives of individuals from minority cultures have all had their influence on the selection of texts for courses. This influence was particularly seen in the number of courses that were specifically related to postcolonial issues.

The continued development and re-assessment of theories around feminism, gender and sexuality is the third area informing the list. As we have seen the inclusion of a more or less equal number of women and men writers on the list is of importance here, although it has to be noted in terms of sexuality that the prevailing trend is still for novels that subscribe to heterosexual relationships and plots despite the importance of Queer Theory in contemporary literary and cultural studies.[15]

Finally, the move away from the structuralism of the 1960s and 1970s has seen an increasing interest in a re-historicising of literary studies, most visibly in the theories around New Historicism and Cultural Materialism. These influential theories appear to be informing the selection of novels that are concerned with exploring the inter-relationship of texts and cultural artefacts, and the penchant for historical fiction (especially that type of historical fiction that shows an intellectual awareness of the relationship between historicity and textuality).

### *5. Conclusions*

As the database is not yet complete, conclusions are provisional at this stage, however, a few speculations may be proposed. It would seem apparent that the canon or canons that are emerging in the present with regard to contemporary fiction are responding to popular themes and concerns within cultural and literary theory. This is not to suggest that the relationship between theory and fiction is hierarchical, rather that there is a parallel interconnection between the two. The contemporary canon that is emerging with regard to those texts being taught in British universities appears to be based on a balance of aesthetic concerns, engagement with contemporary theories in literary and cultural studies and an ideologically informed criticism. This is far from Harold Bloom's fear in the early nineties that future academic curricula would only be based on ideologically informed criteria with little regard to aesthetic judgements.

However, following Eagleton's logic that canons are always culturally and historically contingent, we should not be complacent about the current status of academic syllabuses. Although at present there is a healthy presence of authors and texts that represent marginalised subject-positions (especially with regard to women's fiction and postcolonial/ethnic minority fiction) this could just be a phase, after which a canon based on a more conservative range of texts re-emerges. One observation that is relevant here is that there are now very few courses or texts that openly focus on working class fiction, as there certainly were twenty or thirty years ago. That is not to say that fiction that deals with working class issues or experience is no longer represented, but that it is no longer regarded as important that such texts should be identified or foregrounded within a separate canon. As Guillory points out, it is much easier to make the canon more representative of cultural diversity than it is the university itself.[16] The pluralisation of the canon is negated if the demographic of those taking university English degrees does not also represent the cultural diversity of the nation. In addition, it is problematic to equate the social identity of the author with the identity politics associated with the minority culture to which they belong, for example, how representative of British Asian culture is Salman Rushdie?

One consequence of this research is that it is itself implicated in the construction and maintenance of a canon. In publishing this article in a literary journal it becomes an intervention in the process of canon formation, rather than simply a detached record of what is already there. I do not want to suggest that the 'canon' as a way of teaching literature should be removed, or that we can ever find a definitive list of texts that represents the best of what is being produced at this time. Eagleton's theory teaches us that all canons are contingent. Nevertheless, having a canon is still important in the practical teaching of contemporary fiction: it all depends on our attitude towards canonicity. Personally, I would reject a Bloomean model, because it fails to identify the contingencies of the value system involved in the choice of texts to be canonised. Similarly, Eagleton's discussion of the canon seems contradictory and self-defeating leaving no space or confidence by which to offer a qualitative selection of literary texts on which to maintain a practical programme of literary studies. Frank Kermode's support for the maintenance of the canon for practical purposes (rather than based on any fixed evaluative criteria) is appealing, but I would like to extend this to include a sense in which the concept should be pluralised to reflect the diversity of subject positions in contemporary Western societies. As mentioned earlier, it is tempting to consider a postmodern model of canonicity, although I am suspicious of the complexities of this overused term. A postmodern model, as you might expect, would support a multi-perspectival and self-reflexively partial criteria for the canonization of texts. The monolithic canon would thus be replaced by a series of parallel canons, each of which might set out its particular focus. These canons would not necessarily be competing; they would run alongside each other, with individual texts and authors appearing in different canons. This is essentially the thinking behind ideas such as gynocriticism, and designations like 'black British' writing, but instead of these being regarded as sub-categories occupying a marginalised position with respect to the 'real' canon, I advocate a model that sees, for example, women's writing alongside a canon of men's writing, or of Western European men's writing. This is hinted at in Bloom's addition of that 'Western' in the title to his book on the subject: *The Western Canon*, but in his case this gesture towards geographical difference masks a lack of sensitivity to other subject divisions, such as class, race, gender and sexuality. In the spirit of this postmodern model of the canon I would like to offer a reworded title to Bloom's book; how about: *The Western, Phallocentric, White, Middle-Class Canon*. Not a happy prospect for publishers I imagine, but representative of a specific canon that could take its place alongside other, equally-accurately-defined canons.

## *Notes*

1 Butler (1989: 20).
2 *Ibid.* 26.
3 Bloom (1989: 17).
4 Eagleton (1983: 14).
5 Kermode (2003: 28).
6 *Ibid.*
7 *Ibid.* 29.
8 Guillory (1993: vii-viii).
9 *Ibid.* 38.
10 Bloom (1989: 53-55).
11 For more information please contact me at n.bentley@keele.ac.uk.
12 A full list of those who provided information will be published with the database.
13 I intend to include the year of publication of the text as an additional category in the completed database.
14 Lyotard (1984).
15 Works by Jeanette Winterson and Pat Barker on the list are notable exceptions.
16 Guillory (1993:7-8).

## *Bibliography*

Amis, Martin: *London Fields*, London, 1989.
Atwood, Margaret: *Alias Grace*, London, 1997.
---: *Surfacing*, London, 1994.
Barker, Pat: *Regeneration*, London, 1991.
Barnes, Julian: *England, England*, London, 1998.
---: *A History of the World in 10 ½ Chapters*, London, 1989.

---: *Flaubert's Parrot*, London, 1985.
Bloom, Harold: *The Western Canon*, New York, 1994.
Butler, Marilyn: "Repossessing the Past: the Case for an Open Literary History", in M. Levinson et al. (Eds.), *Rethinking Historicism: Critical Readings in Romantic History*, Oxford, 1989, pp. 64-84.
Carter, Angela: *The Passion of New Eve*, London, 1992.
---: *The Bloody Chamber*, Harmondsworth, 1990.
Eagleton, Terry: *Literary Theory: An Introduction*, Oxford, 1983.
Eliot, T.S.: "Tradition and the Individual Talent", in *The Sacred Wood: Essays on Poetry and Criticism*, London, 1920, pp. 47-59.
Guillory, John: *Cultural Capital: The Problem of Literary Canon Formation*, Chicago, 1993.
Kermode, Frank: "Canon and Period". – In Dennis Walder (Ed.) *Literature in the Modern World*, second edition, Oxford, 2003, pp. 27-31.
Lessing, Doris: *The Golden Notebook*, London, 1973.
---: *The Grass is Singing*, London, 1950.
---: *Briefing for a Descent into Hell*, London, 1971.
Lyotard, Jean-Francois: *The Postmodern Condition*, trans. Geoff Bennington and Brian Massumi, Manchester, 1984.
McEwan, Ian: *Atonement*, London, 2002.
Morrison, Toni: *Beloved*, London, 1997.
Rushdie, Salman: *Midnight's Children*, London, 1995.
---: *Shame*, London, 1995.
---: *The Satanic Verses*, London, 1994.
Smith, Zadie: *White Teeth*, Harmondsworth, 2001.
Swift, Graham: *Waterland*, London, 1996.
---: *Last Orders*, London, 1999.
Winterson, Jeanette: *Oranges Are Not the Only Fruit*, London, 1991.
---: *Sexing the Cherry*, London, 1990.

## *Appendix*

Contemporary Canons Database (extract)

| Author | Title | Nationality | Gender | Module | University | Region |
|---|---|---|---|---|---|---|
| Achebe, Chinua | *Things Fall Apart* | Nigerian | Male | New Literatures in English | Bishop Grosseteste College | England |
| Achebe, Chinua | *Things Fall Apart* | Nigerian | Male | Twentieth Century Literature | Exeter | England |
| Achebe, Chinua | *Things Fall Apart* | Nigerian | Male | Literature in the Modern World | Open University | U.K. |
| Ackroyd, Peter | *Hawksmoor* | English | Male | Contemporary Writing 1 | Sussex | England |
| Ackroyd, Peter | *Chatterton* | English | Male | | Edge Hill University College | England |
| Adair, Gilbert | *A Closed Book* | Scottish | Male | | Edge Hill University College | England |
| Allende, Isobel | *The House of Spirits* | Chilean | Female | | Oxford Brookes | England |
| Allingham, Margery | *The Tiger in the Smoke* | English | Female | Detective and Crime Fiction | Aberystwyth | Wales |
| Amis, Kingsley | *Lucky Jim* | English | Male | Post War Literary Culture | Anglia Polytechnic University | England |
| Amis, Martin | *Time's Arrow* | English | Male | Narrative in Culture | Anglia Polytechnic University | England |
| Amis, Martin | *London Fields* | English | Male | End of the 20th Century | Keele | England |
| Amis, Martin | *The Information* | English | Male | | London Metropolitan | England |
| Amis, Martin | *Other People* | English | Male | Postmodernism | Bishop Grosseteste College | England |
| Amis, Martin | *London Fields* | English | Male | | Oxford Brookes | England |
| Amis, Martin | *Money* | English | Male | Contemporary British Fiction | Staffordshire University | England |
| Atkinson, Kate | *Behind the Scenes at the Museum* | English | Female | Contemporary Fiction | Sheffield Hallam | England |

| Author | Title | Nationality | Gender | Module | University | Region |
|---|---|---|---|---|---|---|
| Atwood, Margaret | *Lady Oracle* | Canadian | Female | | Aberdeen | Scotland |
| Atwood, Margaret | *Alias Grace* | Canadian | Female | | Oxford Brookes | England |
| Atwood, Margaret | *Alias Grace* | Canadian | Female | Contemporary Fiction | Sheffield Hallam | England |
| Atwood, Margaret | *The Edible Woman* | Canadian | Female | Twentieth Century Literature | Exeter | England |
| Atwood, Margaret | *Surfacing* | Canadian | Female | Reading Recent Fictions | Hope | England |
| Atwood, Margaret | *The Handmaid's Tale* | Canadian | Female | | Oxford Brookes | England |
| Atwood, Margaret | *Surfacing* | Canadian | Female | Modern Women"s Writing | Bishop Grosseteste College | England |
| Auster, Paul | *The New York Trilogy* | American | Male | Contemporary Writing 1 | Sussex | England |
| Auster, Paul | *City of Glass* | American | Male | Twentieth Century Fiction: Modernism to Postmodernism | Huddersfield | England |
| Ballard, J.G. | *Crash* | English | Male | Twentieth Century Fiction: Modernism to Postmodernism | Huddersfield | England |
| Ballard, J.G. | *Crash* | English | Male | Literature and Sexualities | Exeter | England |
| Banville, John | *Shroud* | Irish | Male | Contemporary Writing 1 (MA) | Sussex | England |
| Banville, John | *The Book of Evidence* | Irish | Male | Contemporary Writing 1 | Sussex | England |
| Banville, John | *The Newton Letter* | Irish | Male | Critical Theory | Bishop Grosseteste College | England |
| Banville, John | *Eclipse* | Irish | Male | Contemporary Writing 1 (MA) | Sussex | England |
| Barker, Pat | *Regeneration* | English | Female | Contemporary Literature (MA) | Sussex | England |

| Author | Title | Nationality | Gender | Module | University | Region |
|---|---|---|---|---|---|---|
| Barker, Pat | *Regeneration* | English | Female | Contemporary Cultures: Britain 1979-2001 | Exeter | England |
| Barker, Pat | *Union Street* | English | Female | Learning to Labour: Class, Gender and Identity in Postwar Britain | Staffordshire University | England |
| Barker, Pat | *The Eye in the Door* | English | Female | | Aberdeen | Scotland |
| Barker, Pat | *Regeneration* | English | Female | Contemporary Fiction | Sheffield Hallam | England |
| Barnes, Julian | *Flaubert's Parrot* | English | Male | Contemporary Literature (MA) | Sussex | England |
| Barnes, Julian | *Flaubert's Parrot* | English | Male | | Edge Hill University College | England |
| Barnes, Julian | *England, England* | English | Male | Reading in Hyperreality | University of East London | England |
| Barnes, Julian | *A History of the World in 10 ½ Chapters* | English | Male | | London Metropolitan | England |
| Barnes, Julian | *England, England* | English | Male | End of the 20th Century | Keele | England |
| Barnes, Julian | *A History of the World in 10 ½ Chapters* | English | Male | Metafictional Experiments in the Postmodern Novel | Aberystwyth | Wales |
| Barnes, Julian | *England, England* | English | Male | Postmodernism | Bishop Grosseteste College | England |

*Doryjane Birrer (Charleston)*

# Theoretical Fiction, Academic Culture: Contextualising British Novels of the 1980s

C.S. Lewis once said, "There is an inherent absurdity in making current literature a subject of academic study, and the student who wants a tutor's assistance in reading the works of his own contemporaries might as well ask for a nurse's assistance in blowing his own nose."[1] That an entire issue of an academic series is devoted to considering the study and teaching of contemporary British literature is a strong testament to challenges posed over the last several decades to attitudes like Lewis'. Yet Lewis' statement touches on an interesting issue with regard to teaching contemporary texts, as it implicitly questions just what aspects of, for example, a contemporary British novel would demand additional study, and just how students would benefit from the assistance of a teacher like those of us whose work is included in this issue. One assumption Lewis makes with his statement, as Bernard Bergonzi points out, is "that the task of the teacher is removing contextual difficulty – historical, cultural, linguistic – and that a contemporary text will not present any such difficulty, so there is nothing for the teacher to do. Such texts should be instantly transparent and accessible to the reader."[2] Certainly, addressing historical, cultural, and linguistic contextual difficulties is one important aspect of rendering literature of any period more accessible to students. And as an American professor at an American college, addressing such contextual difficulties still plays a prominent role in my own teaching of novels that, to American students, are still somewhat 'foreign' despite their origins just on the other side of what, in this increasingly networked and navigable world, is essentially a very small pond. However, to 'remove' such contextual difficulties is not merely a matter of clarifying British idiom, or giving mini-lectures on British history and culture.

This last idea is true in part because our conceptions of what referents 'history' and 'culture' actually point to (let alone the term 'British' itself) have become more complex given increasingly theoretical orientations toward such terms in literary study since the latter third of the twentieth century. A similar theoretical shift is noticeable in a substantial number of British novels published contemporaneously with the rise of theory in the academy. The combination of these academic and literary trends results in an additional contextual difficulty: a theoretical one (or what many of my students have described as a 'philosophical' one). This, I think, is a contextual difficulty relevant to the teaching of English literature regardless of one's institutional location or citizenship, and this essay is about one mode I have been experimenting with to address it. I have tried to do this in ways that don't intimidate students unfamiliar with literary theory, or frustrate them with a complex argot that seems to many of them to impede, rather than to facilitate, literary conversation; in ways that emphasise the relevance of theoretical questioning to students' own capacities to live more examined lives; and in ways that help students to explore the roles such questioning has played in the development of their literary-critical discipline. In the process, I have hoped students will come to appreciate the extent to which fiction itself plays overt and oblique roles in changing notions (to steal David Richter's handy categories) of why, what, and how we read.[3] The present essay outlines the specific strategies I have used to engage such pedagogical objectives and considerations in the most recent permutations of my "English 357: Contemporary British Literature" course (an upper-division undergraduate course comprised primarily of English majors). I will begin with a general description of the course, which places contemporary British novels of the 1980s in the context of debates about academic culture and the rise of literary theory in the same decade; move on to specific issues relevant to this context that I raise when teaching particular novels; and conclude with a brief consideration of the outcomes of this mode of addressing the theoretical aspects of contemporary British fiction.

The novels that I have taught in "English 357: Contemporary British Literature" fall primarily within a category Mark Currie has described as "fiction with theoretical intent, or theoretical fiction". For Currie, such fiction is essentially a permutation of the novel of ideas, and can be a more productive form for engaging complex ideas than the essay, given fiction's "ability to explore ideas or historical forces as lived by individuals".[4] Theoretical fiction, to loosely summarise Currie, is situated on a substantially blurred boundary between fiction and criticism/theory, and characteristically explores the functions of narrative: not merely fictional narrative in a literary sense, but also narratives personal, national, historical, and so on. Further, theoretical fiction "is a performative, rather than a constative narratology"; in other words, rather than embarking on an extended discourse about a particular kind of narrative, it "enacts or performs what it wishes to say about narrative while itself being a narrative".[5] Drawing on Currie's ideas, and particularly on his conception of theoretical fiction, I titled my course "Fictions of Contemporary Britain" in an attempt to capture the notion that the course would "engage the idea of 'fictions' on numerous levels, from developments in British fictional forms, to fictions – often overlapping – of personal identity, gender, sexuality, region, and nation" (this was the opening sentence of the course description). In order to help ground many of the theoretical aspects of the course in what I hoped would be a productive and interesting manner, I added to the course an engagement with academic culture: "The writers we'll study", the course description reads, "also have a great deal to say about literature's place in academic institutions and its roles in society, so we'll consider what reading literature has to do with our lives as students, teachers, and members of the 'real world.'" Ultimately, I wanted to explore with my students the intriguing interrelationships among fiction and the criticism, theory, and pedagogy that have developed alongside it, as well as some of the ways in which these elements are situated within the realm of academic culture.

I begin the course with at least one highly metafictional novel to set the stage for later discussions of narrative constructions generally (I teach Muriel Spark's *The Comforters* [1957] and/or John Fowles' *The French Lieutenant's Woman* [1969]). However, the bulk of the novels I originally chose for the course were published in the 1980s, including Salman Rushdie's *Midnight's Children* (1981), Graham Swift's *Waterland* (1983), Julian Barnes' *Flaubert's Parrot* (1984), Penelope Lively's *Moon Tiger* (1987), Kazuo Ishiguro's *The Remains of the Day* (1989), and A.S. Byatt's *Possession: A Romance*, written at the close of the eighties and published in 1990. Throughout the course, as we discuss the novels' historical and social contexts and responses to previous literary traditions (such as social realism and modernism), I also situate the novels in the context of contemporaneous debates in the eighties about the nature and purpose of literary study. I chose this decade because with the rise of literary theory and associated cultural politics in the late sixties and seventies, debates in the U.K. addressing the constitution and trajectory of English studies became by the eighties "unusually angry and peculiarly public", and marked a time of "unprecedented strain in literary education".[6] Such highly publicised events as the 'MacCabe affair' at Cambridge in 1981, confrontation between Cambridge-based Frank Kermode and Oxonian Dame Helen Gardner, and fiery polemics sparked by Methuen's *New Accents* series – especially *Re-Reading English* (1982) – prompted heated debates about issues I'm going to categorise, *pace* Richter, rather broadly as follows. First, 'why' literature should be read, or literature's role in society; second, 'what' literature should be read, or the makeup of the British national canon and/or course syllabi; and third, 'how' literature should be read, or interpretive strategies. These issues, of course, have informed discussions about literature as far back as literary creation itself, but the eighties sense of crisis due to widespread disagreement over responses to them perhaps became so intense because not only more tightly bound up with institutional politics, upon which not just professional interests but livelihoods depend, but also with governmental politics: namely, Thatcherite utilitarian anti-intellectualism. The value and purpose of literary study, even the viability of English Literature as a discipline, might well seem under fire in such a volatile climate, as commentary from the eighties in fact indicates.

In order to help students understand some of the concerns at stake in these debates, I've found that it's useful to begin with some background on the history of English studies and literary-critical activity. While I won't thoroughly rehearse the context I provide here, it should be useful to touch on some of the main ideas I try to convey. This is particularly important in order to provide a sense of my own views with regard to English studies in the U.K., views that are necessarily inflected and compromised by my outsider status as an American who has neither lived nor taught overseas. To begin, I refer to the Arnoldian tradition in English literature, and address the idea that English studies had long linked social cohesion and order to literary and cultural order. In a corollary fashion, order in literary criticism was perceived as necessary to the viability of English studies: without order in the discipline, how could order be pursued in the world outside? I talk about how this disciplinary order was imposed obliquely through such means as the rigorous philological scholarship associated with Oxford, and more overtly through the 'Practical Criticism' of I.A. Richards associated with Cambridge. What amounted to the institutionalisation of Richards' system, particularly under the later auspices of F.R. Leavis, would imbue English studies with the 'objectivity' and 'authority' deemed necessary not only for disciplinary order, but also for the academic legitimation of English studies within the university: here could be a discipline rooted in agreed-upon principles through which students could be objectively tested.

I also discuss how the desire for an Arnoldian 'disinterestedness' as manifested in Practical Criticism (and its implicit devotion to the idea of independent aesthetic objects) was accompanied by strong undercurrents from the moral aesthetic aspect of the tradition of English criticism, particularly as expressed in liberal humanist orientations to literary study. To help students come to grips with the tension between dexcontextualised close reading and a desire to better a social world largely excluded from such literary analysis, I have turned to Peter Barry's undergraduate-friendly discussion of English studies, practical criticism, and liberal humanism in *Beginning Theory: An Introduction to Literary and Cultural Theory*, which I excerpt and distribute in class. Barry usefully attempts to formulate a number of underlying tenets of liberal humanism that "comprise the values and beliefs" that originally constituted the "half-hidden curriculum" of English studies. I can't do justice within the scope of this essay to Barry's discussion, but in brief, among those tenets identified by Barry, most relevant to my course are the idea that the meaning of a literary text is self-contained and "doesn't require any elaborate process of placing it within a context" (Barry names here "socio-political", "literary-historical", and "autobiographical" contexts); a belief in the "transcendent subject", or what Barry describes as "the belief that the individual [...] is antecedent to, or transcends, the forces of society, experience, and language"; the attitude that literature's purpose "is essentially the enhancement of life and the propagation of humane values; but not in a programmatic way: if literature, and criticism, become overtly and directly political they necessarily tend towards propaganda"; and finally, the notion that "[a] theoretical account of the nature of reading, or of literature in general, isn't useful in criticism", and would "encumber critics with 'preconceived ideas' which will get between them and the text".[7]

Though the parameters of the course don't allow for detailed exploration of the nuances of twentieth-century literary-critical history, I do indicate to students that additional critical moves were being made in the early to mid-twentieth century. However, overall I emphasise that the Ricardian and Arnoldian-Leavisite modes of formalist and liberal-humanist criticism comprised in tandem the dominant and most influential critical orientation throughout most of the discipline's early history, particularly through the work of Leavis and *Scrutiny* at Cambridge. As I tell my students, although Leavis himself was neither universally nor consistently respected in educational institutions, including his own, a preponderance of literary teachers and scholars since, from across political spectrums, have identified a strongly Leavisite tradition underlying most secondary and tertiary education. I conclude with the idea that it was largely the literary-critical tradition I have just outlined that was dramatically challenged in the early eighties with the rise of new literary theories and, concomitantly, what became increasingly political questions about what, why, and how we read – questions that would truly shake up literature as a discipline.

Terence Hawkes' General Editor's Preface to Methuen's *New Accents* series, begun in the late seventies and in full swing by the early eighties, helps to sum up some of the terms of challenges to 'traditional' literary study, and I distribute it to the class. Briefly, Hawkes addresses the rise of "new methods of analysis", "new concepts of literary forms and modes", and "new views of literature's role in relation to society", and references, for example, crucial incursions from anthropology, sociology, and linguistics; he also alludes to the rise of electronic media and the inception of what would eventually become Cultural Studies. As a whole, Hawkes characterises the time as one of "rapid and radical social change", including "the erosion of the assumptions and presuppositions that support the literary disciplines in their conventional form" with the result, he argues, that "modes and categories inherited from the past no longer seem to fit the reality experienced by a new generation".

Each volume in the *New Accents* series would "seek to encourage rather than resist the process of change".[8] I also draw again on Barry's work to help summarise some of the particular challenges that the rise of theory presented to 'traditional' literary study, and provide for students the short section entitled "Some recurrent ideas in critical theory." Briefly, Barry's list of theoretical ideas covers the social construction of what we often consider "the basic 'givens' of our existence" (in which he includes "gender identity", "individual selfhood", and "the notion of literature itself"); the relativity of 'truth'; the linguistic constitution, rather than reflection, of reality; the instability/contingency of meaning, including within a literary text; and the problems associated with totalising ideas such as 'universal' human nature.[9]

After we've discussed the general ideas outlined by Hawkes and Barry, students generally grasp the tenor of increasing challenges to liberal-humanist assumptions. However, to provide at least a few more specific examples, I distribute excerpts from *Re-Reading English*, the controversial early volume in Methuen's series whose contributors voiced their concerns, variously expressed, that the teaching of English literature at the time of the volume's publication was widely under-theorised, and was underpinned in classroom activities and examination systems by reductive assumptions about, among other things, how literature as both abstract concept and concrete texts should be understood. These excerpts begin with Peter Widdowson's call for a more materialist criticism to combat what he describes as "the largely unshaken dominance of conventional criticism" and Brian Doyle's discussion of English studies and "cultural uniformity". I also include parts of Tony Davies' analyses of Cambridge Tripos examination questions, which he argues are variations on redundant and limiting themes, and Catherine Belsey's arguments for recognising the plurality of texts, particularly in order to challenge Leavis' reading strategies which, she argues, had reduced such textual plurality. I also discuss the work of two additional critics, Chris Baldick and Francis Mulhern, whose discussions in the eighties of the English literary-critical tradition address the close reading associated with practical criticism, and Leavis' work in particular. A primary concern Mulhern has with "English Reading" (Mulhern's term) is what he sees as its goal of "shared vision", a desire to "*pre-scribe* the subjective conditions of seeing" (emphasis in the text),[10] which culminates in what Baldick refers to as "the corroborative mode of criticism".[11] Both Mulhern and Baldick discuss hallmarks of Leavis' rhetoric as problematic in this way, pointing, for example, to his repeated use of "we" – which suggests that the reasonable reader already agrees with him – along with his repetition of phrases along the lines of "This is so, is it not?" (with the "is it not" becoming less and less a real request for alternate opinions). Essentially, Mulhern and Baldick highlight what they see as Leavis' tendency toward tautology, in which consensus visions he strives to create are implied already to exist. Pedagogy rooted in such strategies, following Baldick's and Mulhern's arguments, can result in 'standardised' thinking, or an unreflective ventriloquism of received ideas (particularly for the purposes of exams), even though Leavis himself was passionately committed to fighting the standardization and groupthink he associated with the rise of mass culture.

Overall, I try to paint a picture of the 'crisis' in English studies as an unstable and often polemical but nonetheless exciting transition that demanded of scholars and teachers of all critical orientations more explicit conversations about the implications of literary pedagogy, from more abstract discussions about ideology and canon-formation to practical considerations regarding the relative merits of primarily formalist versus more historicist or materialist and increasingly politically engaged pedagogy. I explain that contributors to the *New Accents* series and those who welcomed work like *Re-Reading English* at that time (to isolate just one group of teachers and scholars) generally saw the 'crisis' in English studies as an exciting opportunity to initiate dialogues about literary study as a discipline, and embraced the potentially protean nature of literary studies to shift shape and develop in response to what they perceived as changing social and cultural needs. I also emphasise, however, that for a considerable number of teachers and scholars, the crisis threatened to undermine what many of them viewed as universal and eternal human values, and the appropriate modes to study that literature which was purported to reflect and support such values. Further, incursions allowing for more interdisciplinary approaches to literature also posed a potential threat to English studies as a discrete component of the university curriculum, raising concerns about such practical but important matters as continued funding and academic posts, not to mention the continued institutional footing of English as a discipline after its proponents strove so diligently to establish it as a central component of a humane and liberal education. It's tricky at this point in class to reflect adequately or fairly the myriad positions within such debates, and I encourage students to think about them in terms of spectrums or webs of responses. However, for heuristic purposes, it's generally been expedient, at least early on in the course, to position the debates between poles represented by broadly humanist and formalist Leavisite criticism on the one hand, and materialist/historicist and more theoretically informed strategies on the other. From here we as a class can begin to talk not so much about specific theories, but about the kinds of questions and assumptions that underlie different approaches to reading, writing, and talking about literature, and that I see as surfacing in a great deal of contemporary British fiction from the 1980s on.

For example, questions about literature's role(s) in society are closely linked to questions about the relationship between fiction and reality, questions that surface overtly or obliquely in theoretical novels. As Patricia Waugh says of metafiction, novels that play with this relationship explore "the possible fictionality of the world outside the literary fictional text" as a corollary of exploring the structures of literary fiction.[12] I expand on this idea in class in relation to individual novels, drawing on strategies typical of what Currie calls postmodern narrative theory, or socio-narratology, which he sees as adding to the moves of earlier, more rigidly formalist narratology a greater awareness of theoretical developments since the eighties such as the constitutive nature of language, the constructedness of individuality and culture, and a greater engagement with historiography. For Currie, this results in "a narratology capable of bringing its expertise to bear on narratives wherever they can be found, which is everywhere".[13] As Currie points out, this last idea has become by now somewhat clichéd, and some of my students have encountered versions of it in freshman composition classes rooted in semiotics and cultural analysis. However, in the context of our course the novels we read represent part of the vanguard of this expanding socio-narratological perspective in the eighties, and they enact and give life to the theoretical questions about individual, social, cultural, and historical narratives becoming more prevalent in the criticism and academic debates of the time.

Throughout the course, then, we explore the power of narrative for good and for ill beginning with three novels that address strikingly similar questions about narrative: Swift's *Waterland*, Rushdie's *Midnight's Children*, and Lively's *Moon Tiger*. Tom Crick, Swift's narrator, talks, for example, about the desire of "man, the storytelling animal" to create order within the chaos of existence and to help make sense of the events of one's life through narrative.[14] Rushdie's narrator Saleem Sinai wants to end up "meaning – yes, meaning – something"[15] through a story that serves in part to establish his notion of personal identity alongside his vision of his nation's history. Finally, in Penelope Lively's *Moon Tiger*, Claudia Hampton meditates on the power of language not only to shape the story of her life, but also to help her "control the world".[16] These novels, however, pit their storytelling protagonists dramatically against external social and cultural forces, including family, region, and nation. With these ideas in mind, one of the discussion questions I hand out to the class asks students to analyse assessments (implicit and explicit) of the functions of storytelling offered by the characters in each novel. With the novels to ground our discussions, as a class we go on to talk about novelists' (and students') perceptions of the powers of narrative generally. Part of the volatility of eighties debates was due to attacks on the humanist notion of autonomous individual identity by theorists who saw lives as largely over-determined by social forces, often negatively associated with Grand Narratives. Novels like Swift's, Rushdie's, and Lively's that pit narratives of personal identity against social and cultural narratives present the terms of these debates imaginatively, and students can therefore witness characters' negotiations with these issues and come to a better understanding of what is at stake in such negotiations, both fictionally and in the 'real world.' How much control, I ask the class, do we have over our own lives: our choices, our allegiances, our beliefs, our impact on the world? To what degree are we affected by social forces and in what ways might we affect them? Despite the prevalence of theories related to the post-structuralist deconstruction of the subject, people still have a sense of being individuals with the drive to be the authors of their own life histories, their own 'stories', and possibly even to influence the stories of the cultural forces that can support and sustain them, but might also threaten to circumscribe them. When we begin to talk about a corollary issue, whether literary texts can actually help shape reality for better or for worse, we've then entered, without needing too much complicated theoretical vocabulary, Leavisite versus post-Althusserian debates about literature and ideology.

Each of these novels also demands engagement with questions about the contingency of meaning and the relativity of truth, two concepts challenging previously more stable literary-critical ideas about objectivity, authority, and the pursuit of knowledge. These novels primarily address these issues through their negotiations with history, and particularly through their characters' linkings of their own personal and family histories to broader historical forces. Tom Crick, a history teacher who connects his family history to the history of the Fens of East Anglia, calls history "a lucky dip of meanings": "events elude meanings", he says, "but we look for meanings", often without a satisfactory result.[17] We compare this description of history to that provided by a nineteenth-century historian: "Human history is a record of progress—a record of accumulating knowledge and increasing wisdom, of continual advancement from a lower to a higher platform of intelligence and well-being."[18] In the context of these differing descriptions, we begin to tie questions about history to earlier analyses of the functions of narrative, and we explore the relationship between subjectivity and historical storytelling. This relationship is particularly clear in *Midnight's Children*, as Saleem Sinai believes himself "handcuffed to history", given his birth at the moment of India's independence.[19] Similarly, as popular historian Claudia Hampton in *Moon Tiger* narrates her own history, she links it to her deathbed "history of the world".[20] We talk as a class about how each narrator tends to view and/or interpret historical events in a personally significant context, and we extend our considerations of historical subjectivity to 'textbook' history. For example, contrasts between Claudia's accounts of historical moments and other accounts (such as schoolteacher Miss Lavenham's glib assertion that she teaches English history to show "how England became a great nation"[21]) highlight the ways in which different worldviews can radically alter the perspective from which history is perceived. We also look at Rushdie's own discussion of *Midnight's Children* in "Imaginary Homelands", with his consideration not simply of differences, as students might expect, between Indian national history and English imperial history, but of the multiple Indian histories involved in any number of "Indias of the Mind".[22] As we explore the narrative aspects of history in relation to these novels, we also explore their implications in terms of debates in the eighties about relativism. While the idea of relative 'truth' with regard to history or any other potential source of human knowledge and understanding can be an exciting one that allows for the revision and redefinition of previously received ideas, an empty or 'anything goes' relativism is extremely problematic. Although many of my students begin discussions with the idea that "everyone is entitled to his/her opinion", their views characteristically become more complex as they decide that they aren't sure whether, for example, the opinion that the Holocaust is a fabrication is an opinion anyone should be entitled to. We can then consider empty relativism versus a potentially more productive pluralism when it comes to debates about competing interpretations not just of literature but also of literary history. And we can do this with a sense of what larger issues might be involved when, to give just one example from earlier in the class, a critic like Catherine Belsey calls for re-readings of 'The Great Tradition', particularly in order to pay greater attention to gender issues.[23]

We can also engage in debates about the canon, and particularly about the implications of canon-formation for contemporary British fiction, starting with the prevalent public arguments in the eighties about English nationalism and England's imperialist/colonialist legacy, both of which inform notions of a 'national' literature and culture. Postcolonial novels like *Midnight's Children* and novels exploring the concept of 'Englishness' itself, such as Ishiguro's *The Remains of the Day*, are productive in this context, since notions of what it means to be English or British helped to buttress a previously more narrowly defined 'national' canon. Mulhern, for example, identifies in Leavis' literary rhetoric the "sovereign *topos*" of the "continuity of Englishness",[24] and Leavis bemoaned in other contexts the loss of the organic community he saw as central to a once readily identifiable English culture.[25] Similar rhetoric abounded in the eighties, such as Cambridge professor Christopher Ricks's heated assertion during the MacCabe affair that "it is our job to teach and uphold the canon of English literature".[26] For many teachers, this largely meant sticking to 'traditional' methods and texts in the face of political incursions in the form of both critical method and canon-busting (the latter represented by increasing demands for representation in courses of previously marginalised groups – particularly women, and later, postcolonial writers). Yet for many, upholding English literature also meant keeping English 'English', or at least 'British', in the most insular sense. We talk as a class about postcolonial nations when we discuss *Midnight's Children* and we address Rushdie's depictions of English colonialism and 'Englishness', particularly when we discuss the character and imperialist behaviour of Englishman William Methwold as he turns over his nominally 'English' estates in Bombay to their new Indian owners. The more extensive and sustained explorations of 'Englishness' and nationalism in Ishiguro's *The Remains of the Day* further illuminate the impetus behind attacks like Edward Said's on the "academy of English letters". Said characterised English Literature as a place where monuments of national literature (often implicitly imperialist) are "canonised into rigid dynastic formation, serviced and reserviced monotonously by a shrinking guild of humble servants".[27] Students are often interested to discover that the terms of such debates date back to the widespread establishment of English as a discipline in the early twentieth century. Critical historians like Baldick and Terry Eagleton, among others, have demonstrated that literary study in England both overtly and covertly served to heighten national unity and pride in the British Empire. While I don't have time to rehearse their extensive arguments in class, I provide excerpts of what Baldick calls the "English literary jingoism" of the 1921 Newbolt Report, *The Teaching of English in England.* These excerpts help demonstrate how literature professors were seen as one important channel through which pride in English language and literature could be spread, helping to foster social community through national unity – in the words of the report, an appreciation of 'English' would "beget the right kind of national pride".[28]

This nationalist legacy is evident in 1980s debates about the Englishness of English literature (as well as, I note, in the revival of little Englandism under Thatcher). Consideration of this legacy helps students understand why teachers across the political spectrum might invest decisions about, for example, curriculum and syllabi with such importance: for some, the integrity of a longstanding 'native' literature and culture was (and is) at stake, whereas for others, 'Englishness' is a limited and limiting concept that at best functions to create an only mythical unity, and at worst serves imperialist ends. Our class discussion of *The Remains of the*

*Day* addresses in part the creation and disruption of mythologies related to Englishness upheld by the dignified English butler, Stevens, in the face of changing cultural values. As we analyse the ways in which essentially feudal master/servant relationships, the institution of the English country house, and a repressive class structure (to provide just a few examples) are eulogised by the nostalgic Stevens, we can explore the often reductive assumptions behind and damaging implications of Stevens' conceptions of 'Englishness' – particularly as borne out through his blind support of his fascist employer. We also consider the fact that Ishiguro himself has a complex 'English' identity. In particular, I summarise for students Steven Connor's discussion of the early reception of *The Remains of the Day*, in which Connor demonstrates reviewers' nearly unanimous belief that the novel must be about the question of Japanese, rather than English, identity, "despite the fact that there is no mention of Japan or the Japanese in the novel".[29] We tie Connor's ideas to our discussion of Rushdie's complex cultural identity as a migrant Anglo-Indian writer who can celebrate his hybrid identity even while he remains at some level an outsider in terms of both cultures, perhaps even more so now that he lives in the States. Our explorations of 'Englishness' highlight the complexity and question the desirability of establishing a fixed national canon. I also remind students that questions in the eighties and since about national identity are not simply the result of the publication of literary texts in English by a greater number of writers from postcolonial nations; rather, they have been inherent in literary study since its inception in terms of the cultural positions, for example, of writers from Ireland, Scotland, and Wales, as well as expatriate writers like T.S. Eliot – the latter often placed somewhat ironically but firmly at the centre of English criticism. Excerpts from Patricia Waugh's chapter "Nation and New Identities" in *Harvest of the Sixties* help provide additional context for exploring these latter ideas in class.

To this point, I've talked primarily about potential contexts for exploring why and what we read, and I'll close with contexts for exploring how we read. Naturally, questions about critical strategies implicitly have been raised throughout the class, both in terms of how characters in the novels 'read' their worlds, and through the strategies we ourselves have been using to discuss the novels. Ultimately, however, we return to these questions more thoroughly and explicitly. In class, discussions about how we read initially often revolve around debates about literature as formal aesthetic object versus both leftist and more conservative permutations of the moral aesthetic. However, students by the end of the course have a broader understanding of the different kinds of approaches to literature that were discussed vociferously in the eighties, and can therefore think about issues of how we read in less binary terms. They also have a better sense of how the debates we've covered thus far are variously manifested in the complex politics of academic culture, and students are by this time well prepared to consider questions about how we read in relation to novels that address literary research and/or academic culture directly. Barnes' *Flaubert's Parrot* provides a productive starting point for discussions of literary research as students trace the progress of protagonist Geoffrey Braithwaite, who has undertaken a quest to understand the 'real' Gustave Flaubert, and faces complications and conflicting textual 'evidence' at every turn. The failure of Braithwaite to 'find' the elusive Flaubert (or his parrot) highlights some of the challenges and limitations of criticism and literary study generally, particularly when it comes to seeking knowledge about a literary figure from the past. Barnes also parodies critical language and literary examinations (the latter a section my students always find highly amusing), and suggests throughout the novel the potential for absurdity if an awareness that there can be no truly 'objective' literary history, or literary interpretation based on that history, is not reflected in critical inquiry. These points tie usefully into our earlier discussions of the narrative aspects of history, the contingency of meaning, and the relativity of 'truth'.

My students have generally enjoyed Barnes' irreverent treatment of literary research, but it also raises questions for them about the potential pointlessness of literary study if Barnes' viewpoint is unequivocally upheld. Our study of Byatt's *Possession: A Romance* has proved a useful way of exploring this latter idea, especially as it addresses academic culture more directly than does *Flaubert's Parrot*. While it might seem that campus novels like those by David Lodge would be an obvious starting point here, I have generally preferred to teach Byatt's novel, in part because in terms of narrative play, *Possession* falls more in line with theoretical fiction. More importantly, however, I see Lodge's novels as in the lampooning tradition of more immediately post-war campus fiction like Kingsley Amis' *Lucky Jim*, or Tom Sharpe's *Porterhouse Blue*. I agree with Adam Begley who argues that Byatt's academic novel epitomises a genre he dubs the "Pomo Postdoc Romance", whose purpose is less consistently focused on "expos[ing] the foibles of the pointy-headed" – although there's plenty of fuel for discussion in this area. Instead, *Possession*, says Begley, "insist[s] upon the magical properties of scholarship, the peculiar obsessiveness required to live for knowledge".[30] As a result, Byatt's novel provides more intriguing scope for talking about not only the institutional negotiations of the scholars and the relative merits and drawbacks of the different modes of scholarship she presents (and often satirises), but also about the reasons why, despite the "foibles of the pointy-headed", literary study might still be perceived as personally fulfilling and socially important. It seems that closing with the discussion of Byatt's novel, published in 1990 after a decade of heated debates about the future of English studies, helps to suggest that despite that plurality of voices in these debates, and the concern, angst, and even at times outright nastiness that variously characterised them, the debates reflected a shared sense (if not shared on the same terms) of the importance of literature and literary study, and a love of engaging literary worlds as well as what's popularly known as the real one.

It's with regard to this last idea that we can revisit, as a class, our changing conceptions of the literary texts themselves both aesthetically and socially, along with our understandings of the literary, critical, and institutional issues we've discussed. Although some students may still be sceptical that what takes place in a novel, in the classroom, or in a critical article might have a significant extensive or even local impact on the 'real world', I've found that most students are willing to believe that there is more to debates about literature and literary study than a bunch of academics pointlessly battling about books or simply trying to find new topics to write articles about (another charge that is levelled – with, I admit, at least some fairness – every time I teach). And students are definitely willing to take stock of their education and to consider their choice of English studies as a major and potentially a career. Questions regarding how and why we attempt to make sense of literary texts – and which texts we choose to try and make sense of – provide an impetus to remind ourselves with regard to literary study of what we are doing, why we are doing it, and whether we are doing it in a way that is in fact valuable to academic culture and to the world outside it. As Timothy Clark recently argued, "What is called the crisis in English might be taken as a direct ratio of its health, its transcendence of being merely an academic discipline." He continues, "Literary study is not only the site for the detailed study and analysis of literary works: it is simultaneously a place in which the kinds of language a culture uses about itself are continually up for reconfirmation or revision. It is a space in which our culture – or cultures – attempt to define what they are or might be."[31] I try to emphasise this point throughout the course by promoting students' thoughtful negotiations with the issues I've outlined here. It's my hope that exploring the implications of literature and literary study through our engagements with literary texts, rather than strictly through critical and theoretical essays and/or abstract discussions, not only helps imaginatively inform such discussions, but also promotes literature's value beyond the boundaries of the page or the classroom.

*Notes*

1 In Bergonzi (1990: 80).
2 *Ibid.*
3 Richter divides the essays in *Falling Into Theory* into these three categories, though he recognises (as I do) the considerable potential for overlap among them.
4 Currie (1998: 51).
5 *Ibid.* 52.
6 Bergonzi (1990. 10).
7 Barry (2002: 16-21).
8 In Widdowson (1982: vii).
9 Barry (2002: 34-36).
10 Mulhern (1989: 251).
11 Baldick (1983: 174).
12 Waugh (1984: 2).
13 Currie (1998: 1).
14 Swift (1983: 62-63).
15 Rushdie (1981: 4).
16 Lively (1987: 51).
17 Swift (1983: 140).
18 In Gasiorek (1995: 150).

19 Rushdie (1981: 1).
20 Lively (1987: 1).
21 *Ibid.* 22.
22 Rushdie (1991: 10).
23 See Belsey's essay in Widdowson.
24 Mulhern (1989: 251, 253).
25 Leavis & Thompson (1964: 93-98).
26 In Walker (1981: 4).
27 In Waugh (1995: 153).
28 In Baldick (1983: 95).
29 See Connor (1996: 107-108).
30 Begley (1993: 36).
31 Clark (1999: 219, 220).

## *Bibliography*


Baldick, Chris: *The Social Mission of English Criticism, 1848-1932*, Oxford, 1983.

Barnes, Julian: *Flaubert's Parrot*, London, 1984.

Barry, Peter: *Beginning Theory. An Introduction to Literary and Cultural Theory*, 2d ed., Manchester & New York, 2002.

Begley, Adam: "Raiders of the Lost Archives", *Lingua Franca* July/August 1993, 36-40.

Bergonzi, Bernard: *Exploding English. Criticism, Theory, Culture*, Oxford, 1990.

Byatt, A.S.: *Possession. A Romance*, London & New York, 1990.

Clark, Timothy: "Literature and the Crisis in the Concept of the University". – In David Fuller & Patricia Waugh (Eds.): *The Arts and Sciences of Criticism*, Oxford, 1999, pp. 217-237.

Connor, Steven: *The English Novel in History, 1950-1995*, London & New York, 1996.

Currie, Mark: *Postmodern Narrative Theory*, New York, 1998.

Gasiorek, Andrzej: *Post-War British Fiction. Realism and After*, London & New York, 1995.

Ishiguro, Kazuo: *The Remains of the Day*, London, 1989.

Leavis, F.R. & Denys Thompson: *Culture and Environment. The Training of Critical Awareness*, London, 1964.

Lively, Penelope: *Moon Tiger*, Harmondsworth, 1987.

Mulhern, Francis: "English reading". – In Homi Bhabha (Ed.): *Nation and Narration*, London, 1989, pp. 250-264.

Richter, David: *Falling into Theory. Conflicting Views on Reading Literature*, 2d ed., Boston, 2000.

Rushdie, Salman: *Midnight's Children*, London, 1981.

---: "Imaginary Homelands". – In S.R.: *Imaginary Homelands. Essays and*

*Criticism 1981-1991*, London, 1991, pp. 9-21.
Swift, Graham: *Waterland*, London, 1983.
Walker, Martin: "English Lit. policy splits Cambridge", *Manchester Guardian Weekly* 25, 1981, 4.
Waugh, Patricia: *Metafiction. The Theory and Practice of Self-Conscious Fiction*, London & New York, 1984.
---: *Harvest of the Sixties. English Literature and Its Background 1960-1990*, Oxford & New York, 1995.
Widdowson, Peter (Ed.): *Re-Reading English*, London, 1982.

*Ruth McElroy (Liverpool)*

# Bringing it Home: Devolution, Multiculturalism and British Students' Voices

This essay aims to explore how the reading of contemporary British writing creates a space for the articulation of ideas of home, place and belonging. Such a trajectory does not entail regarding contemporary British fiction merely as the site for the making of national identity – an example of the role of English Literature in the 'Forging of the Nation' as it were; rather its broader aim is to investigate the occasion for thinking and speaking of location that the readerly relationship with text and other readers offers, specifically within the context of a course in British higher education.[1] The specific analysis below is based upon the experience f teaching one particular class, "Writing Britain", a one-semester module for final year undergraduates at University College Worcester. The plurality of national identity is one reason why British students may find it difficult to articulate and assess the symbolic meanings of Britain and Britishness, a difficulty that in my pedagogic experience is heightened when discussing a specifically English identity. The recent reformulations of the British political state, together with Britain's experience of being a post-imperial state, provides the broader historical context for the current debates on English national identity. 1997, the year that Labour finally came to power after nineteen years of Conservative rule, witnessed devolution referenda in Scotland and Wales, which lead to the establishment of a Scottish parliament in Edinburgh and a Welsh Assembly in Cardiff. In this context, questions of what it meant to be English were routinely aired both in the media and via the publishing industry with a flurry of publications including Julian Barnes' *England, England* (1998), Simon Heffer *Nor Shall My Sword: The Reinvention of England* (1999), Jeremy Paxman *The English: A Portrait of a People* (1998), Michael Wood *In*

*Search of England: Journeys into the English Past* (2000) and Tony Linsell (Ed.) *Our Englishness* (2000). Whilst the politics of English identity and belonging, both within a British and specifically English context, have been debated in public for several years, tensions and confusion endure in their articulation.

One route into negotiating these tensions is to provide spaces for the articulation of different types of talk. These may include the autobiographical mode, which may allow students to establish more forceful, enabling relationships with literary texts that seek to clarify not simplify the cultural dynamics of what it means to live in and write of Britain. Rather than seeing the personal voice as a distraction from the serious business of reading and analyzing literary texts, we might concur with Anthony Easthope in his remark that such shifts of tone are themselves an effect of the subject matter:

> It is no surprise that the topic of nation comes so close to those who write about it that they feel compelled to break the usual decorum of academic impersonality and say something about themselves [...] these lapses into autobiography [...] illustrate how plural national identity is.[2]

## *1. "Writing Britain": The Module and its Concerns*

"Writing Britain" was a one-semester module for final year undergraduates at University College Worcester. It was taught by means of a single three-hour long session that I could divide into lectures, workshops and seminars. Thirty students were registered on the module and all were taught as part of the same single group, as was routine within the department. The students ranged in age from their early twenties to retired students. The presence of a significant minority of mature students shapes the dynamic of any classroom, and in this module functioned both pragmatically – for example, an agreement was reached to begin the class a few minutes later in order to facilitate childcare arrangements – and culturally, as when students could make points of personal connection across the generations of the writers studied. Although Writing Britain was aimed primarily at students following one of several pathways in English literary studies – including taking the subject as a joint or minor element in their BA degrees – it was also open to students from cognate fields including Media & Cultural Studies, Sociology, and Visual Arts. As noted by several contributors to the events and publications of the English Subject Centre, the process of modularization that has occurred in most quarters of British higher education means that we are increasingly likely to find ourselves teaching literature to students who are also involved in the study of other subjects.[3] Modularization may not produce interdisciplinarity, but it does affect a particular kind of multidisciplinary context, one that both tests and enriches the study of contemporary fiction. For example, one mature middle-aged male student, majoring in visual arts, approached me before the first class to discuss his anxieties concerning the module, which would present him with the first occasion in which to study literary texts since having been at school. The experience of English had not been a positive one for him, entailing what he remembered as a prescriptive curriculum of texts and 'proper' readings. Nonetheless he was at pains to point out that 'outside' of the HE context, he was an avid reader and it was this experience of readerly pleasure – together with a desire to overcome such long-standing educational demons – that was driving him to take the module. I mention this example for two main reasons. Firstly, it acted for me as a reminder of how complex our motives are for entering the literary classroom; we approach neither literary texts nor readerly communities without the history of prior encounters, some of which may be painful and difficult to articulate. There is a particular fragility to the moment on any new module when a group constitutes itself for the first time and readers find themselves with both familiar and unknown colleagues. This banal fact matters when engaging with texts – such as Hanif Kureishi's *The Buddha of Suburbia* which we studied on the module – that are themselves reflective accounts of what it means to belong, to be a part of a collective identity and group. Secondly, the perceived gap between reading for a degree and reading as a cultural pursuit is a common experience for lecturers in literary studies and is one which may map onto a hierarchy of on the one hand, canonical set texts that students can easily feel is complete and established, and on the other, texts chosen for the student's own bookshelf, which even if by canonical authors, may be less self-contained and more redolent of the readerly self. The contemporary focus of this module, together with feedback from students even at the early stages of teaching, meant that I was keen to find ways of bridging this gap, of enabling them to speak both to and with a canon still in formation.

This pedagogic concern derived in part from my own research into questions of sexual/national identity and the place of literary texts. My involvement in a project in the late 1990s which resulted in a collection of essays edited by Lynne Pearce entitled *Devolving Identities: Feminist readings in Home and Belonging* (2000) was instructive in seeing how contributors put literary texts to startlingly different uses in their analysis of home and belonging. As Pearce outlines in her editorial:

> Using literature in this way is not a new thing, especially within the realm of contemporary feminist scholarship [...]. What the writings of authors like Butler, Harraway and Probyn have given us, above all, is a new model of how the text-reader relation can be used to make sense of the world(s) we inhabit: and, in particular, the way in which we can creatively combine the texts of others with the textual productions of 'the self' to gain a new perspective on our complex 'locatedness' within contemporary culture.[4]

For some, this may read like a de-aestheticization of the literary text and a move instead towards cultural therapy. Yet, as Chris Weedon argues, the encounter between reader and text is valuable precisely because it offers an imaginative space of encounter that transgresses the bounded divisions of everyday life:

> Fiction is an important medium for exploring questions of identity and belonging. It is also effective in giving readers some sense of what it is like to be the subject of racism, made other in negative ways by white society [...]. Telling and reading stories are key ways in which people make sense of their lives and imagine modes of living different from their own. Fiction allows for the exploration of emotions that are important in understanding racism both from the perspective of its perpetrators and its victims.[5]

"Writing Britain" asked students, "how do contemporary writers represent Britain?". Focusing upon post-war texts up to the present, the module explicitly centred questions of place, nation and belonging. This was a module not only about contemporary British writing, but also about the meanings of Britishness and the experience of inhabiting Britain today in terms both of textual representations, readerly responses and cultural identities. This initial ambition posed challenges. Whilst I had taught contemporary literature previously, the up-front nature of the national and locational focus was something I had never done in England. In preparing the module, I was struck by how frequently I turned back to my summer school teaching in Finland, where, in teaching courses on "Contemporary Wales" and "Multicultural Britain", I felt far freer to really begin from scratch, to trace the specificity of Britain as an object of study and – as importantly – to entwine televisual, filmic, and music texts with literature in a sustained rather than an occasional way.[6] Partly these concerns stem from the sense of pressure caused by the clash between numbers and pedagogy, or more frankly, the difficulties of delivering student-centred learning when there are barely enough chairs in the room. At the same time, however, I am struck how despite 1990s talk of re-branding Britain (the era of 'Cool Britannia'), British Studies *per se* seems not to have impacted substantially upon the English literary classroom, and this stands in contrast with the growth of both American Studies and Postcolonial Studies. In different ways, both these areas may appeal to students as 'something different' in the module marketplace. As Laura Chrisman argues:

> The field [of postcolonial studies] clearly holds a radical potential. It is often the first occasion for English departments to recognise the relevance of imperialism, race and ethnicity for the analysis of British literature. As such, postcolonial studies may provide the only sanctioned opportunity for students to interrogate racial and national identity production within a British and comparative Anglophone literary context.[7]

Of course, teachers of English in HE have been debating matters of nation and national identity across a broad historical spectrum, but it does strike me from where I stand that an avowedly interdisciplinary context for analysing Britain and Britishness seems to exist more strongly outside the UK.[8]

## *2. Managing Difference*

The specificity of generational experience is a striking feature of much contemporary British fiction – think here of the aged friends who people Graham Swift's *Last Orders*, or of the generational conflicts in Hanif Kureishi and Meera Syal's work. Reading generational difference facilitated generational classroom debate, which performed the task of unsettling the kind of consensus that can too readily emerge within British HE seminars. These differences were especially marked in the way younger and older students related to Britain as empire. Whilst most students acknowledged the historical fact of Empire, few seemed to 'take it personally' as it were, expressing no subjective or affective relation to its existence or aftermath. For the majority of younger students, the Empire was a long-distant historical fact; they recalled no mention of it in school or in their family lives and were by turn enthralled and shocked by the tales told by older students (in their late middle years and older) of school celebrations of Empire Day and of the pervasive discourse of imperial and national destiny that shaped their lives. Supported by extracts from Chew and Rutherford's *Unbecoming Daughters of the Empire* (1993) and video material of *The British Empire in Colour*, these exchanges of personal recollections militated against a simple disavowal of Empire that I had previously experienced in the majority white classroom. In talking of Empire, students often find the past to be a foreign country, an England that is 'not ours' but belongs to the past, the world of those 'who did not know better'. This disavowal may take many forms but often entails outright rejection of Empire and what it stood for and /or a bemused, quietly guilty sense of bewilderment at such a vast network of exploitation and complex, cultural discourse. Whilst both stances are re-assuring inasmuch as they signal a rejection of imperial nationalist conviction, they can act as an obstacle to exploring the consequences of Empire for all Britons today. Indeed, the disposition to dispense with Empire – especially as a determinant of one's own subject positioning – may itself be an enactment of white privilege. The testament of older white students made the privilege of 'moving on' from Empire that bit harder to retain, and in this way brought home this point more subtly than my teaching alone could have done.

A key concern in selecting texts for the module was to offer as wide a range of different kinds of places and forms of belonging – national, linguistic, racial and sexual – as could fit into a one-semester course. This left me with a familiar but enduring and uneasy paradox. On the one hand, one of the aims of the module was to explore critically the concepts of 'nation', 'identity' and 'belonging' so as to bring both a precision to classroom debate and thereby counter some of the easy stereotypes that are often to be heard in debates on Britishness and other forms of national identity.

If literature can do anything, it can complicate such simplifications by imaginatively detailing the complexities and ambiguities of our lives. On the other hand, in order to do this I had to select a range of texts to provoke such debates, texts that would inevitably perhaps end up being not only representations but also representative of the diverse locations that comprise the spaces of British cultural and literary belongings. To an extent, these dangers were forestalled by selecting more than one author or text from specific national contexts. So for example, in selecting both Sam Selvon's *The Lonely Londoners* and Hanif Kureishi's *The Buddha of Suburbia*, I aimed to provide students with literary representations of London and her suburbs that made clear the tremendous differences generation, sexuality, class and ethnicity make to fictional narratives of new belongings, to borrow Roger Bromley's phrase. Often I found myself creating mini-anthologies, most especially of Scottish and Welsh writing, in order to provide the heterogeneity of style as well as of politics. Whilst many students commented on their enjoyment of these 'new' texts, in module evaluations they repeatedly cited their relative inaccessibility as a problem. One student wrote, "my only negative comment is an over-reliance on hard-to-find texts is difficult to deal with as a student with little available time to hunt texts down!" The need to provide a diversity of literary materials was one of the more demanding aspects of the module. When asked as part of a group work exercise who were their favourite or most thought-provoking writers from Wales, the group of 30 (of whom all but one visiting French student were English) admitted that none of them had read a single text by a Welsh writer. This exercise both revealed to the students some of their own literary exclusions and revealed to me just how difficult it was going to be to situate Welsh writing in English within such a classroom context.

It is worth pausing here to point out that most English students educated in the state school system in England will not have been required to be taught Scottish or Welsh literary texts. If one takes even a cursory glance at the texts set by the English examination boards the A level (GCE) qualification in English Literature, it is striking that Scottish writers are virtually absent whilst Welsh writing appears only rarely, usually in the form of one or two poets such as Gillian Clarke or Edward Thomas. Black and Asian British writers do not fare especially well either, though the OCR board lists Zadie Smith's *White Teeth* as a set text, appearing however under the heading of 'Post-colonial Literature'.[9] This stands in contrast to the rather rich representation of Irish, American and post-colonial texts cited by the OCR and EDEXCEL which range from the key figures of American drama and fiction including Albhee, Fitzgerald, Miller and Morrison, to Irish writers from Wilde and Shaw to Heaney and Friel, and postcolonial writers such as Achebe, Ngugi and Walcott. The Welsh Joint Education Committee (WJEC) offers a far greater selection of Welsh writers, including poets such as Dylan Thomas, Dannie Abse, and Sheenagh Pugh, and fiction writers such as Emyr Humphreys and Glyn Jones. Nonetheless, Scottish writers remain notably absent which again contrasts with the appearance of Irish and North American writers such as Atwood, Friel, Steinbeck and Wilde, as well as canonical English writers from Shakespeare, Keats, Austen, Eliot and Hardy to Lawrence, Forster and Orwell. Comparisons between UK examination boards are difficult to make inasmuch as the papers vary from year to year. Nonetheless, it is salutary to realise that at the point most young people are choosing whether to study English literature in UK Higher Education, the majority will not have formally studied a Scottish or Welsh writer unless educated in one of these countries, and many will not have studied either a Black or Asian-British writer.

Introducing Scottish and Welsh writing in English to English students demands strategies for overcoming two different readerly tendencies, some of which may be common to first encounters with Black and Asian British writing.[10] One tendency is to regard such texts as indubitably strange. This results in positioning them variously as romanticised Celtic texts (as one student put it 'they are different over there'), or as hostile webs of linguistic and cultural complexity that may intrigue but are more likely to ensnare the unsuspecting reader. A second tendency is readily to incorporate them into the English literary tradition with the effect that the distinctive literary paradigms from which they emerge are eclipsed. The felt need to negotiate such standpoints can be discerned in the opening pages of some critical surveys of contemporary Scottish and Welsh fiction. For example, Cristie March begins her *Rewriting Scotland* thus:

> The picture of 'Scotland' that occurs to many, if not most, people involves kilts, bagpipes, green hills and thick Scottish brogues that appear in films such as *Braveheart* (with the occasional Highland cow thrown in for good measure). Similarly, the picture of Scottish writing that occurs involves Roberts Burns' romanticised visions of rustic love in the heather and Sir Walter Scott's historical novels celebrating the Highlands and Scottish heroes such as Bonnie Prince Charlie.[11]

Meanwhile, Stephen Knight begins his *A Hundred Years of Fiction* by claiming that, "[i]n 1900, Welsh fiction in English was basically a way for English readers to tour Wales without leaving the armchair", before taking us on a critical journey to demonstrate that such articulations were deeply colonial readings of Welsh difference.[12]

Faced with such challenges, my response felt inadequate. Too often I tried to compensate for a lack of knowledge by squeezing in too much material on both literary and cultural factors that shape literary production in Scotland and Wales, from questions of regional diversity and publishing, to matters of language and dialect. Whilst strategies to counter these difficulties were employed – the use of secondary sources on Scottish literature and the use of video interview material with the Welsh playwright Ian Rowlands, for example – the question of how to manage my teacherly self remained a persistent problem.[13] Misidentified by several students as Scottish and correctly identified by others as Welsh, my self could not – and at times, annoyingly would not – remain outside the classroom. This was both a strength and weakness of the teaching experience. Prepared to speak personally in the classroom, I nevertheless wanted to avoid acting or being interpellated as a guarantor of cultural credibility, a kind of 'if she says it and she's Welsh it must be true" scenario. There was then a tension between the authority of my own hierarchical position as tutor and my sense of being subject to a particular form of English discourse that cast all debates about Britishness in strictly English terms. On occasion, the English 'we' of discussions became so routine and forceful that I felt it intellectually and personally necessary to say no, not 'we' but 'you'. Disagreement thus entailed disidentification, and my refusal to sit within the 'we' risked reinforcing a you/me divide that might not only silence students, but also allow my voice greater credence than it would have in a more diverse classroom context. Such pronoun problems were fairly frequent, and the situational identification and disidentification of myself as tutor was a pressing dynamic in my experience of the classroom. Engendering confident and reflective debate within a relatively homogenous national group proved exceptionally difficult.

Finding ways to respond to these difficulties without either diminishing difference or aggrandising it to the extent of silencing students was one of the most challenging aspects of the module. Difference – literary and otherwise – is a difficult concept for students to handle in detail *as they learn* to use and critically reflect upon *in process* and not only after much learning has been done. Writing about the experience of being a gay man teaching gay and lesbian studies to a predominantly heterosexual group of students, Gregory Woods makes a not dissimilar point when he recalls the experience of one student whose response to the difficulties of difference was denial:

> I recently taught a gay cinema course at MA level in which one of the five students present kept returning discussion to the same base line: in her words, "We're all the same, so what's all the fuss about?" No amount of reminding that the majority of the filmmakers we were studying were celebrating difference rather than similarity could shift this student from an implacable liberal line which got us nowhere.[14]

This tendency to deny difference under the guise of liberal enlightenment is just one way in which the subtleties of our cultural locations and readerly selves are flattened. In the classroom context, as elsewhere, a persistent question is how to render what Raymond Williams memorably termed the "intimations of complexity" that shape our belongings and our selves.[15] In the following sections, I shall explore pedagogic examples of how I sought to do this.

## 3. *Mapping*

> That the Science of Cartography Is Limited
>
> – and not simply by the fact that this shading of
> forest cannot show the fragrance of balsam,
> the gloom of cypresses
> is what I wish to prove.[16]

Eavan Boland's poem speaks to the mutability of maps and their partial rendering of place – its contours, memories and meanings. Maps are useful artefacts for the analysis of locational identities and belongings. With this in mind, I began the first seminar of the module with a mapping activity. I asked students to do the following:

1) Draw a map of Britain
2) List 4 keywords, which occur to you when you hear the name "Britain". When you are happy with your choice, write these over your map of Britain.
3) List 2/3 characteristics of contemporary Britain, which you think are the most important or meaningful. These can include the ways in which British culture and society has changed in the past 50 years.
4) List a couple of contemporary British writers whose work you enjoy and/or find interesting. Briefly explain why.
5) Compare your responses to 1-4 with the person next to you. What are the main points of agreement and disagreement? What was the map's effect in terms of how you saw Britain? What struck you about the other person's map and lists?

Despite giggles and protestations of not being able to draw, the exercise engaged students and was a revealing and productive starting point for exploring the links between representation and location. Many students expressed their concern, surprise and often shame at not being able to draw a map of their own country. Many of the maps were substantially inaccurate; Wales, Scotland, Cornwall and East Anglia were frequently distorted in shape and in relation to the rest. Wales and Scotland were often represented as much smaller than in standard maps. I had chosen the term 'Britain' specifically, both because of the module's focus, but also because I feared that the students would unconsciously slip between national, geographic and state terms (Britain, British Isles, England, the United Kingdom) without being aware of the political differences between these terms. Several maps of Britain figured Northern Ireland and a handful drew the Republic of Ireland. Such inaccuracies are unsurprising when we consider that the map of us see most routinely – the weather map on television screens – often shows these islands together.

When it came to the keywords, it was as interesting to note the words where written as what they were. I was struck by how over-written England was and how, in comparison, many students steered clear of writing their words over Scotland and Wales. The words used ranged from cues to stereotypes to actual places such as 'football', 'hooligans', 'countryside' and 'London'. But it was also the case that students wrote 'Multicultural' and 'diverse', as well as 'cool', 'music' and 'Americanised'. A significant minority struggled to write any words and were resistant to doing so, and this in itself, I felt to be legitimate and provocative. When it came to listing authors, the majority listed popular fiction (e.g. various 'chicklit' texts) although many confessed that they had not read that many contemporary British authors. This stood in tension with the reason several gave for taking the module; as one student put it: "I want to get an insight into the writing of where we live."

Overall the exercise rendered the imaginary geographies of the students' minds in ways that would bring home to us the different Britains that we Britons carry in our minds. Rather than looking for homogenous, atlas-perfect renditions, I was interested in seeing how the diversity and mutability of maps might provide a route into exploring the mutability of locational belonging, and of different forms of identity including those based on nation, race and ethnicity. Pedagogically, it was also an attempt to ensure that differences of outlook emerged from the beginning, but in a way that would not entail personal one-on-one disagreement of spoken views, something that many British students are reluctant to undertake, especially when the subject matter lends itself to a personal or subjective stance. Whilst I could have asked students to talk about what they thought of Britain today, their own place and identities within it, I suspect the responses would have been more minimal and guarded than the gregarious response to each other's maps, which deflected critical attention from the personal in favour of the representational. Such potential difficulties are hardly surprising for our identities do not exist, nor are they inhabited, purely at a conscious level of articulation, neither are they singular or settled. Moreover, whilst the demand to tell one's story and situate one's self may be a useful, possibly even a radical pedagogic technique, it may also reproduce the very structures of power that one is seeking to reveal and deconstruct. As Beverley Skeggs argues under the heading, "Forcing the working class to tell themselves", telling stories of one's self need not be either a politically positive or neutral act:

> The concept of the self (in particular, the reflexive, knowing, inner self) is a specific historical production, enabled through particular methodologies: forced telling for welfare for the working-class, and authorial exhibitionism for the middle-class. However, this is not a straightforward story, for feminism, and gay and lesbian politics have employed similar methods of telling in order to make political claims. Notwithstanding this dissident divergence [...] the techniques of telling for the middle-class rely on accruing the stories of others, in order to make them into property for one's self.[17]

Talking about oneself is a culturally framed discourse, as Chrisman reflects in her experience of teaching British students at the University of Sussex:

> The willingness and ability to publicly disclose and discuss subject positioning – something integral to postcolonial studies – does not come easily, I have found, to literature students at Sussex of any nationality other than American. Classroom reticence does not extend to written work; when invited to students in my postcolonial courses usually eagerly seize the opportunity to compose non-assessed written analyses of their subject-positioning and how it relates to the field of study. Within the classroom discussion, however, such disclosures are rare, and this means that discussions of cultural difference, of subalternity and dominance can remain at a fairly 'safe' level of abstraction, a theoretical discourse commanded by the most comfortably metropolitan students.[18]

## 4. *Literature, Talk and the Reflexive Self*

The opposition drawn by Chrisman between the oral and written is familiar but possibly unhelpful. It disaggregates what goes on in the weekly classroom from what gets turned in midway through, or at the end of the course. Regimes of assessment may demand this, but pedagogically we would aspire to maintain a link between the shared development of ideas and the individual assessed work. Otherwise, we are likely to find an insurmountable chasm between a purely instrumental approach to learning and a more enduring critical practice. Though regular seminar contributions (as opposed to oral presentations or papers) are rarely formally assessed in British HE seminars, their value is immense inasmuch as they form the site for the practice of forms of talk that are likely to enable students to make sense of their own subjectivities and analyze their social relations and cultural practices. I want to value highly the oral as well as written contributions of students and not reduce them to the minor pre-cursors of the written work that is deemed more important. Talk – as opposed to telling – also catches the nature of the political debate which these texts engendered and which the students produced in dialogue with one another. In reviewing the module evaluations, what strikes me is how often students refer implicitly to their own talk and the challenges it engendered for them as people and as readers of selected literary texts:

> A very thought provoking module which has really made me question my own beliefs and at this point left me feeling rather confused! Not a module I shall go away and forget! Really appreciated the openness of the assignments; the chance to do some creative writing was good.
>
> The module has been one of the most useful to me in terms of 'education' as a person beyond studying for a degree. Issues of how to negotiate equality and difference are issues I have strong feelings about, and this module has informed and challenged these opinions.
>
> An incredibly interesting module. Felt that it was not trying to be politically correct – but acknowledged the diversity of culture and identity. Thoughtful and provoking. Asked us to challenge and reinvent ideas of identity. Texts challenged preconceived ideas about culture.

As this final comment suggests, challenge, anxiety and a concern as to what was sayable were shared characteristics. A ghost at the feast of our literary readings was 'political correctness'. Without digressing into the political problems thrown up by the advance of this phrase, it is worth noting that students invoked this spectre both from a critical position – the notion of the political right refuting the voices of marginalised authors, for example – but more commonly through a concern of how they themselves should or could speak. Many students stepped gingerly into debates where race, ethnicity and nation needed to be spoken. Such awkwardness may itself be revealing both of white anxieties in talking of race, and of the privilege many white subjects enjoy in not thinking of ourselves as raced at all. Importantly, however, the challenge of how to talk about racial, ethnic and national difference was taken out of the classroom when we went down as a group to visit the British Empire and Commonwealth Museum in Bristol.[19] Here students encountered, through both curatorial talks, display materials and press coverage of the museum's opening, evidence of how the challenge to talk of Britain's imperial history and its enduring legacy was a shared, public concern. Classroom discussion over how authors and readers might represent our identities and sense of belonging (or not) were thus linked to the wider public sphere; students recognised that their literary talk was public, was itself a form of cultural criticism rather than being a mere adjunct to the 'real thing'.

If the museum visit sought to transgress the boundaries between the classroom and so-called 'real' world, then the module also sought to transgress the boundary between authorship and readerly consumption so as to instigate in students a sense of themselves as imaginative authors of British literary representations. For this reason, the first of two assignments on the module (weighted 40% and 60% respectively) offered students the opportunity to engage in a piece of creative writing. The assignment brief read thus:

a) Taking 'Britain, Place and Belonging' as your inspiration, write your own piece of creative writing.
b) Write a self-reflexive piece critically analysing your creative writing. You should explore how it compares/contrasts in its writing of Britain with that of any of the literary texts studies so far.

The first part of the brief was designed to provide a broad focus or prompt for students' writing, without restricting excessively their responses to the module and its thematic concerns. As a reader too, I wanted to avoid endless stories of 'What it means to be British' or 'Living in Worcester today'. The second part of the brief was partly a conservative attempt to forestall problems of how to grade creative pieces on a module that was not about creative writing *per se*. More positively, I used the pairing as a way of trying to foster in students the sense of being a part of a literary exploration. Substantial time was allocated in class to discuss this basic brief in more detail. This included clarifying that any genre of writing was acceptable, and that aesthetic merit would be credited but was not the sole or determining factor in allocating a final grade. It also afforded students time to discuss what a self-reflexive critical analysis might entail, both conceptually and stylistically. In particular, I sought to make clear that the critical analysis should not be a purely descriptive account of what they wrote, but should instead seek to read from the inside the work produced as a textual representation open to the kinds of analysis (of narrative, perspective, character and language) that we might readily employ in reading the set texts. As John Parnham argues, a reflexive pedagogy requires "explanation (in formal sessions) of how to do reflexive work [and] discussion of and openness about its purpose".[20] Many students took some persuading of my openness to their writing; this was understandable inasmuch as many had not written creatively for public view and because these were third-year students whose grades would count heavily towards determining their final degrees classifications. For this reason, I felt it important to preserve the option for students of writing a traditional essay even for this first assignment should they wish to, though in the end, the majority of students did not.

The imaginative license afforded students enabled many to test some of the ideas encountered on the module and to make them their own by forming them in a world of their own making. Most students avoided the more obvious pitfalls of writing purely about themselves (most did not write in the first-person), but sought to draw a social world shaped by differential degrees of belonging. So, for example, Lucie, a visiting French student, wrote a short story based on the friendship of a white Eastern European and Asian immigrant to Britain. It allowed for some careful observation of everyday English life, and provided a space to think about the difference race may make to immigrant experience. A male mature student, Russell, took the question of home as his structuring principle for a visual/poetic series on homelessness, articulating both critical views of local press coverage of homelessness and flagging up local racial divides over welfare provision. Formally balanced and stylistically measured, the series brought home to both author and reader the immediacy of what Jatinder Verma has described as the multicultural abrasions of contemporary British life.[21] The ongoing negotiation over how to speak of racialised conflict in sensitive sites, including in this a hostel where the student worked, extended in far greater depth and subtlety the question of how to speak of difference in a predominantly conservative, white city. For a minority of students, the creative piece entailed an autobiographical reflection upon home and their own former belongings. For example, Susan, a student in her 40s, sought for the first time to write in the Midlands dialect her adoptive family encouraged her to discard as part of her class mobility. Reclaiming this language, Susan's work was formally innovative in its rendering of dialect, and a thoughtful meditation on the costs of moving from a working-class life and community.

In his analysis of teaching in cultural studies, Parnham found the "reflexive project was unsuccessful because coursework was either conventionally theoretical or uncritically autobiographical".[22] Thus:

> I read moving essays that positively affirmed schooling as an escape from family pressures (and expectations). School was viewed as a site for 'personal development', 'self-realization' and the exercise of 'personal choice' away from parental control. Neither perspective, however, reflected on the ideological function of the education system [...] so, for example, a generally excellent presentation on sex education in schools ends up dismissing the political, governmental context as irrelevant because the presentation was about 'our learning and our selves'.[23]

Although some very fine, eloquent and moving pieces of creative writing were produced, many students struggled to produce an equally engaging critical piece. Students who allowed themselves the freedom to write imaginatively in the creative section often displayed a rather plodding and descriptive tone in the critical section. Sometimes students seemed to force connections of affinity rather than difference between their own work and the literary texts studied, whilst others – despite advice to the contrary – regarded the critical section as a slightly more formal continuation of the first. Often, the assignments betrayed a lack of time allocated to the second section, and it may be that it would be better to signal a specific percentage for each of the two components separately and/or to set different deadlines for the submission of each piece. With some exceptions, few students proved to be as astute in reading their own work as they were in reading literary texts.

These difficulties are understandable. It is after all an extremely difficult thing to reflect upon one's own work intellectually, imaginatively and culturally, and this is especially so soon after having first produced it. Many of us may be poor readers of our own work, yet we rarely need to make such a process visible outwith the piece of writing itself. Moreover, finding a voice in which to speak of one's output is itself testing of the self, of the 'I' who is learning to speak. This skilled use of the 'I' was a form of writing that students had not mastered because they had not practiced it, having been rigorously schooled not to use the first person for many years.

## *5. Conclusion*

In the 2004 UK general election, the British National Party put up an increased number of candidates, including in the city where this module was taught. Today, in the metropolitan city where I now teach, another Black teenager is being buried following a racially motivated attack.[24] The need for literary scholars to offer students imaginative and political insights into the lives of all British subjects seems in such a context to be especially pressing. This is not to suggest that the reading and writing of British fiction should be reduced to political tracts devoid of aesthetic pleasures. Moreover, sympathetic engagement alone need not engender substantive transformations of readers' civic practice. As Kimberly Chabot Davis argues in her analysis of Oprah Winfrey's book club, "cross-racial sympathy can often delve into a colonising appropriation".[25] Nonetheless, as she argues, "empathy is an active cognitive process of imagination that can play an important role in catalysing action".[26] Taking the literary texts and talk beyond the confines of the classroom into the realm of public debate, creative reflection, and cultural critique of the categories of differences that form and bind us, is a challenging task routinely undertaken. We need to continue to ask how to make the literary work for us at a time when the question of British belongings are at times matters of life and death.

## *Notes*

1 My use of this term refers to Linda Colley's celebrated volume, *Britons: Forging the nation.*

2 Easthope (1999: 30).

3 The English Subject Centre is part of the Higher Education Academy and supports the teaching of English at this level in the UK. Details can be found at its website [http://www.english.ltsn.ac.uk] (30 August 2005).

4 Pearce (2000: 28).

5 Weedon (2004: 61-62).

6 These summer schools were run by the British Council in conjunction with the Professional Association for Teachers of English in Finland in 1998 and 1999.

7 Chrisman & Phillips (1999: 4)

8 These are of course, merely personal impressions; Mark Addis' and Philip Tew's ongoing English Subject Centre project, "Teaching the contemporary: fiction" will shortly provide more analytic evidence on the state of the subject.

9 The A level is an advanced, non-compulsory qualification normally taken by 16-18 year olds. The Scottish education system's equivalent (which is not identical) is the Advanced Higher Grade. In England, three examination boards are responsible for setting examination papers, Edexcel, OCR and AQA, (details of websites are listed in the bibliography below). In Wales, the exam board is the WJEC but it should be noted that schools in England may opt to set a WJEC paper. Set texts were accessible online only for the Edexcel, OCR and WJEC boards.

10 See the forthcoming English Subject Centre event on "Teaching Scottish and Irish Literature."

11 March (2002: 1).

12 Knight (2004: xi).

13 The video, though aimed at school age students, proved exceptionally useful in countering student assumptions regarding both cultural and authorial questions. The video was part of The English Programme titled Writers from Wales and published by Channel 4 Learning.

14 Woods (2002: 53).

15 Williams (1985: 19).

16 Boland in the *Norton Anthology of Poetry* (fourth edition).

17 Skeggs (2004: 119).

18 Chrisman in Chrisman & Phillips (1999: 9).

19 Details of the museum may be found on its website [http://www.empiremuseum.co.uk] (30 August 2005).

20 Parnham (2002: 476).

21 Verma (2001: 6).

22 Parnham (2002: 475).

23 *Ibid.* 467.

24 Anthony Walker, an 18 year old young man was murdered in Huyton, Liverpool, on July 29th, 2005. Recalling the murder in Eltham, South London in 1993 of Stephen Lawrence, Anthony Walker was waiting (with his cousin and his white girlfriend) at a bus stop when attacked by a group of white men.

25 Chabot Davis (2004: 399).
26 *Ibid.* 404.

## *Bibliography*


Barnes, Julian: *England, England*, London, 1998.

Boland, Eavan: "That the Science of Cartography is Limited" in Margaret Ferguson, Mary Jo Salter & Jon Stallworthy (Eds.) *The Norton Anthology of Poetry*, fourth edition, London & New York 1996, p.1819.

Chabot Davis, Kimberly: "Oprah's Book Club and the Politics of Cross-Racial Empathy", *International Journal of Cultural Studies* 7, no. 4, 2004, 399-419.

Chew, Shirley & Anna Rutherford (Eds.): *Unbecoming Daughters of Empire*, Sydney, 1993.

Chrisman, Laura & Lawrence Phillips: "Postcolonial Studies and the British Academy", *Jouvert* 3, no. 3, [http://social.chass.ncsu.edu/jouvert/v3i3/con33.htm] (22 November 2005).

Colley, Linda: *Britons: Forging the Nation, 1707-1837*, Yale, 1992.

Easthope, Anthony: *Englishness and National Culture*, London & New York, 1999.

Heffer, Simon: *Nor Shall My Sword: The Reinvention of England*, London, 1999.

Knight, Stephen: *A Hundred Years of Fiction*, Cardiff, 2004.

Kureishi, Hanif: *The Buddha of Suburbia,* London, 1990.

Linsell, Tony: *Our Englishness*, Hockwold, 2000.

March, Cristie: *Rewriting Scotland*, Manchester, 2002.

Parekh, Bikhu (Ed.): *The Future of Multi-Ethnic Britain*, London: 2000.

Parnham, John: "Teaching Pleasure: Experiments in cultural studies and pedagogy", *International Journal of Cultural Studies* 5, no. 4, 2002, 461-478.

Paxman, Jeremy: *The English: A Portrait of a People*, London, 1999.

Pearce, Lynne: *Devolving Identities: Feminist Readings in Home and Belonging*, Aldershot, 2000.

Selvon, Sam: *The Lonely Londoners*, London, 1979 [Original: 1956].

Skeggs, Beverely: *Class, Self, Culture*, London & New York, 2004.

Smith, Zadie: *White Teeth*, London, 2002.

Swift, Graham: *Last Orders*, London, 1999.

Verma, Jatinder: "Braids and Theatre Practice", *EnterText* 2, no. 1, 2001-2002 [http://www.brunel.ac.uk/about/acad/sa/artresearch/entertext/issues/entertext2_1] (30 August 2005).

Weedon, Chris: *Identity and Culture: narratives of Difference and Belonging*, Maidenhead & New York, 2004.

Williams, Raymond: "Wales and England". – In John Osmond (Ed.): *The National Question Again: Welsh Political Life in the 1980s*, Llandysul, 1985.
Wood, Michael: *In Search of England: Journeys into the English Past*, London: 2000.
Woods, Greg: "Educationally Queer: Teaching Lesbian and Gay Studies", *Changing English* 9, no. 1, 2002, 47-57.

*Robert Bond (London)*

# Culture, Materialism and Contemporary Democracies: Teaching Recent British Fiction

## *1. Introduction: The Theory of Teaching Recent British Fiction*

This article addresses some of the tensions that I have experienced teaching contemporary British fiction – at London South Bank University and at the University of Westminster – from a broadly cultural materialist perspective, soon after preparing my doctorate – in Cambridge, on the contemporary London writer Iain Sinclair – from a broadly cultural Marxist viewpoint. The transition from studying and applying the neo-Marxist theoretical insights of Theodor Adorno and Walter Benjamin, to teaching along the lines of a cultural materialism such as Alan Sinfield's, is not an unproblematic shift to effect; and it has made me reflect in particular on my conception of our contemporary democracy. Whereas the cultural Marxism in which I was trained tends to stress our shared unfreedom under capitalism, Sinfield's *Literature Politics and Culture in Postwar Britain* (1997) emphasises that some social groups are more unfree than others, and prompted in me the anxiety that a cultural Marxism which aims for the critique of a monolithic, totalised domination may be insufficiently attentive to the complexity, for instance of the experiences of varying sexualities and ethnicities, which constitutes our contemporary democracy. What I want to suggest in this article, though, is that the potential opposition between a cultural materialism alert to the social complexity of our contemporary democracy, and a cultural Marxism which is largely inert or unresponsive to it, is a false and misleading opposition, and one that we can move beyond when teaching recent British fiction.

Many of these concerns crystallised in our class on Malcolm Bradbury's *The History Man* (1975). Bradbury's novel is of course deeply antipathetic to Marxism, and sets out to expose the degeneration of the promise of social liberation which the Left made in the late 1960s, into an extremist vulgar Marxism, which is embodied by the sociologist Howard Kirk. Bradbury suggests that the potential for social freedom is now replaced by an authoritarian form of academic sociology, and has the student George Carmody complain that in Kirk's classes there is no longer any democracy. The 'consensus model' – which, for Sinfield, would legitimate the postwar, welfare-capitalist stage of liberal democratic society – is suggested by Carmody to be in tatters within the Marxist classroom: "But better not conflict with Dr Kirk. Oh no, it's not a consensus model for his classes all right. I mean, we're democratic, and we vote, but no dirty old conservative standpoints here. Sociology's revolutionary, and we'd better agree. "[1] The prevalence of Marxist sociology is thus blamed by Bradbury for the collapse, within the university setting, of the "consensus model" which structures our contemporary democracy. The classroom is in fact not 'democratic' really, and the individual's vote has become an irrelevance, Bradbury suggests. Indeed *The History Man* also attributes the supposed decline of the liberal humanist concept of individualism, to the rise of Marxist sociology. The novel satirically seeks to contest Kirk's vulgar Marxist reduction of individuals' contingent, plural and complex experiences to their determination by invariant socioeconomic forces, and shows that, though Kirk is a stern critic of liberal individualism and private property, he still keeps his van locked safely and the manuscript of his book *The Defeat of Privacy* carefully out of sight.

My worry is that a Bradbury-like accusation that Marxism in the university threatens the liberal humanist concept of pluralist individualism – which supports the consensus model of our democracy – could continue to determine the way we estimate our potential to teach from a Marxist viewpoint. The argument could certainly be made that it was precisely fear of vulgar Marxism *à la* Howard Kirk, which contributed to the rise of cultural materialism *à la* Sinfield; and I worry that a continuing fear of Kirk may continue to make us resist – or fail to develop – cultural Marxist methods. For perhaps there is indeed a residual, semi-conscious confusion of cultural Marxism with vulgar Marxism to which we are prey, which programmes us to conceive of cultural Marxism as no more than a species of socio-economic determinism, and so to think of Adorno's methods, say, as being just as unsympathetic to the complexity of plural individualities which constitutes our contemporary democracy, as Kirk's were shown to be. It is worth repeating, therefore, that the rebellion against sociological determinism, and the emphasis on the autonomy of culture, are fundamental to the project of philosophical aesthetics, which Adorno initiated in his *Aesthetic Theory*. Further, in Adorno's attempt to rescue the modernist artwork's illusory claim to be nonexchangeable, or to resist the reduction of the work to the status of a commodity bound and reified within the system of capitalist exchange, we can perhaps identify a model for our own attempt to free our plural, autonomous individualities from their reifying reduction to labour value, and from the web of property relations within which we remain absorbed.

We could also wonder whether the methods of cultural materialism truly are responsive to the complexity of plural individualities which constitutes our contemporary democracy, and sufficient for the liberation of our autonomous identities from their pre-set, reified functions within the capitalist economy. Sinfield's 1981 article "Against Appropriation" appeared to propose a method which could be concerned to release autonomous identities, when it argued that "the real relevance of literature (variously defined) resides precisely in its *otherness*", and asserted the value of literature as "a perfect vehicle for [...] cultural anthropology". Yet by the time of *Literature Politics and Culture in Postwar Britain*, I would argue, Sinfield's cultural materialism, rather than attending to literary texts as expressions of other identities, and emphasising the works' varying formal autonomies, instead simply reduces those works to their sociological relation to a normative social context. In 1997 Sinfield wrote, quite uncomplainingly, that after the failure of welfare-capitalism "cultural materialists have been led to insist that art and literature contribute to the processes whereby cultural norms come to seem plausible, even necessary – the processes through which the prevailing power arrangements are legitimated and called into question"[2] For cultural materialism now, art's function has become entirely sociological, reactive and truly lacking in autonomy: to be that which props up (or occasionally seeks to undermine) a given, normalised and normative social landscape: the 'cultural norms'. The absolute indivisibility of 'cultural norms' from 'prevailing power arrangements' – Sinfield's subsumption of culture within domination – of course itself further contributes to the quietening of autonomous creativities within the sociologising model of cultural materialism.

We can argue, then, that whilst cultural materialism claims to reflect and uphold the complexity of plural individualities which constitutes our contemporary democracy, it in fact reduces our individualities to a fixed array of stabilised and normalised social identities – hence erasing precisely the '*otherness*' within ourselves – and replaces cultural criticism with identity politics. Looking back on the first edition of *Literature Politics and Culture in Postwar Britain* in his 1997 essay "The Politics and Cultures of Discord", Sinfield presents his book as a celebratory description of the rise of identity politics – the "more political dynamic" – which was attendant upon the post war collapse of the liberal cultural consensus.

> I described how, in the 1960s and 1970s, youthful, class-mobile impatience with the solemnity and triviality of leisure-class culture collaborated with commercial pressures to undermine the consensual cultural hierarchies that had masqueraded as 'universal', and to replace them, either with a more political dynamic (as in feminism, ethnic subcultures and lesbian and gay subcultures), or with an allegedly undifferentiated postmodernist collage [...]. Lately, these tendencies have accelerated.

The significant difficulty is that Sinfield unquestioningly assumes that, *in itself*, identity politics is "more political", or more radical than left-liberalism: he simply *assumes* that it offers an effective critique of the capitalist system. For Sinfield "the collapse of the post war consensus exposed the vulnerability of many customary left-liberal assumptions, while opening the way for a broader critique of the cultural apparatus". But does Sinfield's study really offer such a broader critique – for instance of the 'commercial pressures' which, in the 1960s and 1970s, structured the atomization of authorised culture into the commodities offered by competing identities? Perhaps within cultural materialism it is precisely the unreflective reliance upon identity politics, or the foregrounding of a reified array of stabilised and normalised social identities, which *inhibits* a broader critique of the cultural apparatus. Drew Milne, voicing Adorno's position, has noted that such an unreflective celebration of particular identities fails to recognise the way in which all identities are warped by social unfreedom, and so can only reinforce that unfreedom: "particularity is a general category the celebration of which prematurely sustains the generality of an unreconciled totality."[3]

Sinfield's cultural materialism gestures toward the commercial pressures which sparked the cultural production now undertaken by particular identities competing within the global market, but cultural materialism cannot effectively critique that market, so long as it continues itself to reify particular identities as pre-set interest-groups of producers and consumers. Whilst these lines of Adorno's from "Cultural Criticism and Society" (1967) could be accused of a sociologising impulse too, their identification of the reduction of "private life" to "an appendage of the social process", works as a critique of the reification of contemporary identities into stabilised interest-groups, which cultural materialism simply endorses:

> The illusory importance and autonomy of private life conceals the fact that private life drags on only as an appendage of the social process. Life transforms itself into the ideology of reification – a death mask. Hence, the task of criticism must be not so much to search for the particular interest-groups to which cultural phenomena are to be assigned, but rather to decipher the general social tendencies which are expressed in these phenomena and through which the most powerful interests realise themselves.[4]

Whereas Adorno here recommends a truly critical uncovering of the socio-historical processes which are expressed in cultural artefacts, the Gramsci quotation with which Sinfield opens his book – as a pointer towards his own intended cultural materialist method – recommends instead an uncritical, fundamentally complicit tracing of the reifying historical process which has moulded fixed, essentialised identities:

> In acquiring one's conception of the world one always belongs to a particular grouping which is that of all the social elements which share the same mode of thinking and acting. [...] The starting-point of critical elaboration is the consciousness of what one really is, and is "knowing thyself" as a product of the historical process to date which has deposited in you an infinity of traces, without leaving an inventory.[5]

The particular cultural materialist call for recovery of particularist identities – 'what one really is' – is unhelpful, I believe, because without also offering an effective critique of the reification or stabilization of those identities within the capitalist economy, it can only further consolidate the reifying process. The market-led dissolution of our contemporary democracy into fixed, competing interest-groups of producers and consumers becomes visible within the contemporary fiction classroom when, already separated outside the classroom, students of differing ethnicities, let us suppose, are disinclined to collaborate with '*otherness*' – with ethnically-other students – within this pedagogic environment. This difficulty in the classroom does not seem to be fundamentally altered by instructing students to read Sinfield and 'know thyself'. It might just begin to be solved by helping students to think more critically about the society, the theory and the fiction which would continue to reify our identities.

## *2. Classroom Conventionalities: Smith, Rushdie and the False Freedoms of Migrancy*

We could, for instance, note that one important way in which current cultural materialist methods in fact reconfirm for students the stabilization of our social identities, and precisely whilst claiming to provide students with exemplary images of fluid, unfixed, de-reified identities, is by uncritically endorsing the treatment of migrancy and rootlessness within recent novels such as Salman Rushdie's *The Satanic Verses* (1988) and Zadie Smith's *White Teeth* (2000). Smith's novel contains this well-known exchange:

> "And then you begin to give up the *very idea* of belonging. Suddenly this thing, this *belonging*, it seems like some long, dirty lie . . . and I begin to believe that birthplaces are accidents, that everything is an *accident*. But if you believe that, where do you go? What do you do? What does anything matter? "
>
> As Samad described this dystopia with a look of horror, Irie was ashamed to find that the land of accidents sounded like *paradise* to her. Sounded like freedom.[6]

The viewpoint of Smith's *alter ego* Irie remains shaped by the sort of postmodernist celebration of migrancy, and of an attendant relativistic hybridity, propounded in Rushdie's 1990 essay "In Good Faith", where he described *The Satanic Verses* in these utopian terms:

> *The Satanic Verses* celebrates hybridity, impurity, intermingling, the transformation that comes of new and unexpected combinations of human beings, cultures, ideas, politics, movies, songs. It rejoices in mongrelization and fears the absolutism of the Pure. *Mélange*, hotchpotch, a bit of this and a bit of that is *how newness enters the world*, and I have tried to embrace it. *The Satanic Verses* is for change-by-fusion, change-by-conjoining. It is a love song to our mongrel selves.[7]

Aijaz Ahmad's *In Theory: Classes, Nations, Literatures* (1992) saw that the eclectic cultural hybridity foregrounded within Rushdie's writing in fact resembles the modes of cultural hybridity which characterise both European high modernism, and the commodity culture of contemporary global capitalism.

> How very enchanting, I have often thought, Rushdie's kind of imagination must be for that whole range of readers who have been brought up on the peculiar 'universalism' of *The Waste Land* (the "Hindu" tradition appropriated by an Anglo-American consciousness on its way to Anglican conversion, through the agency of Orientalist scholarship) and the 'world culture' of Pound's *Cantos*. [...] One did not have to belong, one could simply float, effortlessly, through a supermarket of packaged and commodified cultures, ready to be consumed.[8]

Students could be led to consider whether Rushdie's celebration of migrancy – a phenomenon which in itself is usually nothing other than an effect of global socioeconomic forces – is instinct with capitalism's own advocacy of the efficiently speedy global movement of commodities and labour. Rushdie's novel can be said to be fully complicit with the *mélange*-logic of global capitalism, insofar as the sort of fusion of cultures on offer in *The Satanic Verses* can be seen to represent just another supermarket. A student could also be led to ask whether, precisely to the extent that she does not 'have to belong' to any of the cultural identifications on offer within Rushdie's writing, and can instead simply float through his eclectic fusion of various global cultures, Rushdie's work in fact only bolsters the market-driven fragmentation of global society into fixed, competing interest-groups of producers and consumers. The student may then begin to sense that the reification of her own identity is related to her alienation from alternative identities, now that all (cultural) identities are increasingly reduced to exchange-value and frozen within the status of a commodity.

As if to cloak the actual reifying stabilization of our identities within global capitalism, Rushdie's foregrounding of the concept of migrancy in *The Satanic Verses* generates within the novel a persistent thematization of mutation and metamorphosis; of the "strange fusions" described by Rushdie in his 1985 essay "The Location of *Brazil*".

> The effect of mass migrations has been the creation of radically new types of human being: people who root themselves in ideas rather than places, in memories as much as in material things; people who have been obliged to define themselves – because they are so defined by others – by their otherness; people in whose deepest selves strange fusions occur, unprecedented unions between what they were and where they find themselves. The migrant suspects reality: having experienced several ways of being, he understands their illusory nature.[9]

Rushdie's particular conceptualization of migrancy hence contributes to his writing's postmodern relativisation of cultural realities. Rushdie illogically argues that because the migrant's cultural realities are multifarious they are therefore all somehow 'illusory'. Influenced by magic realists such as Italo Calvino and Gabriel Marcia Marquez, in *The Satanic Verses* Rushdie tempers the presentation of social actuality with fantasy and fairy tale narrative elements. This stress on the 'illusory nature' of our experience, so that London in the novel, for instance, becomes a magic realist city – Saladin Chamcha's "dream-city, *ellowen deeowen*" – can result in a troubling detachment from concrete sociohistorical actuality, and an apparent unwillingness to confront the lived realities of the migrant's experience in a new city. One striking marker of Rushdie's discomfort with relaying lived urban specificities in *The Satanic Verses*, is the way in which the novel gives the real names for all areas of London, *except for* the Spitalfields or Whitechapel area (which, with a tentative glance at Brick Lane, is re-named "Brickhall"[10]) – as if in suspicion or evasion of the reality of the specific area where so many of the novel's migrant characters actually live.

Dominic Head, in his article on *White Teeth*, described the problematic alienation from lived place which accompanies Rushdie's particular conceptualization of migrant identities:

> [Salman Rushdie] does not participate in the attempt to reclaim a particular geographical place, whether urban or rural, or to rethink national identity in relation to it. Rather, Rushdie is the chronicler of the unfettered migrant sensibility, that version of post-colonialism which unhooks historical tradition from place [...This sort of re-writing of official colonial history can result in a] turning away from the particular difficulties inherent in the actual geographical experience of the migrant self in post-war Britain.[11]

Rushdie's celebration of an 'unfettered' migrant experience, it could certainly be added, simply reflects his own globe-trotting class position within the world capitalist economy. Yet whilst it is Rushdie's class privilege that enables him to an extent to disregard the 'particular difficulties' and disabilities experienced by other 'mongrel selves', Smith can disregard them for a different reason. As Head suggests, from Smith's Londoner's perspective a term such as 'mongrel' is itself too charged, too fraught and too outdated, to be of much relevance as a description of her own identity. Yet Smith's writing can therefore disregard the migrant's struggles, I would go on to argue, precisely because it is so well rooted in, or so complicit with, the experience of the capitalist metropolis. As Head notes, "Zadie Smith seems to speak for a third generation of post-war Black British experience, a generation for which the concepts of 'migrancy' and 'exile' have become too distant to carry their former freight of disabling rootlessness."[12] The difficulty with the supposedly fluid, enablingly rootless multi-ethnic society propagandised by Smith's novel, is that it is in fact rooted and assimilated, in real economic terms, within a capitalist city which continues to reify our identities.

The novel's younger characters seem to me to be exemplary, in that they are grounded in their present territorial location considerably more than in their ethnic origins.[13] Yet the tension between the benefits of locationality – adolescent north-west London can be a very privileged territory indeed, as the absence of any reference to Smith's subsequent Cambridge education on her novel's dust-jacket seeks to deny – and the social unfreedom of capitalist society, persists. Hanif Kureishi's *The Buddha of Suburbia* (1990) registered this tension in its opening paragraph. In a way that recalls Smith's novel, the seemingly fluid, post-migrant identity of Kureishi's hero – who contains an "odd mixture of continents and blood" – is in fact fixed within the experience of the reifying city. As a London suburbanite, Karim Amir benefits from a rebellious location, and can quite rightly claim to be "not proud" of England and its capitalist heritage. Yet like any good fledgling Thatcherite he suffers from the delusion that he is "going somewhere", as well as from the condition of being "restless and easily bored" within consumerism.

> My name is Karim Amir, and I am an Englishman born and bred, almost. I am often considered to be a funny kind of Englishman, a new breed as it were, having emerged from two old histories. But I don't care – Englishman I am (though not proud of it), from the South London suburbs and going somewhere. Perhaps it is the odd mixture of continents and blood, of here and there, of belonging and not, that makes me restless and easily bored. Or perhaps it was being brought up in the suburbs that did it.[14]

Students could look more closely into the dialectical relation apparent in recent Black British fiction, between the benefits of locationality – or the (not entirely artificial) sense of integration or community afforded by metropolitan experience – and the ongoing unfreedom and alienation of the capitalist context of that experience. As Philip Tew has noted, Kureishi's novel is focussed on "a very specific location (suburban and subsequently central London in the main)";[15] yet the wider society, shortly to be Thatcher's Britain, is seen within *The Buddha of Suburbia* to be a "bitter, fractured country [that] was in turmoil".[16] It is such a society which circumscribes, and in a sense redefines, the pockets of (sub-) urban privilege that are highlighted within recent Black British fiction. We could consider, too, the stark contrast between Smith's utopian projection of a successfully achieved post-migrant community in *White Teeth*, and the treatment of social fragmentation within Sam Selvon's seminal West Indian London novel *The Lonely Londoners* (1956).

*White Teeth* only very rarely acknowledges lived alienation. "Darcus had come over to England fourteen years earlier and spent the whole of that period in the far corner of the living room, watching television." Smith believes that she is "going somewhere", and consequently can do little more than mock the routine enforced diminishment of the first generation immigrant's experience to a barren "lifelong affection for the dole, the armchair and British television". The novel simply sneers that Darcus was "admittedly, never the most vibrant of men"; as if to suggest that his difficulties could be resolved readily, with an invigorating injection of Thatcherite individualist self-responsibility and self-reliance. Smith's writing offers the reader no explicit consideration of the particular historical and class determinants of Darcus's alienation. The novel neglects to explicate the social fragmentation, and other material causes (amongst which the stultifying effect of British television itself is just one), which programme Darcus's "most incredible lethargy".[17] His alienation from the codes of capitalist productivity would in fact become entirely *credible*, thoroughly believable, if we were to consider the politico-economic processes which have shaped it. Yet in the novel Darcus simply remains a frozen migrant, his alienated identity fixed and reconfirmed in its reification by Smith. It is at this point that we can turn to Tew's important recent study *The Contemporary British Novel* (2004), and his valuable twinning of a critique of the postmodernist and cultural materialist claim to "offer a challenge to universalising subject positions", with a new call for "a return to material referents".[18]

## *3. Transitionality and the Critique of Reification*

*The Contemporary British Novel* starts from the recognition that "more recently and even more comprehensively, postmodernism is being seen as insufficient for explaining or even describing fragmentation, differentiation and plurality. " Tew's study identifies "hybridity" and "the explicit notion of a culture in transition" to be key "dominant cultural themes" characterising British fiction since the mid-1970s.[19] The term 'transitionality' is adopted by Tew throughout his book, to "reflect a contemporary culture that is aware that both the national and the intellectual landscape undergoes constant transformation".[20] Crucially, a stress on the category of transitionality enables "seeing society as intersubjective, as combining changing, often transitional identities and subjectivities".[21] Tew feels that we are already beginning to reshape the reified homogeneity of bourgeois British cultural identity: "creatively and culturally both the nature and deconstruction of the overarching Britishness that concealed a heterogeneous reality is [...] compelling."[22] The concept of transitionality is instinct with the attempt to effect a de-reification of identity, since it enables us to stress our capacity for historical transformation and social change. Here it is worth recollecting the Gramsci quotation with which Sinfield opened *Literature Politics and Culture in Postwar Britain*, which, as we have seen, recommended an uncritical, fundamentally complicit tracing of the reifying historical process which has moulded fixed, essentialised identities. I have suggested that the cultural materialist call for recovery of particularist identities – for "what one really is", in Gramsci's words – is unhelpful, because without also offering an effective critique of the reification or stabilization of those identities within the capitalist economy, it can only further consolidate the reifying process. *The Contemporary British Novel* contains a valuable alternative quotation, taken from Kevin Davey's *English Imaginaries: Six Studies in Anglo-British Modernity* (1999), which helps us to begin to reformulate Gramsci's and Sinfield's conception of identity, "what one really is", in terms of transitionality:

> An identity is an unstable, aspirational point of identification, an attempt to position oneself, or construct a group – in relation to others – through ever-changing representations of a shared or distinguished culture, history, memory or set of utopic longings. [...] Notions of identity, authenticity, essence, where they do gain a footing, have to be created, buttressed, recreated.[23]

The contemporary texts considered within *The Contemporary British Novel* were selected, Tew writes, "to exemplify an idea of a transitional, changing textual culture, but one that is eventful and based within a complex historical reality in transition". Tew's recognition of the need for historical contextualization of literary works leads on to an advocacy of the identification of the shifts within contemporary identities generated by an ever-transforming present. Such an emphasis on the re-creation and re-shaping of identity contributes to what, in my opinion, is the crucial insight suggested by Tew's study: the idea that a new concept of hybridity, *qua* transitionality, can emerge out of precisely a developed critique of reified bourgeois identities. As Tew observes, "an interrogation of the reflexivity of the traditional middle classes has become an aesthetic consciousness for the British novel, part of the review of the dimensions of a British culture and an awareness that contributes to the literary and critical inflection of hybridity."[24] A sustained historicization of the destabilization of British bourgeois identity since the mid-1970s (and before), would contribute significantly to the de-reification of all our identities. Tew's call for a reclamation of material referents and re-invention of class critique, alongside the transitional subject's interrogation of "universalising subject positions", I want to argue, suggests that the classroom study of fiction reflecting marginalised, non- (or anti-) bourgeois metropolitan identities, such as Selvon's or B.S. Johnson's or Iain Sinclair's for instance, may turn out to be more instructive, productive and potentially liberating for students, than the study of bourgeois metropolitan fiction such as Rushdie's or Smith's. It is worth stressing that metropolitan experience is an increasingly important point of reference and identification for students now. Contemporary British fiction courses can easily begin to resemble London writing courses, because as a generator of identities the capitalist metropolis is at once the seedbed and a constricting container of forms of transitionality. As Tew writes, "if the contemporary novel has done anything consistently since the mid-1970s it has been to radicalise traditional understandings of the late capitalist cityscape and urban environment."[25] Unfortunately however, some of the most politicised, technically sophisticated and intellectually rewarding recent fictions of the city – the novels of Iain Sinclair in particular do not typically feature yet on most contemporary fiction reading-lists. To close this article, I want to address now a twin denial – of both class-consciousness and radical urban modernist experimentalism – which, I believe, explains this neglect of some of the most significant recent British fiction.

*The Contemporary British Novel* exemplarily points towards a classroom consideration of multi-ethnic transitionality, and class critique, *in conjunction.* Tew declares that "for fiction and culture more generally, I also see as progressive informed postcolonial critiques, notions of radical hybridity, and of a revived class consciousness".[26] Crucially, the necessary integration and centralization of transitional ethnic and sexual identities within the newly defined, contemporary British canon – and instead of a tokenistic supplementation of an outdated canon *with* these identities – is seen by Tew as instinct with the critique of bourgeois British conceptions of literariness. It is at this point that we could return to Adorno's attempt, in his *Aesthetic Theory*, to resist the reduction of the literary work to the status of a commodity bound and reified within the system of capitalist exchange, so as to begin to identify a model for our own attempt to free our plural, autonomous individualities from their reifying reduction to labour value, and from the web of bourgeois property relations within which we remain frozen. Tew did not turn to Adorno, but he wrote:

> In the past black or post-colonial fiction and women's fiction were awarded separate consideration as an ideological affirmation, but given that both now constitute a significant contribution to mainstream literary culture, this factor must shape my critique throughout. Hence I intend to integrate such writing rather than marginalise it in my critique and they will not be critiqued as discrete fields. Such an emphasis might help to reshape an aesthetic of Britishness in its broadest sense [...]. Set against any radical impulse is a middle-class occlusion, an ongoing self-obsession that distorts our notion of what constitutes significant literariness. Gradually this aesthetic distortion is in the process of being challenged by writers who reflect a range of experiences and viewpoints that explore other identities. This is a process this study wishes variously to detail, acknowledge and enhance.[27]

I would suggest that a classroom project of exploring the class divisions of our transitionally hybrid democracy, which would "reflect a range of experiences and viewpoints that explore other identities", could begin to de-reify our identities. Tew explicitly recommends an interrogation of the "class bias inbuilt into the literary-critical field". He notes that, because traditionally it has been the self-obsessed and self-interested middle class which has defined the constitution of "significant literariness", "objective merit" has hitherto often been replaced by "other issues of ideology and partiality of taste",[28] when decisions have been made about "the kinds of texts that were traditionally chosen for publication and academic study".[29] When we consider the continuing exclusion of outstandingly talented, metropolitan neo-modernist novelists such as B.S. Johnson or Iain Sinclair from university syllabuses, it becomes clear that a residual resistance to radical urban modernist experimentalism amongst the British bourgeoisie, represents one significant ideological issue expressive of ongoing class bias.

Wyndham Lewis's challengingly transitional class identity, along with the metropolitan Vorticist aesthetic to which he contributed (and it is worth remembering that the London Vorticists, such as the working-class, Whitechapel-based David Bomberg, represented the only integrated modernist avant-garde formed in Britain), continues to animate Sinclair's neo-Vorticism.[30] The removal of neo-modernist aesthetic techniques – many of which are derived from other European and American pioneers such as William Burroughs – from the canon of contemporary British fiction, can only consolidate the reification of all our identities, because experimental neo-modernist novelists too – and arguably exemplarily so – "reflect a range of experiences and viewpoints that explore other identities".

Interestingly, in *The Contemporary British Novel* Tew traces one significant recent "shift in the focus of British literariness" – the integration of Scottish working-class writing within the canon since the 1980s – to "devolution and the strengths of local publishing opportunities"[31] (such as provided by Canongate and Rebel Inc.). The capacity of students now to learn from, for example, James Kelman's neo-modernist reformulations of subjective identity, can be related back to a historical shift which twinned political decentralization, democratic plurality, with the freedom of the small press self-publisher from overarching conceptions of a commodified British culture. Kelman's life-work, just like Sinclair's writing issued from his Hackney-based Albion Village Press and Hoarse Commerce, is grounded in an urban, communal, late modernist self-publishing practice which seeks to resist the reduction of the literary work to the status of a commodity reified within the system of capitalist exchange. Yet the ongoing stabilization of British bourgeois identity continues to forestall the assimilation of Sinclair's heightened urban experimentalism within the university syllabus. For, as I suggested in the opening part of this article, whilst cultural materialism *claims* to reflect and uphold the complexity of autonomous creativities which constitutes our contemporary democracy, it in fact reduces our plural individualities to a fixed array of stabilised and normalised social identities: thereby erasing the '*otherness*' within ourselves.

*Notes*

1 Compare Sinfield (1997: 16): "welfare-capitalism aspires to legitimate itself by claiming that it is what people want"; Bradbury (1990: 134).
2 Sinfield (1981: 182, 194); Sinfield (1997: xxiii).
3 *Ibid.* xv, ix; Milne (1991: 41).
4 Adorno (1997: 30).
5 Sinfield (1997: 1), quoting from Gramsci (1971: 423).
6 Smith (2001: 407-408).
7 Rushdie (1992a: 394).
8 Ahmad (1992: 128).
9 Rushdie (1992a: 124-125).
10 Rushdie (1992b: 37, 184).
11 Head (2003: 110).
12 *Ibid.* 107.
13 I grew up in a very similar environment to that documented within *White Teeth*, and hence I tend to agree instinctively with Smith's contention that northwest London represents the closest thing to a successfully achieved post-migrant community, perhaps on the face of the earth.
14 Kureishi (1990: 3).
15 Tew (2004: 31).
16 Kureishi (1990: 259).
17 Smith (2001: 30-31).
18 Tew (2004: 21).
19 *Ibid.* 21.
20 *Ibid.* 1.
21 *Ibid.* 2.
22 *Ibid.* 30.
23 *Ibid.* 21, 1, 2, 30, 1 (quoting from Davey (1999: 7)).
24 *Ibid.* ix.
25 *Ibid.* xi; for an extensive development of Sinclair's social criticism, see Bond (2005); on Johnson's metropolitan marginality, see Bond (forthcoming a); Tew (2004: xi).
26 *Ibid.* xiii.
27 *Ibid.* 15.
28 *Ibid.*
29 *Ibid.* 14-15.
30 *Ibid.* 15, 14-15; for an introduction to Sinclair's neo-Vorticism, see Bond (forthcoming b). I am currently preparing a book-length study, *Star-Cult City*, in this area.
31 Tew (2004: 14).

## *Bibliography*


Adorno, Theodor W.: "Cultural Criticism and Society". – In T.W.A.: *Prisms*. Trans. Samuel & Shierry Weber, Cambridge, 1997, pp. 17-34.

Ahmad, Aijaz: *In Theory. Classes, Nations, Literatures*, London, 1992.

Bond, Robert: *Iain Sinclair*, Cambridge, 2005.

---: "Pentonville Modernism. The Fate of Resentment in B.S. Johnson's *Albert Angelo*", *Literary London. Interdisciplinary Studies in the Representation of London*, 3.1 (March 2005) [http://homepages.gold.ac.uk/london-journal/Bond.html] (forthcoming a).

---: "'Servant to the Stars' Non-Form in Iain Sinclair's Essay Form". – In Robert Bond & Jenny Bavidge (Eds.): *City Visions. The Work of Iain Sinclair* (forthcoming b).

Bradbury, Malcolm: *The History Man*, London, 1990.

Davey, Kevin: *English Imaginaries. Six Studies in Anglo-British Modernity*, London, 1999.

Gramsci, Antonio: *Selections from the Prison Notebooks*. Ed. Quintin Hoare & Geoffrey Nowell Smith, London, 1971.

Head, Dominic: "Zadie Smith's *White Teeth*". – In Richard Lane et al. (Eds.): *Contemporary British Fiction*, Cambridge, 2003, pp. 106-119.

Kureishi, Hanif: *The Buddha of Suburbia*, London, 1990.

Milne, Drew: "'The Function of Criticism'. A Polemical History", *Parataxis. Modernism and Modern Writing* 1, Spring 1991, 30-50.

Rushdie, Salman: *Imaginary Homelands. Essays and Criticism 1981-91*, London, 1992a.

---: *The Satanic Verses*, Dover, DE, 1992b.

Sinfield, Alan: "Against Appropriation", *Essays in Criticism* 31, no. 3, July 1981, 181-195.

---: *Literature Politics and Culture in Postwar Britain*, second edition, London, 1997.

Smith, Zadie: *White Teeth*, London, 2001.

Tew, Philip: *The Contemporary British Novel*, London, 2004.

*Katharine Cockin (Hull)*

# Chicks and Lads in Contemporary British Fiction

In a climate where arguments about feminism frequently provoke unease or derision, it is significant that an extremely popular brand of contemporary fiction has emerged, primarily concerned with the dynamic state of gender relations. In this paper I will be drawing on my experiences of teaching seminars on chick lit and lad lit on the MA Contemporary Literature and Film at the University of Hull, UK. The primary focus of the seminar was the exploration of shifting ideas about fatherhood, gender and work, and a comparative analysis of the figure of the 'lad' and the 'chick'. The seminar group investigated the possible relationship between chicks and lads in contemporary literature, with reference to such novels as Helen Fielding's *Bridget Jones's Diary* and Tony Parsons's *Man and Boy*. These novels are self-consciously contemporary.

In the middle of the nineties, an apparently new phenomenon in popular fiction appeared in the UK and USA. The publication of Nick Hornby's *Fever Pitch* (1992) and the launch of the men's magazine, *Loaded* (1994) marked the beginnings of lad lit, while chick lit has been associated specifically with the year 1996,[1] when publication of Candace Bushnell's *Sex and the City* and Helen Fielding's *Bridget Jones's Diary* coincided with the first performance of Eve Ensler's *The Vagina Monologues* and the founding of the Orange Prize for new fiction by women writers.[2] Although the commercial success of chick lit and lad lit novels is indisputable, their cultural meaning, social function and literary value have been a matter of some debate. In reminding the reader of their timeliness, engaging with the dynamic state of gender relations and registering new generational ruptures, these novels also appropriate particular notions of literariness. The terms 'chick lit' and 'lad lit', which enforce rigid gender differences and designate formulaic comic, romantic narratives, have been applied to a diverse group of texts. However, the relative complexity or predictability of these texts is usually less significant than the social and ideological effects of the boundaries these texts are used to demarcate. The term 'chick lit' is often deployed to categorise women's writing generally, in a manoeuvre which is neither formally accurate nor ideologically neutral. Helen Falconer protested recently, "Far too much writing by women is cheaply dismissed as 'chick lit'", asserting that women's writing today is excluded from the category of literature:

> [...] there is a vast sea of books by female authors out there that are too well-written by women and quirky to be trashed, but which by their nature (written by women, about women, for women) do not qualify as literature.[3]

Chick lit and lad lit bear closer inspection, not least because they occupy a site of literary canon formation. Often dismissed by literary critics at first sight, the ensuing debate tends to expose the criteria for policing the boundaries of literature, outside which chick lit and lad lit are invariably located. In a rapidly expanding sector of the publishing trade, these novels are eagerly consumed by readers but their apparent familiarity can present an obstacle to analysis. Chick lit has engaged with feminism, gender and pleasure in diverse and contradictory ways. If chick lit is a genre – it has been described as a form of romance – the conventions and narrative formulae prove to be unexpectedly diverse.[4]

Chick lit and lad lit creates for the reader a sense of the immediacy of youth and the strangeness of maturity imbued with an awareness of its inevitable onset. Literariness is positioned in the middle distance, alongside the 'proper job', mortgage and parenthood. In the comic, picaresque, autobiographical novel-manqué, *Dave Gorman's Google Whack! Adventure* (2004), the plot is driven by procrastination and the addictive pursuit of serendipity. It is about the novel which Gorman does not write and, evidently, writing a novel is a grown-up thing for a lad to do. Like the new beard which won him its publishing contract, the novel was intended to mark his maturity. Although chick lit and lad lit are associated with the single status of the characters, it is parenting which poses a crisis, putting both the narrative formulae and gender ideology under strain. Chick lit has grown up, prompting what Kate Dorney describes as a 'new generation' of chick lit.[5] The neologisms 'mumlit' and 'dadlit' raise questions about the territory, and the relevance to the novel of a focus on only one family member. The emphasis on sexual difference, rather than parenting in general, is especially the case in the work of Tony Parsons which argues for the equal nurturing potential of the father while simultaneously reinscribing essentialist ideas about women, work and the biological drive to propagate.

In chick lit, the citation of the writer's lifestyle in both the construction of the protagonist and the figure of the author serves to exploit writing, deadlines and publication as a means of self-distraction, self-definition, self-promotion and rite of passage. Writing is something the chick does on the hoof, in confessional mode. Chick lit authors have learnt on the job as journalists or at university. By contrast, reading is evidenced in chick lit by literary citation but is otherwise clearly a drag, a displacement activity. Readers of chick lit may have a relaxed attitude to their choice of reading material because they are aware of the differing function and status of different texts. Literary critics, however, have tended towards a less flexible approach to chick lit. Indeed, chick lit has been cited to establish the discrete boundaries of literature. Some of the debates about the Orange Prize for fiction concerned the quality of women's writing.[6] These concerns were revived on the occasion of the Booker prize in 2001, when the criticism of chick lit by various famous female authors was formulated in condemnatory and dismissive terms. When reported in the *Guardian* by John Ezard under the by line "Bainbridge tilts at chick lit cult", the debate was framed as jousting tournament to exorcise religious deviants.[7] Beryl Bainbridge described chick lit as 'froth', while Doris Lessing designated such novels "instantly forgettable".[8] Pat Barker charged the readers of chick lit with juvenility: "Young people, because they have an insecure sense of their own identity, love reading books which confirm that identity. I think as people get older they need that from their reading less and less, and most of us end up much broader-minded about what it is we are prepared to read."[9] The perceived inferior status of chick lit is reinforced both through the discourse of age by these older writers and by Jeanette Winterson when she designates chick lit as 'entertainment', claiming for her own work 'high art' status.[10] The persecution of chick lit follows familiar terms of engagement which have a long tradition in the history of women's writing.[11] Mary Wollstonecraft similarly had the best interests of women's education in mind when she blamed the sentimental novel for reinforcing the association of women with emotion and distracting them from the concerns of the wider world.[12] Many of the arguments about chick lit are involved in speculation about readers and their engagement with texts which the research of Janice Radway, Jean Radford and Tania Modleski should have made redundant.[13]

The infantilisation of popular fiction, its readers and writers, is ubiquitous. Posy Simmonds's cartoon, "Nurse Tozer helps Dr Derek with an unexpected case" proscribes the reading of chick lit as bad for the health.[14] The body politic is represented by a sickly beach babe, rescued from the after-effects of her holiday reading – *Les Miserables* – which proves to be too rich for someone used to a diet of 'junk (fashion, celebrity gossip, low-grade chick-lit)'.[15] Nurse Tozer giver her medical opinion:

> that sort of fodder is very highly processed – anything hard has been taken out … it's pap! It's minced up into little spoon-sized paragraphs … it slides down effortlessly … your system needs to do no work whatsoever ... and it becomes lazier and lazier – that's why you can't stomach something meaty like "Les Miserables".[16]

The jokes depend on the belief that the political and social impact of the consumption of reputedly low cultural forms is damaging and that readers of popular fiction need to control their bad habits in order to maintain good (carnivorous) health. Even Paula Dique, the editor of a British website devoted to chick lit, regards examples, such as Allison Pearson's *I Don't Know How She Does It* (2002), as a sign of maturity in the genre: "as the original chicklit writers grow up, meet partners, have babies and experience the working motherhood dilemmas of their own, the lead characters are going to become more interesting, more complex and more enthralling."[17] There is a conflation of author and character implied here, as well as a teleological drive towards complexity, as authors experience the rite of passage towards literature. At the end of a radio programme about chick lit, featuring Elaine Showalter, Mike Gayle, Marian Keyes, and Mariella Frostrup, the latter mounted a rebellious defence: "we have to stop apologising for what we write and read" but it is not clear to whom the apology has been addressed.[18] The confidence and purchasing power of the general reader has been promoted, outside the institutions of higher education, by book groups and television programmes such as the Oprah Winfrey Show, Richard and Judy and Page Turners, which seek opinions on their chosen canon (denoted by bookshops with discrete bookshelves and labels) from actors and celebrities as well as the studio audience rather than literary critics.

The literary critical reception of chick lit is often hostile and thereby reveals the process of canon formation. This may be related to the social status of its authors as much as any formal characteristics of the narratives they produce. The neologism 'chickerati', apparently coined in Scarlett Thomas's article 'The Great Chick Lit Racket',[19] neatly blends 'literati' and 'chick lit' but exposes the ideological conflict ordinarily keeping those two categories separate. For Thomas, the 'chickerati' are Helen Fielding, India Knight, Wendy Holden, Jane Green, Marian Keyes and Allison Pearson.[20] There is a fertile traffic between chick lit, journalism, film and television. Many chick lit authors have worked as journalists and two of the founding texts, *Bridget Jones's Diary* (1996) and *Sex and the City* (1996) developed from their authors' newspaper columns. The anxieties about the value and status of chick lit, and to a lesser extent lad lit, also surface in the blurb, prelims and book jackets where biographical details nervously cite higher education credentials and former employment as writers on leading newspapers and magazines. The almost mandatory page of acknowledgements and photograph confirm that the author really is a chick or lad. Wendy Holden has been deputy editor of *Tatler* and worked for *Harpers & Queen, Sunday Times, Sunday Telegraph* and *Mail on Sunday*.[21] Georgina Newbery worked for five years on *American Vogue*.[22] Helen Dunne, a Liverpool University graduate, was associate city editor for *Daily Telegraph*.[23] Matt Beaumont was a copywriter whereas Mark Barrowcliffe, a University of Sussex graduate, has been a sub editor.[24] Freya North "holds a Masters Degree in History of Art from the Courtauld Institute".[25] Chick lit novels have been free gifts in magazines such as *New Woman* and *Cosmopolitan* and even acted themselves as product placement in television advertisements.[26]

The tension and anxieties concerning literary evaluation and the commodification of the book are played out more significantly in many chick and lad lit novels through the indirect definition of characters. The range of explicitly branded purchases and possessions (the Manolo Blahniks and Jimmy Choos) locate the characters in specific groups in marketing terms. In a quantitative analysis of brands cited in four novels (*My Life on a Plate* (2000), *Shopaholic Abroad* (2001), *Bridget Jones's Diary* (1996) and *High Fidelity* (1995)) Kate Dorney has proven that there is considerable "product placement in chick/lad lit texts" and that this seems to function in different ways.[27] Dorney finds that lad lit tends to "reinforce those gender stereotypes and help to maintain these hegemonic assumptions".[28] However, characters are also defined indirectly as particular kinds of readers and writers and through the recurring motifs of different kinds of writing. These literary citations, like those of the shoes, frequently carry the weight of a brand in product placement. Dorney notes briefly that, in *High Fidelity* (1995), Rob congratulates himself for his "liberal Kundera and *Guardian* reading matter",[29] but it seems most significant that when he signals to the reader that his understanding of these texts is superficial, this confession interpellates a sympathetic response.

However, in chick lit, the female protagonist's superficial engagement with reading and writing, even when it is part of her job, is made explicit to the reader as the sign of inadequacy, of deficiencies in her education. She also has a hazy notion of women's history and feminism, which is frequently both derided and asserted. In *Bridget Jones's Diary* (1996) and *My Life On a Plate* (2000), Mrs Pankhurst is a reference to a necessary but now outmoded or marginalised politics.[30] As Jo Knowles has pointed out, the relationship between chick lit and feminism has dominated critical debate.[31] Imelda Whelehan has recently identified a mechanism which, when it is adopted in chick lit, appears to promote much ambivalence and confusion. This is "a certain mode of address which proposes an ironic distance from the chief character, yet, which encourages simultaneous identification with her".[32] There are particular points in *Bridget Jones's Diary* where the reader is both alienated from Bridget and offered a position of superiority in relation to her. The exposure of Bridget's poor spelling coupled with her status as an English literature graduate provides a comic relief and critical distance from Bridget after the episode of office flirting which has deployed a cynical attitude towards sexual harassment. Bridget is observed at her desk composing an electronic message (the equivalent of an email) to her employer who has commented on the length of her skirt as well as her poor time keeping and spelling:

> Skirt is demonstrably neither sick nor abscent [*sic*]. Appalled by management's blatently [*sic*] sizist attitude to skirt. Obsessive interest in skirt suggests management sick rather than skirt. Jones
>
> Hmm. Think will cross last bit out as contains mild accusation of sexual harassment whereas v. much enjoying being sexually harassed by Daniel Cleaver [...] Must work on spelling, though. After all, have degree in English.[33]

Bridget's poor spelling persists even though she acknowledges it as a difficulty. Often overlooked is Fielding's careful placing of Bridget in the novel as a woman with a lot to learn. The interpretation of Bridget's character as an ideal heroine may derive from the film adaptation of the novel which fails to convey some of the subtleties of Fielding's narrative perspective on Bridget. In the novel the reader is offered an intellectually superior position. In Jenny Colgan's *Amanda's Wedding* (2000), another character, Fran, claims this position in relation to the protagonist whose choice of reading matter – women's magazines – while waiting for the prodigal ex-boyfriend at the airport is condemned, implicitly placing them in the longer tradition of conduct literature, self-help and advice literature: "Oh, now there's a good idea for someone as sad as you. They're full of articles on 'How to keep that pathetic cheating low-down pigdog in your life happy'."[34] The victimisation of women in the reproduction of gender in popular culture is cited, acknowledged but ultimately refused by Colgan. The potential for resistance (and disastrous collusion) appears in the form of supportive friends rather than family figures. Similarly, Fielding presents an occasional critique of Bridget Jones and extracts rich comic moments from the debates Bridget has with her female friends where a vast library of self-help books provides their only frame of reference. The function of comedy in chick lit is not straightforward; it deals with fears but does not always satisfactorily dispel them. Sometimes it engages in a playful, almost postmodernist irony. As Angela McRobbie notes in *Postmodernism and Popular Culture* (1994) Susan Sontag's "Notes on Camp" (1967) provides an insight into the "knowing audience [...] capable of detachment".[35] In chick lit there is some diversity in characterization, plot and interpellation of the reader. It is not homogeneous and provides a relatively contradictory rather than consistently conformist position in relation to femininity.[36] Imelda Whelehan has found that "chick lit expresses such a high level of ambivalence about feminism" but that ultimately with its "self-deprecating" humour it expects "resignation" in "a celebration of stasis".[37]

The attempt to universalise the experience and values of the female protagonist of chick lit novels is culpable of reproducing the hegemonic force of a very specific, affluent, metropolitan group based in London or New York. This was at risk when the Chick Lit Writers of the World formed their own separate chapter of the Romance Writers of *America* [my emphasis], claiming that: "Chick lit is a global phenomenon. It's multicultural. It's international. And that's how our chapter should be."[38] Elsewhere in the USA, chick lit is presumed to be specifically located in the UK. Translation is therefore perceived to be necessary. A website devoted to this purpose, Chick Lit USA, presents itself as "your link to Britain's best selling modern romance fiction, affectionately known as chick lit",[39] and in "A Yankee Girl's Guide to Brit Chick Lit" Annie Hills Holland provides a glossary to enable readers to 'speak chick lit!', a canon with some surprising names (Jilly Cooper and Joanna Trollope) as well as a star system relating to the social class of, variously, the characters, the author or the expected reader.[40] The cultural differences identified here are particularly apparent in the understanding of social class. Jo Knowles has recently examined the specific location of many chick lit novels in London, mentioning the exposure by Cleaver of Bridget Jones's limited geographical knowledge.[41] The moment when Bridget needs to consult a map for the location of Germany is defining not merely for Bridget's character but also for the interpellation of the reader, who is assumed not only to know where Germany is but also to be as familiar throughout the novel with London as is a long-term resident.[42] A similar invocation of an Anglocentric perspective occurs in *My Life on a Plate* (2000), in Clara's offensive attitude towards Irishness which is passed off as a humorous aspect of her character.[43] In addition to the anxieties about the body and the life and loves of the single, middle-class woman, homophobic and racist ideas emerge in Fielding's novel, through her characterization of Bridget's mother and in the feminising of the ubiquitous gay friend. These uncontrolled elements let loose in the narrative of chick lit are perhaps the most interesting as they expose the varying ideological positions which cannot quite hold, signalling incoherently the need for social change without identifying any means of achieving it.

According to Clare Hanson, Bridget Jones's "shadowy double" is the single mother.[44] The contentious "politics of reproduction" especially the "economics of motherhood" are, Hanson argues, dominant issues in 'non-feminist texts' such as *Bridget Jones's Diary.*[45] In those novels which explore the other side of the rite of passage into parenthood, the parent's pursuit of pleasure is experienced as thwarted by the arrival of children. In mum lit, reading becomes a significant cultural activity. In India Knight's *My Life on a Plate* (2000), reading exposes the implicit choices made by the working mother, the impact on the forms of pleasure available to her and the positioning of the child as an obstacle to some of these pleasures. The working mother apparently has no time to read for work or pleasure but must make time to read the bedtime story. When Clara Hutt, "a part-time [...] magazine writer" interviews the ballet dancer, Sam Dunphy, for the magazine *Panache*, she fails to do the necessary reading to prepare for the interview and has little to fall back on: "Unfortunately my knowledge of ballet comes, in its entirety, from a slim tome entitled *Angelina Ballerina*, a book about a gifted young mouse that was most popular with [her son] Jack until he recently decided that ballet was 'for girls' and abandoned it in favour of *Know Your Stegosaurus.*"[46] Although the "faxed biography" about Dunphy has been unread, used as hamster bedding, and the interview is a disaster, Clara's attitude towards the reading she does with her children is different. It must be taken more seriously and is skimped or avoided at a parent's peril. Similarly, Allison Pearson emphasises the subjugation of parent by child in the reading process in *I Don't Know How She Does It:*

> [Emily] is so exhausted that I calculate I can turn over three pages of the bedtime story without her noticing. Must get on with that e-mail backlog. But just as I am skipping the pages, a suspicious eye snaps open.
>
> "Mummy, you made a mistake."
>
> "Did I?"
>
> "You left out the bit where Piglet jumps in Kanga's pocket!"
>
> "Oh dear, did I?"
>
> "Never mind, Mummy. We can just start at the beginning again."[47]

Kate Reddy's time needs to be managed carefully. Her new personal organiser advertises itself with the promise of more time freed up for its owner's hitherto deferred pleasures: "Have sex with your husband while you finish that great Carol Shields novel you started some weeks into your first pregnancy."[48] Reddy is defined in contrast to other characters by her literacy and her appreciation of literature: "My favourite character in literature is Rosalind in *As You Like It*; Candy's favourite character in literature is the guy in Elmore Leonard who wears a T-shirt that says, 'You've Obviously Mistaken Me For Someone Who Gives a Shit'."[49] Reading for pleasure – the Carol Shields novel – is something that the working mum has sacrificed for her baby. Its memory shapes her character and she mourns it.

The new father in John O'Farrell's *The Best a Man Can Get* (2000), is acutely aware of the changes to his life brought about by the new baby and appears willing to vocalise an extreme sense of her encroachment on his sense of self: "Millie was supposed to fill me with joy and fulfillment, but my strongest sensation was an overwhelming anxiety. It was anxiety at first sight. I wasn't in love with the baby, I was 'in worry' with it.'"[50] The experience of losing in a competition with the mother and being usurped by the baby is conveyed by Farrell in a powerful but horrifying metaphor:

> One day I came home late and crept into the room that I had persisted in clinging to as my recording studio. Then I saw it. A whole wall had been covered with Wind in the Willows wallpaper. Where there had previously been a Clash poster of Joe Strummer smashing a guitar, now there were little nursery drawings of Ratty and Mole in tweeds and plus fours. That was my parenting Kristallnacht, the moment I knew I was being driven out.[51]

In this alignment of the new baby with the Nazis, the father claims an equal position with the persecuted Jews, yet this is significantly described in gender neutral terms, as "my *parenting* Kristallnacht".[52] The most morally reprehensible historical events are invoked here to disguise this father's inadequate response to his own anxieties. The reader is invited to accept this unfounded and disproportionate sense of subjugation as an appropriate ethical response to the new baby. In lad lit, the anxieties produced by parenting surface in different ways, often concerning the uncertainty of the male character about how, once he finds he is a father, he should engage with performing this role and how (as apparently it must be) distinguished from mothering. These anxieties are usually given credence within the terms of the narrative and are ultimately only minimally threatening to the male protagonist's sense of his own identity.

Tony Parsons' *Man and Boy* (1999) explores more abstract ideas about fatherhood, engaging with inherited notions from parents: "My father was a strong man who had learned to be gentle, a man who had seen enough of death to fully appreciate life. And I couldn't compete, I just couldn't compete."[53] This sense of inadequacy is inflected with the masculine assumption that a father-son struggle is inevitable. In the ensuing episode, an attempt to redraw the picture of fatherhood for his young son, follows the father's culinary disaster:

> "I know I'm not a very good cook, Pat. Not like Granny or Mummy. But I'm going to try harder, okay?" "Daddies can't cook." "That's not true at all." "You can't cook." "Well, that's true. This daddy can't cook. But there are lots of men who are great cooks – famous chefs in fancy restaurants. And ordinary men, too. Men who live alone. Daddies with little boys and girls. I'm going to try to be like them, okay?"[54]

The poignancy of this didactic moment for the boy's development and the apparent humility of the father's repeated acknowledgement of his culinary failure is offset by the overriding assertion that Harry Silver is adaptable, able to cope with the new demands of single-parenting with a child of an age capable of reasoning and negotiation. In another memorable crisis faced by Harry, when his son has an accident in the playground which takes him to hospital, Harry's perspective is altered and he has a sense of acquiring, or activating some innate, inherited patriarchal perspective but the explicit conclusion focuses on parenting: "Maybe I would make a mess of being a parent just as I had made a mess of being a husband. But for the first time I saw that being a man would have nothing to do with it."[55] It is this reliance on the wisdom of other men which seems to dominate lad lit, rather than a reliance on the reading of self-help manuals. Publishers have responded to and endorsed, if not created and exploited, the anxieties of being a father, by producing a number of self-help books,[56] and a magazine, *Fathers' Quarterly* or *FQ* which, in its first issue featured articles about David Beckham as a model father and a survey of baby buggies, using the discourse of blokes' gadgets and fast cars.[57] The popularity of lad lit with male readers is uncertain in the UK although in the USA some popular fiction is successfully marketed specifically for men, such as Harlequin's Stony Men series.

The exploitative aspects of the publishing industry, superficial reading and the cynically formulaic writing of bestsellers are central to the plot in Wendy Holden's *Fame Fatale* (2002). Those employed in publishing and marketing are interested in almost anything but reading and the books they are producing. The organisers of the literature festival, with which the novel opens, misunderstand what one book is about. No-one has even read the synopsis provided in the press release, let alone the book itself: "Um, I suppose we sort of focused on the title – you know how busy things get, no one has time to read a whole release – and, um, well, I suppose we sort of leapt to conclusions. A note of embarrassment had crept into his voice."[58] Consequently, *Sucking Stones* (the book about travels in the Himalayas) is thought to be about the relationship between the Rolling Stones and their groupies. A combined publicity event has therefore been scheduled with *The Clitoris Chronicles*. Attention has already been drawn to the titles of books when two characters played a drinking game called 'worstsellers': "think of an unsuccessful version of a famous book. *Alice in Sunderland*, for example, instead of *Alice in Wonderland.*"[59] Ironically, the titles of Holden's novels themselves employ slightly defamiliarised idioms such as *Bad Heir Day* (2000). Holden's *Fame Fatale* treats the commercial market for popular fiction with satirical scrutiny. In *Fame Fatale* the marketing of authors and the construction of literature by the publishing industry are both exposed and deployed. There is a self-conscious self-referentiality at work. The *roman a clef* mode is ironised by the inclusion of the disclaimer in the prelims: "All characters in this publication are fictitious and any resemblance to real persons, living or dead, is purely coincidental."[60] Yet Holden uses numerous famous names, including J.K. Rowling and Louis de Bernières, as characters. Eve Ensler's *The Vagina Monologues* (1996) is easily recognizable.

However, the notion that Holden's readers apparently need to be protected is indicated by the unselfconscious censoring of one particular word: "'C**t, c**t, c**t,' the women inside the Spiegeltent were shouting. Egged on by Marilou Honigsbaum, they were evidently well on the road to closure with their clitorises."[61] The use of swearing to define female characters as rule-breakers is common in chick lit and has a longer tradition in the radical popular fiction of second wave feminism. Freya North, in her novel *Sally* (1996), for instance, includes an explicit allusion to Erica Jong's *Fear of Flying* (1974): "This time it'll be Erica Jong who's proud of me. I am going to pursue the Zipless Fuck."[62] Wendy Holden's reproduction of a censored language distinguishes her work from the free-ranging experimentation of the literary text. It also, coincidentally, aligns her with the values of the USA Christian chick lit authors, brought together by Faithfulreader.com to debate the conventions of the genre which they seek to revise in accordance with Christian principles, omitting sexually explicit scenes, drinking, and swearing.[63]

Chick lit often takes the form of witty romantic narratives about the single woman's experiences finding a satisfactory sexual relationship and job, in which pursuit she is supported by a circle of friends rather than family. In chick lit there are often unresolved conflicting values at work: women's independence and pursuit of pleasure are desired but the relationship with higher education, literature and feminism provoke anxieties. In these novels, reading and writing, in various contexts, function as citations of lifestyle. They contribute to the definition of character. However, they also expose the uneasy relationship chick lit has with literature, literary value and the commercial market. The automatic rejection of chick lit by some literary critics and authors and the deployment of the term to designate women's writing generally may be motivated by different sentiments. An entrenchment of conservative values supportive of an exclusive literary canon relegates popular fiction and culture but the reiteration of the high/low culture debates rejects (or fails to acknowledge) the dispersal of cultural power unleashed by the Internet, satellite and digital television, the increased purchasing power of readers and the impact of book groups on publishers. Some negative reactions to chick and lad lit are also concerned with the confused, contradictory and often conservative positions they present through their protagonists. Thus authors of chick and lad lit, together with those whose writings are elevated by literary prestige as contemporary fiction, are engaging with changing social structures and a crisis in gender relations which becomes most apparent in the changes to the family and work. In their use of contradiction, ironic wit and ideological vacillation, chick lit and lad lit have elicited diverse responses of intense identification and alienation, proving to be a surprisingly long lasting phenomenon, provoking debates about aesthetic value and contemporary ethical questions.

## *Notes*

This research began with my teaching on the MA Contemporary Literature and Film at the University of Hull, and developed into conference papers I gave at the Lifestyle Narratives conference at Liverpool John Moores University 22-23 November 2003, at the Teaching Contemporary Fiction conference at University of Westminster 29 May 2004, and a research seminar paper at the Centre for Women's Studies, University of York, 9 May 2005. I am grateful to these audiences for their encouraging response.

1 See Imelda Whelehan: 2000.
2 See Emma Parker (2004: 1-15).
3 Helen Falconer (2005: 28).
4 A six-week online course, available for just under $400 entitled "Chick lit: writing women's literature", assumes that chick lit is a genre related to both romance and the literary, "something in between ... and a little of both". [http://www.mediabistro.com/courses/salon/chiclit.asp] (4 May 2005).
5 Kate Dorney (2004: 13).
6 See Parker (2004: 1-15).
7 John Ezard (2001).
8 Beryl Bainbridge quoted in *ibid.*
9 Pat Barker quoted in *ibid.*
10 Jeanette Winterson quoted in *ibid.*
11 George Eliot (1856: 442-461).
12 Mary Wollstonecraft (1982).
13 See Janice A. Radway (1987); Tania Modleski (1990); and Jean Radford (1987).
14 Posy Simmonds (2003).
15 *Ibid.*
16 *Ibid.*
17 www.femalefirst.co.uk/celebrity/chick_lit_grows_up.php (19 May 2003).
18 Mariella Frostrup in "Open Book", BBC Radio 4, broadcast 23 February 2003.
19 Scarlett Thomas: "The Great Chick Lit Racket", *Independent on Sunday* 2002 [www.enjoyment.independent.co.uk/books/features/story] (19 May 2003).
20 *Ibid.*

21 Wendy Holden (2000).
22 Georgina Newbery (1998).
23 Helen Dunne (2001).
24 Matt Beaumont (2000); Mark Barrowcliffe (2000).
25 Freya North (1999).
26 Whelehan (2000: 7).
27 Kate Dorney (2004: 12).
28 *Ibid.*, 17.
29 *Ibid.*
30 See Katharine Cockin (2004: 17-32).
31 Jo Knowles (2004: 2).
32 Imelda Whelehan (2004: 29).
33 Helen Fielding (1996: 24-26).
34 Jenny Colgan (2000: 37).
35 Angela McRobbie (1994: 19).
36 Two anthologies published in the USA understand chick lit in terms of postfeminism; see Chris Mazza & Jeffrey DeShell (1995); and Chris Mazza & Elisabeth Sheffield (1996).
37 Imelda Whelehan (2004: 5-8).
38 [http://www.Chicklitwriters.com] (4 May 2005).
39 [http://www.Chicklit.us] (4 May 2005).
40 [http://www.Chiclit.us/News3] and [chicklit.us/diction] (both 4 May 2005).
41 Jo Knowles (2004: 41).
42 *Ibid.*
43 India Knight (2000: 31).
44 Clare Hanson (2004: 16-27).
45 *Ibid.*, 23-24.
46 Knight (2000: 29).
47 Allison Pearson (2003: 31).
48 *Ibid.*, 122-123.
49 *Ibid.*, 20.
50 John O'Farrell (2000: 48).
51 *Ibid.*, 54.
52 My emphasis; *Ibid.*
53 Tony Parsons (2000: 140).
54 *Ibid.*, 115-116.
55 *Ibid.*, 140.
56 See Ian Sansom (2005); Marcus Berkmann (2005); Jon Smith (2005); Joe Kelly (2005); James Douglas Barron (2005); Spencer Johnson (2005); Steven Giles (2005) reviewed in Nicholas Lezard (2005: 10-11).
57 See Ross Leighton (2003: 28-34) and (2004: 29-37).
58 Wendy Holden (2002: 40).
59 *Ibid.*, 27.
60 Prelims, Wendy Holden (2002).
61 *Ibid.*, 41.
62 Freya North (1997: 127).

63 The Chick Lit Roundtable recorded in detail the views of Judy Baer, Tracey Bateman, Kristin Billerbeck, Lori Copeland, Penny Culliford, Sharon Dunn, Robin Jones Gunn, Neta Jackson, Annie Jones, Allie Pleiter and Laura Jensen Walker [http://www.faithfulreader.com] (4 May 2005).

## Bibliography


Anon: "15 Essential Items for New Dads", *FQ*, Spring 2004, 29-37.

Barron, James Douglas: *She's Had a Baby ... And I'm Having a Meltdown*, London, 2005.

Beaumont, Matt: *e*, London, 2000.

Berkmann, Marcus: *Fatherhood. The Truth*, London, 2005.

Cockin, Katharine: "Inventing the Suffragettes. Anachronism, Gnosticism and Corporeality in Contemporary Fiction", *Critical Survey,* 16, no. 3, 2004, 17-32.

Colgan, Jenny: *Amanda's Wedding*, London, 2000.

Dorney, Kate: "Shop Boys and Girls! Interpellating Readers as Consumers in Chicklit and Ladlit", *Diegesis. Journal of the Association for Research in Popular Fictions*, 8 Winter 2004, 11-21.

Dunne, Helen: *Trixie Trader*, London, 2001.

Eliot, George: "Silly Novels By Lady Novelists", *Westminster Review* 6, 1856, 442-461.

Ezard, John: "Bainbridge Tilts at Chick Lit Cult", *Guardian*, 24 August 2001.

Falconer, Helen: *Observer*, 30 April 2005, 28.

Fielding, Helen: *Bridget Jones's Diary*, London, 1996.

Frostrup, Mariella: "Open Book", BBC Radio 4, broadcast 23 February 2003.

Giles, Stephen: *From Lad to Dad*, Newton Abbot, 2005.

Hanson, Clare: "Fiction, Feminism and Femininity from the Eighties to the Noughties". – In Emma Parker (Ed.): *Contemporary British Women Writers*, Cambridge, 2004, pp. 16-27.

Holden, Wendy: *Bad Heir Day*, London, 2000.

---: *Fame Fatale*, London, 2002.

Johnson, Spencer: *The One-Minute Father*, London, 2005.

Kelly, Joe: *The Pocket Idiot's Guide to Being a New Dad*, London, 2005.

Knight, India: *My Life on a Plate*, London, 2000.

Knowles, Jo: "Editorial", *Diegesis. Journal of the Association for Research in Popular Fictions*, 8 Winter 2004, 2-3.

---: "Material Girls. Location and Economics in Chicklit Fiction, Or, How Singletons Finance Their Jimmy Choos Collections", *Diegesis. Journal of the Association for Research in Popular Fictions*, 8 Winter 2004, 36-41.

Leighton, Ross: "Beckhams United", *FQ*, No. 1, January 2003, 28-34.

Lezard, Nicholas: "Invasion of the Pregnant Dads", *Guardian*, 26 January 2005, 10-11.

Mazza, Chris & Jeffrey DeShell (Eds): *Chick-Lit. Postfeminist Fiction*, Tallahassee, 1995.
---- & Elisabeth Sheffield (Eds): *Chick-Lit 2. No Chick Vics*, Illinois, 1996.
McRobbie, Angela: *Postmodernism and Popular Culture*, London, 1994.
Modleski, Tania: *Loving With a Vengeance. Mass-produced Fantasies for Women*, London, 1982 (1990).
Newbery, Georgina: *Think Pink*, London, 1998.
North, Freya: *Sally*, London, 1996 (1997).
---: *Cat*, London, 1999.
O'Farrell, John: *The Best A Man Can Get*, London, 2000.
Parker, Emma: "'The Proper Stuff of Fiction'. Defending the Domestic, Reappraising the parochial". – In E.P. (Ed.): *Contemporary British Women Writers*, Cambridge, 2004, pp. 1-15.
Parsons, Tony: *Man and Boy*, London, 1999 (2000).
Pearson, Alison: *I Don't Know How She Does It*, London, 2003.
Radford, Jean (Ed.): *The Progress of Romance. The Politics of Popular Fiction*, London, 1987.
Radway, Janice A.: *Reading the Romance. Women, Patriarchy and Popular Literature*, London, 1984 (1987).
Sansom, Ian: *The Truth About Babies*, London, 2005.
Simmonds, Posy: "Nurse Tozer helps Dr Derek with an unexpected case", *Observer*, 26 July 2003, 3.
Smith, Jon: *The Bloke's Guide to Pregnancy*, London, 2005.
Thomas, Scarlett: "The Great Chick Lit Racket", *Independent on Sunday* 2002 [http://www.enjoyment.independent.co.uk/books/features/story] (19 May 2003).
Whelehan, Imelda: *Overloaded Popular Culture and the Future of Feminism*, London, 2000.
---: "Sex and the Single Girl. Helen Fielding, Erica Jong and Helen Gurley Brown". – In Emma Parker (Ed.): *Contemporary British Women Writers*, Cambridge, 2004, pp. 28-40.
---: "High Anxiety. Feminism, Chicklit and Women in the Noughties", *Diegesis. Journal of the Association for Research in Popular Fictions*, 8 Winter 2004, 5-8.
Wollstonecraft, Mary: *Vindication of the Rights of Woman,* London, 1982 [1792].

*Mike Doherty (London)*

# Anarchy in the Classroom: Pop Music and Teaching Contemporary British Fiction

> [F]or us lot the likes of Rotten, Strummer, Pursey and Weller were the best writers, producing the sort of literature that dealt with our lives. They didn't need to fake anything, do any research, just wrote what was already festering inside them and connected with millions of other people who felt the same way. These people were the contemporary, everyday authors we've hardly ever had in England, writing about life through music because they never thought about doing it in book form, firmly outside the literary class and without the classical reference points. And that was what made these people so special, their reference points the same as ours, right there in our own lives.[1]

One of the pleasures of teaching contemporary fiction set in contemporary times is that it is bound to contain cultural reference points that students will appreciate immediately. Since the 1960s, Britain's best-known cultural export has been its pop music, which figures prominently in the work of many of the country's writers. Students who have never been to Britain are likely to recognise references to styles of music that British bands helped to popularise, from sixties pop to progressive rock to punk to New Wave to rave and electronica. Although a number of recent novels focus directly on music and fictional music-makers (e.g. Iain Banks's *Espedair Street* [1987], Geoff Nicholson's *Flesh Guitar* [1999], Jeff Noon's futuristic and experimental *Needle in the Groove* [2000]), those which interweave non-fictional musical references into their texts and use music as a cultural marker can be particularly rewarding to teach. When a course connects the history of British pop, punk and beyond to the social and political movements which gave birth to them, students can derive a sense of the complexity hidden behind what seem at first glance to be simple concepts.

In my experience, North American students' understanding of contemporary Britain can be vague. Many, if not most, students have seen the movie *Trainspotting*, for instance, but few will know that it presents a hidden side of Edinburgh. Students will have heard of Britain's class system, but they will tend to equate class with money. Tony Blair is known as an ally to George W. Bush, but his background, as well as the ideological division between Old and New Labour, and the potentially confusing affiliation between New Labour and conservatism, are not well known. I have found it particularly useful, in this respect, to introduce students to Jonathan Coe's *The Rotters' Club* and Irvine Welsh's *Trainspotting*, which use musical references as a device to demonstrate their characters' tastes and leanings, in the service of functioning as condition-of-England and condition-of-Scotland novels respectively.

*The Rotters' Club* is a coming-of-age novel about a group of friends and their parents in 1970s Birmingham, set against the background of miners' strikes, IRA bombings, and pop culture. Coe writes his depiction of the recent past as a historical novel; in its frame narrative, two of the protagonists' children meet at the turn of the twenty-first century and set out to tell each other what they know of their parents' lives. Sophie introduces the main narrative to Patrick:

> Just think of it! A world without mobiles or videos or Playstations or even faxes. A world that had never heard of Princess Diana or Tony Blair, never thought for a moment of going to war in Kosovo or Afghanistan. There were only three television channels in those days, Patrick. Three! And the unions were so powerful that, if they wanted to, they could close one of them down for a whole night. Sometimes people even had to do without electricity. Imagine![2]

As bizarre as it may seem to Patrick to postulate a first-world society where unions are so powerful and mass movements of committed citizens can effect change (viz. the Stop the War coalition's million-person march on Trafalgar Square in 2003, which failed to have any effect on Blair's decision to support the American invasion of Iraq), the power of unions in 1970s Britain is even less comprehensible to North American students. Students may find themselves slightly bewildered at the presence of a frame narrative which seems to have so little to do with the novel's main story (although this connection becomes much clearer in the sequel, *The Closed Circle*); I find it useful to stress how one of Coe's aims in his intergenerational narrative seems to be to cast a relatively contemporary time in a historical light, and to illustrate how the seventies gave birth to our current age. *The Rotters' Club*, as a multiple-character Bildungsroman, is unsentimental, expressing not only the loss of illusions but also disillusionment. Coe's view is echoed by that of Nick Kent, who wrote for the New Musical Express in the seventies: "After the utopianism of the sixties, there was the decadence of the seventies.[…] Peace and love in the sixties; let's be totally selfish and stab our friends in the back in the seventies."[3]

For all of Coe's focus with serious social upheavals in the 1970s and his occasional inclusion of shocking passages and events, his novel displays an engaging panoply of characters in often amusing situations. This makes it a particularly enjoyable novel to teach, as opposed to, say, its slyly satirical but relatively dour counterpart, Margaret Drabble's 1977 novel *The Ice Age*. Coe's saga focuses on a group of Birmingham schoolboys, one of whom, Doug Anderton, gives a speech in 1999 where he looks back on the seventies and addresses the issue of utopian optimism. Doug, whose father is a union leader, recounts to a London audience his friend Philip's abortive attempt to form a progressive rock band called "Gandalf's Pikestaff", and observes that Philip's

> ludicrous attempt to squeeze the history of countless millennia into half an hour's worth of crappy riffs and chord changes suddenly seemed no more Quixotic than all the things my dad and his colleagues had been working towards for so long. A national health service, free to everyone who needed it. Redistribution of wealth through taxation. Equality of opportunity. Beautiful ideas, Dad, noble aspirations, just as there was the kernel of something beautiful in Philip's musical hodge-podge. But it was never going to happen. If there had ever been a time when it might have happened, that time was slipping away. (193-194)

Music in the novel takes on an allegorical dimension, as Coe suggested in a public interview in Toronto in 2003, when he mentioned his view that Thatcherism "killed off" Labour (and its attempts at reconciliation with unions) in the same way punk killed off the dinosaurs of progressive rock. In *The Rotters' Club*, Gandalf's Pikestaff (named after a character in *The Lord of the Rings*, by J.R.R. Tolkien, who lived in Birmingham for a time) collapses after half a rehearsal when three of its members spontaneously form a punk group.[4] Progressive rock chronicler and musician Ed Macan explains that fantasy works such as Tolkien's sagas of Middle Earth have been important to the genre because they "depict societies far different than our own, and to the hippies' way of thinking, far more desirable: pastoral and linked to the earth in a way that we are not, sharing a sense of community and possessing a spiritual insight that we have lost".[5] Likewise, Philip's musical idea is symptomatic of impractical utopian idealism. Philip takes as his model the group Yes, whose album *Tales from Topographic Oceans* he lauds in his school's paper. His review reads, in part:

> Hailing from Accrington, Lancs., Anderson has always had an affinity with Eastern spiritualism and philosophy. Inspired by Paramhansa Yoganda's 'Autobiography of a Yogi' (nothing to do with Jellystone National Park!) the album is a double album with four sides, each containing only one long song, comprising four long songs in total.[...] Some songwriters [...] just write pop lyrics, but it would be nearer the truth to say that Jon Anderson writes poetry and sets it to music. Take this couplet of lines from his song 'The Memory' [sic]:
>
> "As the silence of seasons on we relive abridge sails afloat / As to call light the soul shall sing of the velvet sailors course on." What does this mean, the listener wonders? Who are the velvet sailors, and where is the bridge that sails afloat? Jon Anderson is too profound a poet to give us pat answers and soapbox slogans. In the enigma lies the message. (67-68)

Besides serving as a potential clinic for students about how not to write an essay, Philip's review of *Tales* can illustrate important aspects of his character. Students are unlikely to have much knowledge of Yes beyond their 1983 #1 hit (and critical and commercial revival), "Owner of a Lonely Heart". In order to contextualise Philip's ardour for the band, I explain that while *Tales from Topographic Oceans* topped the English charts in 1973, it would become one of the most critically ridiculed releases ever. Shortly after Yes released the album, "[h]eadlines such as 'Over The Edge', 'Wishy Washy Tales from the Deep' and 'Adrift on the Oceans' ran in the same music papers that had recently hailed them as the best band in the world".[6] Over time, the album's reputation has not been resurrected; surely, Coe makes reference to it because of its notoriety, but also because of its provenance – not only from the Midlands, but also from a band whose singer, Jon Anderson, a milkman's son from Accrington (best-known to students of British literature as the down-at-heel mining town where Jeanette

Winterson grew up, and which she portrays in *Oranges Are Not the Only Fruit*), was decidedly working-class. Some critics have argued that progressive rock's preoccupation "with utopian-hippie visions of an egalitarian and cool society are hypocritical, coming as they did in some cases from musicians who depended on a good deal of advanced technology and who came from fairly well-off backgrounds".[7] This line of criticism is not only facile but also, in some cases, entirely ill-founded. In *The Rotters' Club*, Philip, the son of a busdriver and would-be prog symphonist, is perhaps the most earnest character in the novel.

On one hand, Philip's admiration for Yes springs from a dubious fascination with the "enigma" of lyrics which seem crafted for their euphony and their power of suggestion rather than any decipherable hidden meaning. Guitarist Steve Howe, who wrote most of *Tales* with Anderson, has admitted:

> People got obsessed – everything we did was spacey, cosmic – and yet, the interesting thing for me was that I wrote songs much more down to Earth, because I was much more affected by Bob Dylan than fantasy writers. I used to write things like, "Close to the Edge/Down by the river." And to me, that was fine. Jon heard it, and ... he'd take something that was in your face, but try and colour it [...] he'd take it out of the personal and direct statement into the more vague.[8]

The lyrics which Philip cites, from the beginning of the 21-minute song "The Remembering – High the Memory", are set to a floating, pastoral tune set in the irregular metre of 7/4. I recommend playing this excerpt, as well as musical examples I will be discussing later, in the classroom; students who hear it will perhaps notice that it sounds both gentle and rather 'noodly', its lyrical indirection matched by a musical one.[9] In the liner notes to this piece, the members of Yes wrote: "Hopefully we should appreciate that given points in time are not so significant as the nature of what is impressed on the mind, and how it is retained and used."[10] Philip's approach to music and life is, fittingly, more focused on the abstract than the concrete.

Yes's aesthetic was also reflected in their stage design and album covers, much of it designed by artist Roger Dean. David Watkinson's coffee-table book *Yes: Perpetual Change* contains many photographs and reproductions of album covers from Yes's heyday. Lecturers may wish to show their students some of this artwork in order to illustrate progressive rock's sometimes outlandish sense of spectacle.

Progressive rock was famously countered by punk in the late-seventies; the upstart genre's aesthetic was seemingly entirely opposed to that of bands with epic ambitions such as Yes, King Crimson, and Emerson, Lake, and Palmer. Ed Macan explains:

> The counterculture had already entered a period of fragmentation by the early 1970s; punk rock delivered a deathblow to the series of assumptions which had sustained it. Punk countered the counterculture's largely discredited message of optimism and brotherhood with a chilling nihilism[...]. The punks saw little concrete progress resulting from the hippies' credo of peace, love, and understanding; instead, they saw the counterculture as having fallen victim to exactly the kind of self-indulgent materialism and hypocrisy that the hippies themselves had once so vehemently denounced.[11]

In *The Rotters' Club*, Doug, like his friend Philip, writes for the school paper, but their musical tastes differ greatly. In 1976, he ventures to London with the intention of writing a piece for the *New Musical Express*. Students may be familiar with the paper, but it was once, like Rolling Stone, a more combatively written and "edgy" publication. In 1976, it was advertising for "hip young gunslingers" to cover punk music (*Inky Fingers*, 2005).[12] Once again, musical references carry an ideological weight: Doug turns down the opportunity to review a gig by prog-rock band National Health (who are named after a concept which he will dismiss later, in his flash-forward speech, as unworkable). He is assigned to a "Rock Against Racism" concert, but gets lost and ends up at a gig by The Clash instead, where he has a life-changing experience. Doug sees the band's lead singer Joe Strummer "shouting, screaming, singing, howling into the microphone" (171-172), and he gets lost "in the sea of chords and sweat and beer and feedback and pounding bodies throwing themselves manically up and down in a distant approximation to the rhythm of the music" (171). After the concert, he encounters a secretary from the publication *Horse and Hound*, the "preposterously named" Ffion Ffoulkes (174); she and Doug repair to "the studio on the King's Road her father had impulsively bought for her one weekend", and they make passionate love, or at least lust, throughout the night (174). In the process, Doug loses "something [...] to do with his sense of self, his sense of belonging, his loyalty to the place and the family he came from. In the space of a few hours, a lifelong allegiance was severed, and a newer, more tenuous one formed. That night, in short, he became enamoured of the upper classes" (174).

One might be led to think that Doug has lost his left-wing ideology, but this is not borne out by the rest of the novel, which sees him remaining politically active, for the same causes he had espoused before. Coe portrays a fluidity which questions the kind of hard and fast class divisions North American students would expect to find. Julie Burchill, self-proclaimed proletarian prophetess and, during the seventies, one of Doug's *NME*-writer idols, wrote in *The Guardian* in 2002:

> I've never had a problem with the posh; they're thick, they're dying and they know it. The middle class – that's another story. They're everywhere. They're eating the world! Chewing each mouthful 50 times, of course. Touching everything that was once lively and vital in our culture, from food to football, with the dead hand of their dreary, desiccated, deracinated taste. [...] People from my teachers to Tony Blair have held up this state of disgrace as something to aspire to![13]

Joe Strummer seems not to have upheld "being middle class" as an aspiration, seeing as he himself was the son of a diplomat who was educated at boarding school in Surrey. Doug sees the band perform the song "London's Burning", in which Strummer sings: "The wind howls through the empty blocks looking for a home / I run through the empty stone because I'm all alone / London's burning with boredom now... / London's burning dial 99999." A suitably uproarious version (albeit one with slightly different lyrics) can be found on the 1999 compilation *From Here to Eternity: Live*. Unlike in Yes's "The Remembering", there is no "enigma" here – the message of disaffection is delivered loudly, if not always, in Strummer's case, clearly. Playing one excerpt after the other and asking students to articulate the differences they find between the two should elicit some worthwhile responses, particularly to do with energy and emotion, both of which punk exploited, and which captivates Doug; students may also find that, for all their confrontational aspect, punk often employed catchy melodies with easily remembered lyrics and, in their three-chord tunes, a degree of musical conservatism. Moreover, while in The Clash, Joe Strummer was aided by the Brixton-raised, working-class guitarist and singer

Mick Jones, the sound of rebellious, disillusioned youth does not necessarily equate to a class revolution. Simon Frith writes, provocatively:

> British rockers' radical proletarianism comes, primarily, from rock's social association with lumpen leisure, and punk's cultural significance was derived not from its articulation of unemployment but from its exploration of the aesthetics of proletarian play. This was the source of punk politics; punk was not the voice of unemployed youth but a strident expression of the bohemian challenge to orderly consumption.[14]

Coe brings play and leisure to light in Doug's short-lived liaison with Ffion Ffoulkes. While she fails to tell him she is engaged until after they have made love, he neglects to mention that he is still a schoolboy until after her revelation (176). Instead of being concerned, each one is amused by the other's revelation. There is nothing "orderly" about The Clash's gig or its aftermath; Doug admires the "cluttered Bohemianism" of Ffion's flat, and becomes "enamoured of the upper-class ways of eating, drinking, waking the neighbours up with deafening music, taking drugs and, of course, having sex, which he had never realised could be so boisterous, cheery, polymorphous or strenuous an experience" (175). In a sense, and in a way which may at first seem strange to students conditioned by popular literature to see vast gulfs between princes and paupers, the upper and working classes make not-so-strange bedfellows.

In his eve-of-the-millennium "flash-forward", Doug remembers the night when Margaret Thatcher was elected in 1979, when Paul Trotter, a member of the school's self-appointed right-wing think tank, the Closed Circle, celebrated by holding up a sparkler that was fizzling out and said it symbolised "The death of the socialist dream" (193). In a scene set in the seventies later in the book, Paul cycles down the street past his brother Ben and Philip (222). He is "singing to himself at top volume [...] in an excruciatingly tuneless boy soprano/*I am an anti-CHRIST/I am an anar-CHIST*" (222). The song, of course, is The Sex Pistols' vitriolic "Anarchy in the U.K.", as found on their one and only album, *Never Mind the Bollocks*. Paul's singing it may seem rather startling, since he is an unabashed capitalist. Even though the Sex Pistols were best-known for causing havoc and swearing on live TV, their last gigs in the UK were in support of the families of striking firemen in Yorkshire – a heartwarming scene in the documentary *The Filth and the Fury* shows John Lydon, or Johnny Rotten, singing at one of these gigs, surrounded by little girls wearing *Never Mind the Bollocks* t-shirts, playfully smothering him with pie. After showing this excerpt to my students, I explain to them that it displays a degree of self-mythologization. The Sex Pistols were like Thatcherism in being both radical and conservative at the same time. While Thatcher was economically libertarian but politically reactionary as she sought to crush the unions, the Pistols deployed royalty-baiting shock tactics and quasi-Situationist images and slogans at the same time as being fairly musically staid.

It became clear shortly after the band's breakup that Lydon was disaffected. Rock critic Simon Reynolds explains:

> Punk seemed to be "over" almost before it had really begun. For many early participants, the death knell came on 28 October 1977 with the release of *Never Mind the Bollocks*. Had the revolution come to this, something as prosaic and conventional as an album? *Bollocks* was product, eminently consumable. Rotten's lyrics and vocals were incendiary, but Steve Jones's guitar sound and Chris Thomas's superb production – thickly layered, glossy, well organised – added up to a disconcertingly orthodox hard rock that gave the lie to the group's reputation for chaos and ineptitude. Lydon later blamed McLaren for steering the rest of the band towards "a regressive mod vibe", while admitting that his own ideas for how the record should have sounded would have rendered it "unlistenable for most people because they wouldn't have had a point of reference".[15]

Punk's appeal was much more immediate and visceral than that of "prog", but the same could be said of generic hard rock. It was only in the post-punk era, where bands such as A Certain Ratio, New Order, Gang of Four, and The Clash themselves married punk's stripped-down ethos with elements of dance, funk, reggae, and dub, that the legacy of punk became, in its own way, musically progressive – this post-punk movement would give rise to current, popular UK bands with which students should be well-acquainted, such as Bloc Party, The Futureheads and Franz Ferdinand. It was only in the post-punk era, as well, that punk's occasional displays of latent racism were convincingly swept away.[16]

Fittingly enough, as is hinted in *The Rotters' Club* and made explicit in its sequel, *The Closed Circle*, Paul eventually becomes a New Labour MP. In the 1997 election, Tony Blair's campaign was strong enough even to bring together Britpop's arch-rivals, Noel Gallagher of Oasis and Damon Albarn of Blur, in support against John Major. As illustrated in the 2003 documentary *Live Forever*, which lecturers may want to recommend as a contextual resource to their students, the rockers' subsequent disillusionment with New Labour's policies indicates what they see as the collapse of a value system they believed in, the ebbing away of a youthful force, the strongest indication of the shift in policy from Old Labour to New Labour. Coe makes his point subtly but forcefully by looking at the appropriation of rock idealism for self-serving gain.

A second wave of punk musicians, who were rigidly musically conservative and sometimes racist National Front sympathisers, formed oi! bands. Coe appears to be referencing the seeds of this development when he writes about the punk band The Maws of Doom, which spins off from Gandalf's Pikestaff at their first rehearsal. They take their name from a repeated incantation delivered by schoolboy prankster Harding, who delivers a mock by-election speech at a school Debating Society meeting by affecting an aged demeanour and reading a National Front leaflet verbatim (188). Doug remarks, in his flash-forward: "It became so absurd that a few people did start laughing, nervously.[…] But some of us were beginning to feel that Harding's humour, if that's what it was, was taking us to some pretty strange places lately" (189). The musicians in Gandalf's Pikestaff, rebelling against Philip's magnum opus, play "riotous three-chord thrash" while "an aggressive little character called Stubbs" screams "The very maws of doom!" with "a kind of demonic exhilaration, fuelled by sheer, unpolluted delight in trashing something, kicking something over" (192-193). At this point, the nascent punk band seems to bear out Stewart Home's view that punk tapped "into a reservoir of social discontent and create[d] an explosion of anger and energy. PUNK [sic] wasn't offering a solution, it was simply a genre of novelty music being hyped on the back of the manic and frequently pointless exploitation of social tensions." In the hands of a few bands like the infamous Skrewdriver, this "pointlessness" would be channelled into a very ugly form of white supremacist rock.[17] In *The Closed Circle*, the prankster Harding has lost his sense of humour and become the kind of unreconstructed racist he seemed to be parodying in *The Rotters' Club*, and helping to finance a record company that signs skinhead bands that promote race hatred. He has become a caricature of his former, caricaturing self. Similarly, although to much less pernicious effect, The Sex Pistols reformed well after Sid Vicious's death for their *Filthy Lucre* tours, playing up the fact that they were in it for the money – as, in all fairness, they probably were the first time through.

Coe's use of musical references should reinforce the complexity of the British class system for students, and show how music can be integral to people's perception of themselves as both individuals and members of social groups. Welsh, in *Trainspotting*, similarly uses forms of popular music to illustrate the vicissitudes of the British political and social situation, especially in the late eighties, when the book is set. Its down-at-heel underclass characters affect a kind of gutter dandyism and see themselves self-consciously as being defined by their musical tastes.

While Doug's revelation at a Clash gig in *The Rotters' Club* is portrayed as being ultimately positive, Tommy, in *Trainspotting*, has a dark revelation while stoned and drunk at an Iggy Pop concert in Glasgow. He has just fought with his friend Mitch, in an example of the kind of Scottish infighting that the novel's protagonist, Mark Renton, consistently decries. To add injury to injury, he is head butted at the concert, obviously a rather violent affair, but he makes his way to the front nonetheless. Tommy reflects: "Iggy Pop looks right at me as he sings the line: 'America takes drugs in psychic defence'; only he changes 'America' for 'Scatlin', and defines us mair accurately in a single sentence than all the others have ever done."[18] I play Pop's song "Neon Forest" for students and ask them to listen for the mockery in Pop's voice; the song provides a satirical indictment of America's consumer and advertising culture, in which he strikes out against George Bush (The First) just as the Pistols repudiated Thatcher. The singer, whose raw, working-class rock with Detroit band The Stooges in the late sixties and early seventies has been seen as a precursor to punk, gives voice to the disenfranchised in his song by ironising the middle-class consumer capitalism that leads Renton and his mates to justify their drug use – they are dropping out of a culture they cannot respect, and following the self-destructive path that Iggy Pop took in his early years. Tommy, after attending the gig, begins to follow this path as well, taking up heroin use and ending up as an invalid. In his more despairing moments, Renton reflects on the entrenched inferiority complex that leads him and his friends to believe that, as Johnny

Rotten sings in "God Save the Queen", there is truly "no future" for those faced with a "fascist regime". America, at least, managed to throw off English rule, while Renton views Scotland as being "colonised by wankers [...] We're ruled by effete arseholes. What does that make us? The lowest of the fuckin low, the scum of the earth. The most wretched, servile, miserable, pathetic trash that was ever shat intae creation" (78).[19] "Neon Forest" also suggests, with its lyrics, "Do you have any money? Are you anybody?", that Americans in the late eighties were letting themselves be defined by their material worth; Renton and his junkie mate Sick Boy see this occurring in Scotland under Thatcherism, and seek to define themselves by other, more aesthetic, standards.

Renton is a social chameleon who is so adept at passing himself off in different situations that he manages to convince a judge that he was stealing books for his own edification by giving a discourse on Kierkegaard's proto-existentialist philosophy (165-166). It is significant, therefore, that he is a fan of the musical chameleon David Bowie – so much so that he owns every album the singer has ever made, "[t]ons ay fuckin bootlegs n aw" (17). When Renton reflects on this, he is listening to the song "Golden Years", from the 1976 album *Station to Station*, played on a Walkman by a girl sitting across from him on a bus. Students will likely have heard the song, but may not be aware that its reassuring lyrics belie the fact that Bowie, at the time he recorded it, was a paranoid cocaine addict; he has since "confessed he was so addled that he can hardly remember making the album".[20] I tell students about the disjunction between Bowie's image and his private life in the seventies in order to illustrate the model which Renton uses to construct a façade of control. Renton's reaction to hearing the song is to reflect, "Ah dinnae gie a fuck aboot him [Bowie] or his music. Ah only care aboot Mike Forrester, an ugly talentless cunt whae has made no albums. Zero singles" (17). In the throes of heroin withdrawal, Renton is obsessed with scoring from his dealer. In temporarily renouncing his model, he is coming, ironically, closer to him.

In *Porno*, *Trainspotting's* sequel, Renton reflects about his time hanging out with Sick Boy: "we both knew that decadence was a bad habit for council tenants. A ridiculous habit in fact. The *raison d'être* of our class was simply to survive. Fuck that; our punk generation, not only did we thrive, we even had the audacity tae be disillusioned."[21] Once again, punk connects the upper and lower classes, in its embrace of excess, however unhealthy that may be. In a review of *Trainspotting* for the now-defunct music web site Addicted to Noise, Johnny Walker (Black) wrote perceptively:

> *Trainspotting* depicts a "low," gutter existence which has far more in common with the elevated world of the rich than it does with the day-to-day treadmill of the middle management classes: both groups, high and low, shun the middle's notion that a successful life involves the infinite deferment of pleasure and mere accumulation of material goods, these philosophies being unwelcome offshoots of the filthiest four-letter word which appears in the novel: WORK.[22]

The irony, however, is that in *Trainspotting*, Renton and Sick Boy are about ten years too late to be part of the real "punk generation"; their generation is that of acid house, and of a very different kind of musical and cultural rebellion. While punk was confrontational, the rave scene was seen to strive for communion through ecstasy, a much more social drug than heroin, which after all killed Sid Vicious. It is difficult for North American students to imagine exactly what impact the acid house scene had on youth culture in Britain in the late eighties.[23] Turner Prize-winning artist Jeremy Deller explained that his 1997 work *Acid Brass*, in which a brass band plays arrangements of acid house classics, was a "potent form of resistance to Margaret Thatcher's government"[24] – how, one wonders, could this be true? It is a symbolic, rather than an open, act of revolution. Using the brass band, an emblem of military precision, order, and tradition, to play music which is, as the 1994 Criminal Justice and Public Order Act would have it, "wholly or predominantly characterised by the emission of a succession of repetitive beats",[25] is a method of thumbing one's nose at a Conservative government which uses as much irony as the Sex Pistols but much less vehemence. A club track from 1991 by the short-lived group V.I.M., called "Maggie's Last Party", well illustrates their strategy of getting the enemy to join you if they cannot beat you. It features cut-up samples of Margaret Thatcher, who had stepped down the year before but whose policies were being largely continued by her Tory successor John Major, saying such things as "[t]his, Mr. President, is a remarkable record", "the bass goes on", and "come to the party / come to the rave" in time to an infectious breakbeat loop and nasal synthesiser riffs. Inevitably, students' reaction to this record is to laugh – as a protest song, it is certainly more humorous than those of Iggy Pop or The Clash, and it illustrates an effective way of (literally) appropriating the voice of the administration and using it against itself.

In *Trainspotting*, Renton and his disenchanted, disaffected and disconnected mates find themselves too caught up in an earlier ideology of "outsiderness" to take part in a more communal or positive protest. Margaret Thatcher famously said, "there is no such thing as society",[26] and in *Trainspotting*, while Renton and his mates turn their backs on the Iron Lady's economic ideology, they also give in to the fragmentation she espouses. Renton quotes his dealer, Johnny Swan: "'We are all acquaintances now.' It seems tae go beyond our personal junk circumstances; a brilliant metaphor for our times" (11). Taking drugs as psychic defence, especially an antisocial drug like heroin, involves shutting out the pain others can inflict on you. The combination of acid house and ecstasy, however, can be redemptive, if only for fleeting moments. In Welsh's 1995 novel *Marabou Stork Nightmares*, the profoundly antisocial protagonist Roy Strang goes to a club and drops a tab of E with a couple of his co-workers, and he feels for the first time a sense of hope, well-being and fellowship. Renton himself, in *Porno*, has become a more or less better-adjusted character since investing in a dance club in Amsterdam. Welsh does not see ecstasy as a panacea, but his portrayal of drug culture, with the nuances between ecstasy and heroin, between community and fragmentation, between punk and acid house, can help to give students some indication of the cultural and political forces shaping Britain's history.

Playing music in the classroom, of course, can provide a useful break from the routine of lectures and discussions, but it can also serve at once to demonstrate the inevitable influence that popular music has had on contemporary literature, and to provide an extra dimension to students' appreciation and understanding of contemporary novels. Furthermore, an examination of interconnections between fiction and music can help students derive a sense of the contemporary novel as something more than an individual and isolated artefact – a part of a larger, interdisciplinary cultural dialogue. Certainly the way characters express appreciation for certain musical styles (and even identify with their practitioners) can reveal much about them; an understanding of the cultural weight of these musical styles will often help students make connections between these characters' musical preferences and larger historical and thematic issues which the novels explore, whether implicitly or explicitly. Music can serve as a vehicle for readers to enter texts set in unfamiliar times and places, and as an intermediary for characters to deal with social events which appear at first too vast or complex to comprehend. As *The Rotters' Club*'s protagonist Ben reflects: "It was the world, the world itself that was beyond his reach, this whole absurdly vast, complex, random, measureless construct, this never-ending ebb and flow of human relations, political relations, cultures, histories [...] How could anyone hope to master such things? ... It was not like music. Music always made sense" (108).

*Notes*

1 King (2000: 195). *Human Punk* is, like *Trainspotting* and *The Rotters' Club*, a Bildungsroman of sorts tracing the life trajectory of a music fan. It makes a good companion piece to both books in its exploration of the punk ethos, particularly from a working-class point of view. However, unlike the other two novels, John King's book is narrated entirely by one character; Joe's forcefully expressed points of view about music and society admit for less complexity than those expressed in Welsh and Coe's more polyphonic texts.

2 Coe (2001: 6). Further references to this novel will be included in the text.

3 *Inky Fingers* (2005).

4 For a readable overview of the upheavals in 1970s rock in America and the UK and a number of its predominant practitioners, please see Frank Moriarty's *Seventies Rock* (2003).

5 Macan (1997: 80).

6 Watkinson (2001: 38).

7 Martin (2002: 71).

8 Howe (2001).

9 Another worthwhile piece of music to play to students in conjunction with the opening of "The Remembering" is the pastoral, wispy "Galadriel", one of the best-known songs by a second-tier progressive rock band, Barclay James Harvest. The band, which formed in Oldham in Greater Manchester in the mid-sixties, is a favourite of Philip's; in the frame narrative, his son Patrick mentions, "[t]he last album he bought was by Barclay James Harvest" (3). The song is named after an Elvish princess in *The Lord of the Rings*, and despite its surprisingly short length of three minutes, its soporific nature and obscure provenance mark it as being decidedly far removed from punk. There is perhaps

another significance to Coe's having Patrick mention Barclay James Harvest at this point: he does so in a revolving restaurant in Berlin just "as the vast, brightly lit glass-and-concrete extravagance of the new Reichstag came into view" (3). Barclay James Harvest's biggest concert occurred in 1980, at the Reichstag (Domone 2005).

10 Quoted in "Tales from Topographic Oceans".

11 Macan (1997: 180).

12 The 2005 BBC Four television documentary *Inky Fingers*, which follows the history of the NME from the sixties to the present, includes a segment on the struggle that the weekly paper faced when confronted with punk's meteoric rise, and gives an idea of how a slightly bewildered staff may indeed have hired a young, fresh face like Doug to write for them.

13 Burchill (2002: n.p.).

14 Frith (1983: 267).

15 Reynolds (2005: 5). This book is the first to tackle the post-punk era comprehensively.

16 As Roger Sabin has shown, "punks were angry about lengthening dole queues, the privileges of royalty, the anguish of boredom, and police brutality. But they were also angry about 'Pakis' moving into their neighbourhoods, Arabs buying everything in Harrods, Puerto Ricans nicking their girlfriends, and there being too many Jews for their liking" (1999: 212).

17 Home (1995: 23, 93-105).

18 Welsh (1993: 75). Further references to this novel will be included in the text.

19 Interestingly enough, this is similar to Welsh's spoken-word description of Edinburgh Hearts football fans in his 1995 musical collaboration with Primal Scream and Adrian Sherwood called *The Big Man and the Scream Team Meet the Barmy Army Uptown*: "In every hick town in Caledonia, across this pseudo-nation, you can see the most fucked-up scum that were ever shat into creation, where a blue McEwan's lager top equals no imagination" (Welsh 1996).

20 Pegg (2000: 224).

21 Welsh (2002: 365).

22 Walker (1996: n.p.).

23 Matthew Collin's *Altered State* (1998) and Simon Reynolds' *Energy Flash* (1998) (also published in the U.S. as *Generation Ecstasy*) are two excellent books on the subject of the cultural history of rave culture.

24 Quoted in "Osama's House" (2004).

25 Quoted in Collin (1998: 223).

26 Quoted in Keay.

## *Bibliography*


Burchill, Julie: "Call Me Middle-Class and I'll Punch You", *Guardian Unlimited*, 12 April 2002 [http://www.guardian.co.uk/g2/story/0,3604,682857,00.html] (12 April 2002).

Clash, The: "London's Burning". *The Clash*, Epic, 1977.

---. *From Here to Eternity: Live*, Sony, 1999.

Coe, Jonathan: *The Closed Circle*. 2004, Harmondsworth, 2005.

---. *The Rotters' Club*. 2001, New York, 2003.

Collin, Matthew: *Altered State: The Story of Ecstasy Culture and Acid House*, second edition, London, 1998.

Domone, Keith & Monika: "Biography", Barclay James Harvest Original Home Page [http://www.bjharvest.co.uk/bjh-biog.htm] (30 July 2005).

Frith, Simon: *Sound Effects: Youth, Leisure, and the Politics of Rock*, London, 1983.

Home, Stewart: *Cranked Up Really High: Genre Theory and Punk Rock*, Hove, 1995.

Howe, Steve: Telephone interview, 22 July 2001.

*Inky Fingers*. Dir. Chloe Thomas, BBC Four, 4 July 2005.

Keay, Douglas: Interview with Margaret Thatcher (excerpt), *Margaret Thatcher Foundation* [http://www.margaretthatcher. org/speeches/displaydocument.asp?docid=106689] (30 July 2005).

King, John: *Human Punk*, London, 2000.

*Live Forever*. Dir. John Dower, Passion Pictures, 2003.

Macan, Ed: *Rocking the Classics: English Progressive Rock and the Counterculture*, Oxford, 1997.

Martin, Bill: *Avant Rock: Experimental Music from the Beatles to Björk*, Chicago, 2002.

Moriarty, Frank: *Seventies Rock: The Decade of Creative Chaos*, Lanham, MD, 2003.

"Osama's House Makes Turner Prize Shortlist", *Times Online,* 18 May 2004 [http://www.timesonline.co.uk/article/0,,1-1114906,00.html] (30 July 2005).

Pegg, Nicholas: *The Complete David Bowie*, London, 2000.

Pop, Iggy: "Neon Forest", *Brick by Brick*, Virgin, 1990.

Reynolds, Simon: *Energy Flash: A Journey Through Rave Music and Dance Culture*, London, 1998.

---: *Rip It Up and Start Again: Postpunk 1978-1984*, London, 2005.

Sabin, Roger: "'I Won't Let That Dago By': Rethinking Punk and Racism". – In R.S. (Ed.): *Punk Rock: So What? The Cultural Legacy of Punk*, London,1999, pp. 199-218.

Sex Pistols, The: "Anarchy in the UK". *Never Mind the Bollocks*, EMI, 1977.

---. "God Save the Queen". *Bollocks*.

"Tales from Topographic Oceans", *Yesworld* [http://yesworld.com/lyrics/TalesFromTopographicOceans.html] (30 July 2005).

V.I.M.: *Maggie's Last Party*, Oak Lawn, 1991.

Walker, Johnny (Black): "Rock and Roll (Writing) Saved by Welsh", *Addicted to Noise*, May 1996 [http://web.archive.org/web/20020211173629/www.addict.com/issues/2.05/Sections/In_Print/Trainspotting] (30 July 2005).

Watkinson, David: *Yes: Perpetual Change*, London, 2001.

Welsh, Irvine: *The Acid House*, 1994, London, 1995.

---: *Ecstasy*. 1996, London, 1997.

---: *Marabou Stork Nightmares*. 1995, London, 1996.

---: *Porno*. London, 2002.

---: *Trainspotting*. 1993. New York, 1999.

---: On-U Sound and Primal Scream. "Full Strength Fortified Dub", *The Big Man and the Scream Team Meet the Barmy Army Uptown*, Creation, 1996.

*Anja Müller-Wood (Mainz)*

# Enabling Resistance: Teaching *Atonement* in Germany

## *1. Introduction*

My article is inspired by observations made over the years I have spent teaching English Literature to students at different levels in two German universities. Whenever I assign contemporary texts I am struck by students' ambiguous reaction to them. While intuitively they find fiction published from the 1990s onwards both more interesting and more accessible than texts from the "traditional" canon, they would, if they had the choice, write about *Jane Eyre* rather than *The Eyre Affair* any time. Contemporary fiction seems to be just as strange to students in their early twenties as are, say, nineteenth-century texts, requiring a similar amount of explanation and contextualisation. This is not surprising. After all, while 'classics' are available in annotated editions where arcane diction and oblique references are clarified by explanatory material, your ordinary version of *Bridget Jones's Diary* comes 'naked', as it were – leaving not only political, historical or literary allusions but also everyday banalities and in-jokes unexplained by merciful footnotes.[1] Thus, my experience in Germany supports Doryjane Birrer's argument in her essay in this volume, which challenges, from an American perspective, the critical prejudice that contemporary fiction does not deserve specific scholarly attention because its meaning is perfectly transparent to its readers. The apparent accessibility of contemporary fiction is deceptive; especially when taught in a non-native context (but not only there) 'new' novels are no less in need of explanation than canonical texts.

In turn, contemporary fiction raises the question of how we approach literature in the classroom much more pointedly than texts around which a critical tradition has already developed. Since contemporary novels are as yet not bolstered by authoritative interpretations, it is we, the teacher-scholars working with them, who lay the foundations for a critical perspective on these texts. While participating in this formative process is in itself one of the most rewarding aspects of teaching contemporary fiction, it is also a potential problem. Engrossed in ploughing these untilled literary fields, we might, in teaching them, get caught up in the process of textual and contextual exegesis without considering the way we transmit this information. As a result, it is more likely that we impose interpretations upon our students than foster their active and critical engagement with the texts in question. Granted, in an assessment-based institutional context some degree of top-down teaching is unavoidable. Nevertheless, at times we seem to forget that our task, beyond the teaching of factual information, is also to teach methods – transferable skills that transcend the narrow limits of a single text and enable students to become independent sophisticated readers who can come to terms with any text, literary or non-literary.

I became aware of the dilemmas of contemporary fiction when teaching Ian McEwan's *Atonement*: a complex and challenging novel that can be approached from multiple points of entry. One, the novel can be investigated for its historical content. Its first three parts are anchored in factual historical contexts with particular relevance for British national identity: the anxious pre-WWII period, the Dunkirk episode and the experience of the Blitz. Two, the novel can be explored for its dense web of explicit and implicit intertextual references to different literary genres (drama and prose), styles (realism and modernism) and literary protagonists associated with these genres and styles. Finally, the novel invites rigorous textual investigation, particularly of narrative perspective, and explores the question of textual reliability. This stylistic feature has inevitable repercussions for our reading of the book, whose concluding epilogue exposes the previous three parts of the novel to be a text by narrator-protagonist Briony Tallis, thus emphasising the strategic and intentional nature of what we have read. In light of the epilogue, *Atonement* immediately metamorphoses from an apparently straightforward historical novel into a historiographical critique of the uses of history in personal and collective mythology. Although its different dimensions may be prised apart and investigated independently, the novel's meaning lies in their interaction. As an 'innocent' reading of the novel's historical dimension is impossible, we need to investigate the impact of structure and style on content and context to do justice to the text. This need becomes all the more pressing when *Atonement* is taught outside of Britain, where the novel's contextual significance can only ever be explained in a very limited way, to the extent that contextualisation may be counterproductive, merely affirming students' distance from the text rather than enabling them to grasp and, potentially, challenge it.

On the whole, *Atonement* was a success amongst my students, who liked it as a psychological drama raising complex moral issues (such as crime, guilt and punishment) and inviting them to take sides. Far less obvious and, above all, interesting was the cultural significance of the novel's specific historical locations, which they saw as a mere decorative backdrop for the book's personal story. In saying this, I do not mean to accuse my students of ignorance or unwillingness to respond to my teaching. To the contrary, their reactions not only suggested that I might have to rethink the way I teach the text, they also altered and extended my general view of the novel. Their resistance to my approach raised crucial questions: about the process of reading and interpreting, the incalculable enjoyment factor that shapes this process, as well as the enduring relevance of presumably outmoded notions like 'authorial intention'. More specifically, my students' resistance to the novel's thematic and contextual concerns made me wonder to what extent this reaction might be a part of the author's politics.

*Atonement* is arguably McEwan's most 'British' novel to date (even the recently published *Saturday*, although exclusively set in London, returns to a more cosmopolitan, global perspective), apparently reiterating the perennial assertion that Britain – at its most isolated but also finest hour – could and would take it. While the associations evoked by the novel are of continuing relevance to Britons 60 years after the end of the Second World War, even to those who were born decades after the event, they potentially baffle a continental reader whose associations with the war, while no less potent, are simply different. However, far from only testifying to the cultural divide that separates German students of English Literature from the texts they study, the sense of bafflement experienced by non-British readers of the novel might be the result of the exclusionary potential of its historical setting, the implied emotional significance of which may forever remain closed to readers with a different cultural background. Since to focus on historical content would affirm this exclusion, especially when the book is read and taught outside Britain, a conscious focus on narrative and perspective may ultimately have a more lasting educational effect. At the risk of appearing counterintuitive, especially in view of the apparent popularity of historical fiction in current curricula (see the data collected by Nick Bentley, this volume), I suggest that in teaching McEwan's novel one ought to initially disregard its historical content and focus on its linguistic specificity: its *textual politics* rather than the *political issues* to which it makes reference, the form of its historiographic critique rather than the historical objects of that critique. While contextualisation potentially reduces students to mere receptacles of the explanatory reference material brought to the novel, 'textualisation' responds to the need to make them more independent readers. A conscious focus on the novel's narrative strategies not only brings students closer to McEwan's novel, it also immunises them against the narrative strategies employed by the narrator-protagonist to assert her dominance. As I will argue, this readerly resistance against the text not only entails a clear political dimension, it also is an effect produced by the novel itself.[2]

## *2. Content and Context*

A few summative remarks about *Atonement* may be in order before identifying possible didactic entryways into the text.[3] McEwan's four-part novel is the story of Briony Tallis, an upper-middle class girl guilty of unjustly charging her childhood companion Robbie Turner with the rape of her cousin Lola. Her false accusation leads to Robbie's conviction, imprisonment and separation from his lover, Briony's older sister Cecilia. *Atonement* portrays Briony at different moments in her life: as an adolescent, a young adult and an ageing woman recently diagnosed with vascular dementia. While in part one, set in a country estate in the South of England on a blistering summer's day in 1935, we witness the events leading up to Briony's fatal accusation from a variety of (contradictory) perspectives, part two, set in the Northwest of France at the time of the evacuation of the British Expeditionary Force and part three, set in London during the Blitz, are dedicated to Robbie and Briony respectively, illustrating their individual experiences of the war. Part three climaxes in a cathartic encounter between Briony, her sister Cecilia, who had broken off all contact with the family after Robbie's imprisonment, and Robbie, during which Briony apologises for what she has done and promises to rehabilitate her victim(s) by recanting her first, false statement.

Up to that point, this is a romantic tale of star-crossed lovers finally rewarded by fate (or rather: by the remorse of a repentant perpetrator). This happy ending, however, is not to be. Part three ends with the tell-tale signature "BT London, 1999", which leads over into the novel's final part, set in the present, by identifying the previous three sections as fiction. In this part, we learn that the text we have read is in fact Briony's book, the final version of a life-long attempt to atone for her guilt by retelling the story in ever-new ways. What this epilogue also identifies are some of the changes Briony had made to the facts, the most manipulative of them being her denial of the deaths of Robbie and Cecilia and the fictional depiction of the apology she never made. Nevertheless, subsequent to her confession she defends her fictionalisation of reality not only as a necessary act of remembering that guarantees Cecilia's and Robbie's survival, she also describes it as a merciful transformation of fact into a comforting fiction for the sake of the reader:

> [...] I can no longer think what purpose would be served if, say, I tried to persuade my reader, by direct or indirect means, that Robbie Turner died of septicaemia at Bray Dunes on 1 June 1940, or that Cecilia was killed in September of the same year by the bomb that destroyed Balham Underground station. That I never saw them that year. That my walk across London ended at the church on Clapham Common, and that a cowardly Briony limped back to the hospital, unable to confront her recently bereaved sister [....] How could that constitute an ending? What sense or hope or satisfaction could a reader draw from such an account? Who would want to believe that they never met again, never fulfilled their love? Who would want to believe that, except in the service of the bleakest realism? (370-371)

In short, what we have read is the melodramatic transformation of a tragic tale of love lost, things unsaid and actions never taken into a heroic romance with a blissfully happy ending. With her final confession, Briony appears to admit – from the perspective of an elderly woman recently diagnosed with a fatal degenerative disease – boldly and self-critically to her manipulation of the past. Her belated acknowledgement of her lifelong manipulative need to tamper with reality also affirms her earlier self-depiction that she is "one of those children possessed by a desire to have the world just so" (4). This desire becomes apparent not only in her meticulous arrangement of the toys in her bedroom (5), it also expresses itself in her attitude to writing and provides the reason for her abandoning her early dramatic experiments in favour of prose, as the incalculability of performance undermines the aims and intentions of her play texts. In part one, the shambolic rehearsals of her melodrama *The Trials of Arabella* challenge her authorial intentions. The interference of her cousins, whom she grudgingly allows to perform in her play, leads her to acknowledge that "the self-contained world she had drawn with clear and perfect lines had been defaced with the scribble of other minds, other needs" (36). The act of writing prose, by contrast, allows Briony to assert her dominance and power because writing relies on an unencumbered and near-telepathic transmission, or so she believes: "by means of inking symbols onto a page, she was able to send thoughts and feelings from her mind to her reader's" (37).

However, the adult's self-accusation cannot undo the child's past failure to act; on the contrary, it is part of Briony's larger plan. Presenting herself as manipulative and selective, Briony is as strategic as she is when she describes the reader as greedy for harmony. As such, Briony's strategic self-critique draws attention to the fact that *Atonement* is essentially a novel about the narrator's protracted non-atonement, underlining her cowardice, dishonesty and desire to dominate. What is more – and this ought to be a central aim when teaching the novel – it invites the reader to understand and to resist Briony's strategy of obfuscation and dominance.

On one level, Briony establishes her dominance by various intertextual or contextual references. The novel's topographies – country house, Dunkirk and London during the Blitz – have a near mythical status in the collective memory of Britain: symbols of national unity, they constitute a symbolic code directed at an exclusive circle of readers to whom its significance is immediately transparent. The Tallises' house, a mansion built on the site of an eighteenth-century building destroyed by a fire, within extensive grounds complete with country house accoutrements like a temple, a fountain and well-kept lawns, invokes the positive associations of harmonious coexistence associated with the seventeenth-century poetic genre that triggered off this enduringly popular cultural discourse.[4] The background of European conflict against which this setting is placed heightens these ideals. The Dunkirk chapter conjures up notions of working-class solidarity and bravery, which are played out not only against the callousness of the German fighter planes overhead, but also the stoically indifferent and/or potentially dangerous French peasants on the ground. Part three shows Briony as a nurse doing her bit on the home front like a latter-day Florence Nightingale. Functioning as stages for individual and national bravery, these environments (or Briony's use of them) endorse the popular notion that the Second World War was "the people's war", during which Britain, despite all class and gender divisions, closed ranks against (and thus vanquished) a common enemy.

However, although *Atonement* here seems to buy into a particularly resilient popular discourse, the novel eschews the media Anglocentrism of TV channels like UKTV History. The novel's epilogue, questioning the reliability of the text we have just read as well as, by implication, all narratives, diverts our attention from the historical set pieces through which Briony affirms her identity to the ideological uses to which these are put. The epilogue thus urges us to investigate the historiographic depths underneath the novel's historical surface, above all the disturbing analogy between individual and national heroism, established also by the uncanny aural similarity of "Briony" and "Britain". In a nutshell, the novel is about the stories we tell ourselves, as individuals and nations, the reciprocal relevance of such stories – as well as their failure. As such, it participates in the critical reassessment, taking place in recent years, of the function of the Second World War in the British imagination and the politics of its representation.[5]

The question for the teacher is how to make the novel's critique of historical myths transparent without becoming Briony's accomplice by repeating her strategies. This complicity may arise if we focus on theme and context rather than the novel's textual strategies. Unfortunately, this is exactly what I did in teaching the text for the first time in an undergraduate course called "Studying the Novel". Rather than focusing on the text, I started off with the context – not least because I thought that the students would find this more interesting. On the basis of short, purely informative and fact-based presentations by students, we approached McEwan's novel through a variety of topics (such as its historical background as well as the relevance of World War II in British Culture, the intertextual dimension of the text as well as their postmodern premises) Although these topics are immediately relevant to the book, looking back at the course I think that a more textual approach to the novel would not only have been more rewarding for students, but also closer to the critical perspective of McEwan's novel.

### *3. Matters of Perspective*

The starting point for a truly productive reading of the novel is its final deconstructive section: the epilogue, which overshadows the book's meaning and hence any interpretation of the text. Other than critics who have seen the epilogue as cheap "postmodern gimmickry" on the part of McEwan (on that charge see Finney), I take it as a serious signal inviting the reader to withstand the fiction created by Briony in parts one to three, asking them to recognise and deconstruct her strategy. This is best achieved through the close analysis of key scenes in which this strategy becomes apparent, whether they are selected for or by the students.

One of these scenes is when Briony witnesses an exchange between her sister Cecilia and her childhood friend Robbie by a fountain in the garden, where they seem to struggle over a vase. Although apparently in the powerful observer position, Briony claims not to grasp what is really going on. Seeing her sister, in response to what she describes as an "imperious gesture" (38) by Robbie, strip near naked to retrieve the vase from the fountain where it had slipped, she reacts with confused consternation:

> The sequence was illogical – the drowning scene, followed by a rescue, should have preceded the marriage proposal. Such was Briony's last thought before she accepted that she did not understand, and that she must simply watch. Unseen, from two storeys up, with the benefit of unambiguous sunlight, she had privileged access across the years to adult behaviour, to rites and conventions she knew nothing about, as yet (39).

Despite the precociously self-confident tone of the passage, its inherent contradictions serve to express confusion: Briony's self-image shifts from experience ("privileged access") to innocence ("as yet") and thus shapes the way we perceive the scene: as a display of adult rites and conventions which seem positively dangerous. The narrative makes obvious who is victim and perpetrator here, its underlying juxtaposition of masculine force ("imperious") and feminine innocence already evoking notions of violation and rape. Briony's claim that she does not judge the scene because it does not fit her scheme of things, therefore, is a deliberate misrepresentation. The passage foreshadows a later moment of misinterpretation by Briony, when she reads her sister and Robbie's passionate embrace as an act of violence. Here, Robbie fulfils the image of the "maniac" as she had imagined him earlier, his embrace of her innocent sister "with her bare shoulders and thin arms so frail" (123) a violent, physical attack. This instance of sibling solidarity also entails a clear gender dimension, uniting the two different female characters against a common male enemy.

An instance later that day, when Briony, again from a window above, sees Robbie crossing the lawn towards the house, similarly conjoins the accusation of an other with the defence of herself:

> Some time after five, when there was talk of breakfast being prepared [...] the word flashed through the household that a figure who might be Robbie was approaching across the park. [...] At first they saw nothing, though Briony thought she could make out the tread of shoes along the drive. Then everyone could hear it, and there was a collective murmur and shifting of weight as they caught sight of an indefinable shape, no more than a greyish smudge against the white, almost a hundred yards away. [...] No one could quite believe what was emerging. Surely it was a trick of the mist and light. No one in this age of telephones and motor cars could believe that giant seven or eight feet high existed in crowded Surrey. But here it was, an apparition as inhuman as it was purposeful (181-182).

As in the earlier scene, Briony invokes and yet defies the link between sight and power: although looking out on the park, she claims that she is unable to identify the approaching object. In the absence of clear vision, hearing initially supersedes sight; once the shape emerging from the darkness has become more visible, it becomes a site of projections and interpretations. With Briony's sense perceptions fooled by the darkness, she resorts to child-like associations with fairy tales or horror stories. At the same time, these associations are duplicitous and strategic. Identifying the dehumanised "thing" on the lawn as dangerous, while defending the person observing it, these depictions channel the reader's perception. Briony again claims to be not guilty, while surreptitiously accusing Robbie of a deed he did not commit. However, rather than the inhuman creature Briony imagines, it is her narrative that is purposeful here, reinterpreting her limited perception as a sign of innocence, the inability to interpret as a lack of capacity.

Briony also asserts her innocence in yet another way. Asked by the police inspector investigating Lola's rape whether she is convinced that it was Robbie she had seen in the garden near where the scene of the crime, a significant exchange develops, in the course of which Briony will accuse an innocent man while simultaneously denying this:

> "I know it was him."
> "Let's forget what you know. You're saying you saw him."
> "Yes, I saw him."
> "Just as you see me."
> "Yes."
> "You saw him with your own eyes."
> "Yes. I saw him. I saw him" (181).

Rather than asking questions, the policeman here makes suggestive statements, literally putting words in Briony's mouth. Although the line "You're saying you saw him" clearly gives her some responsibility for her false evidence, the passage as a whole suggests that an outside force is involved in her misrepresentation of the facts. Here, the assertion of innocence is extended, as Briony suggests that getting things wrong is human. Suggesting that to make mistakes is part of the human condition, the above exchange transforms Briony from an exception into the norm, making her part of a larger group of people united by their guilt.

The novel's changeable narrative perspective (notably in part one, where it shifts from chapter to chapter) serves to underline this strategy. The different viewpoints that orchestrate Briony's story[6], most of them limited and/or incorrect, not only create the impression of multiperspectivity (and hence appear to express a sense of tolerance), they also suggest that misinterpretation is ubiquitous and unavoidable and hence cannot be blamed on Briony alone. For instance, Cecilia's take on Robbie is contradictory to say the least. On seeing Robbie work in the garden, she dismisses his horticultural interests as "his last craze but one" and his plans for a medical career "pretentious" and "presumptuous" – "since it was her father who would have to pay" (19). A little later there is the suggestion that there might be more behind these dismissive statements, as Cecilia describes herself as "exasperated" by Robbie's "affectation of distance" (22) towards her. Her view of her younger sister is equally contemptuous, as she describes her writing as "an enveloping obsession" and the rehearsals of her play shaped by "her frenetic vision" (21). Even presumably responsible adults are subject to misperceptions. In a way that is typical for McEwan's work (especially novels like *The Cement Garden* and *The Child in Time*) Briony's parents are shown to be figures of authority bereft of their superior vision: while Mr Tallis is away on mysterious assignments in London, Briony's mother keeps to her bed nursing a migraine. Weak witnesses both, they nevertheless join in – and thus legitimise – the collective attack against Robbie.

Of course, as the determining perspective behind these depictions is that of Briony, they too form part of her attempt to diminish her guilt. Cecilia's criticism of her sister, for instance, literally invites disagreement on the part of the reader, who is thereby summoned to Briony's defence. Furthermore, Briony disturbingly includes Robbie in the circle of misinterpreters. In a crucial passage, she has him describe "a white shape which seemed, at first to be part of the pale stone of the parapet. Staring at it dissolved its outlines, but within a few paces it had taken on a vaguely human form" (93). Only somewhat later does he realise that this vague shape is in fact Briony. The fact that this scene anticipates Briony's fantastic depiction, cited above, of Robbie as a destructive machine not only serves to legitimise her misinterpretation by revealing that others (even Robbie) are prone to mistakes, too; in a way that is typical for her self-defensive strategy the passage collapses Robbie and Briony, victim and perpetrator, the innocent and the guilty, into one another.

While the multiple perspectives in part one create the impression of a microcosm in which human beings are united by their fallibility, in the subsequent parts the broad spectrum of human perceptions and misinterpretations narrows as the text zooms in on Briony, Cecilia and Robbie. At the same time as suggesting their fundamental relatedness as heroic others against the world, the reader is here told where to direct her or his sympathies. In the Dunkirk episode, the former outsider Robbie is depicted as a person of natural authority and superior communicative skills. Similarly, the sloppy Cecilia is shown to be resourceful, authoritative and hard working. And even Briony, who initially retains her role as a social outcast, especially when she begins to work in a London hospital, manages to develop the practical side of her personality. What unites these characters is their sense of integration rather than exclusion, adaptability rather than egocentricity. Essentially, what Briony depicts in parts two and three is an intimate circle of war heroes united by their struggle against a callous enemy, although these experiences take place independently. These individual acts of heroism are rewarded when the three characters are finally reunited in the emotional, almost cathartic showdown in London, in which Briony promises repentance.

In reality, of course, this fantasy expresses Briony's helpless attempt at undoing something that she cannot change. Nor can she forget it – not until she herself "fad[es] into unknowing" (355) as her mental faculties decay. Nevertheless, despite the futility of her imagined atonement, her appropriation of history to manage personal crisis is emblematic of any form – collective or individual – of identity construction. Because as such it implicates non-British (and specifically German readers) in a particular way, it deserves special attention.

## *4. Conclusion*

One of the most crucial insights to be gleaned from Briony's textual self-creation is that the self always needs an other to define itself against, that identity relies on difference. Whereas in part one of McEwan's novel that other is Robbie, in parts two and three Briony's imagined circle of war heroes is united by their commitment against another, more real outside force: the Nazi enemy. However, although it would seem that *Atonement* moves from the domestic to the public sphere, from the petty concerns of the country-house microcosm towards a larger, apparently more relevant framework, the public is already used in part one to judge individual characters. The cousins who come to live with the Tallises because of their parents' divorce are initially described as "refugees from a bitter domestic civil war" (8); on arrival, however, the victims soon metamorphose into a dangerous force of invasion. Lola, in particular, the oldest of the three, soon appears as a powerful competitor potentially annihilating Briony, who ponders ominously that "the advance of Lola's dominion" was "merciless and made self-pity irrelevant" (15).

Students could be asked to identify, categorise and assess other scenes in the novel which similarly establish a sense of conflict and difference. For instance, in the Dunkirk section, even Robbie's relationship to his fellow soldiers is shown to be complex, however admirable their mutual support. The fact that he speaks French and his gentlemanly demeanour single him out as different, a stranger within his own class. The retreating British army is presented as a motley crew: the down-at-heel privates, of whom Robbie is one, feel shamed by the "discipline and cohesion" (241) of a spick and span platoon of Welsh Guards; Scottish soldiers in kilts and with bagpipes are ridiculed by the British infantry (218). In Dunkirk, the rage of the ordinary soldiers against the RAF, by whom they feel to have been betrayed, climaxes in a violent attack on one of them (250-254). Class conflict does not spare Briony and her sister: while the former is scolded for her upper-class naivety by her superiors in the London hospital where she is being trained, Cecilia is confronted by her nagging landlady, to whom she responds with a tone of haughty superiority (334).

It would seem, then, that Briony's account of British wartime experience, in tune with recent historical scholarship, complicates the typical image of "the people's war" – from which process she does not even exclude her own family. A revealing passage in part one summarises the Tallis' family history, identifying them as middle-class arrivistes whose wealth stems from their grandfather's canny exploitation of the fears and suspicions of an emerging risk society: a locksmith turned industrialist, he provided those who desired an ever greater seclusion from the world with the relevant products. Yet despite their social ascent, the Tallises are quite clearly not up to the world they strive to enter: their house is not only a graceless imitation of the eighteenth-century model that once stood on the site, it is also far from the harmonious haven with which the country-house myth had always, falsely, associated these estates. Like seventeenth-century England, which saw the emergence of country-house poetry as a homogenising ideology against groundbreaking social changes in which poets were ambiguous participants (Wayne 78-80), Briony's world is one of transformation. If, in early modern country-house poems, it is the newly emerging mercantile middle class taking over the splendid aristocratic estates, here it is the working class – represented by Robbie – staking out its claims in a world now dominated by capitalist lords of the manor. Briony's fatal accusation is only one way of putting a stop to this daunting intrusion, as the figure of Paul Marshall suggests. A friend of Briony's brother, Marshall is the owner of a sweet factory whose chocolate bar, appropriately and cynically called Amo Bar, is a cheap synthetic snack included in the troops' kitbags – fodder for cannon fodder. If the Tallis family demonstrates that new money is fake, not to be trusted, the figure of Marshall serves to suggest that it also callously profits from death and destruction.

Again, in light of the epilogue, Briony's vision of a disunited Britain is less evidence of her differentiated (if not disillusioned) worldview than part of her strategic self-defence. Fairness and honesty, it is suggested, are scarce in a world overshadowed by internal conflicts and misconceptions; small wonder, therefore, that she did what she did. And yet the different fronts of this divided Britain quickly close ranks in the face of a common enemy – be it a promising working-class upstart or the Germans – enabling the creation of a superficial sense of unity. Craving this sense of unity, Briony herself sets up the strategic divisions that maintain it, causing a not inconsiderable collateral damage in the process. However heroically she may act after her false accusation of Robbie, these actions are dwarfed by her inexcusable guilt.

It is here that Briony's self-portrait reaches out to the novel's readers, notably those who would find themselves on the other side of the divisions she has set, inviting comparison with other novels by McEwan. *Atonement* is unusual in so far as it skirts the European concerns and contexts that characterise so much of McEwan's work. *The Innocent* is set in post-war Berlin, *The Comfort of Strangers* in the unnamed but recognisable Venice, *Black Dogs* in post-reunification Berlin and contemporary France. A world away from the tourist and culinary curiosity for the European continent in the novels by Peter Mayle or Joanne Harris, McEwan's European settings point to the vital necessity of the European project as well as its problems in the face of a history of conflict. *Atonement*, by contrast, written from an exclusively British perspective, is clearly more one-sided and reduces the historical others on which British national identity relies (such as the nameless German soldiers in their planes bombing the French countryside and London, the French civilians as well as Briony's French husband Thierry – who mentioned only once and in passing) to marginal extras in the narrator-protagonist's heroic pageant. By extension, Briony's non-British readers, too, are left out of this narrative, relegated to observers of her procession of myths, lacking the information to understand what she casually assumes to be common knowledge.

As a final interpretive gesture, therefore, it is relevant to address student readers' own exclusion from Briony's fictional world and the function and significance of that exclusion. Rather than enabling students' grasp of the historical facts that make McEwan's novel meaningful, the task of the teacher is to embarrass the narrator who resorts to these facts by inciting their readerly resistance to them. Rather than providing them with the relevant information to understand what the narrator-protagonist takes as given, or by pointing them towards topics they may research, a more appropriate way of studying the novel might be to get students to formulate their own role in Briony's strategic narrative, for instance by confronting them with straightforward questions about their own relationship to the text. What is it you do not know, and why might that be the case? Why should these issues be relevant to you? Is there another, more universal tale entailed in this novel, which might be worth investigating? And especially: whose tale is it: Briony's, or McEwan's? It is by paying particular attention to the narrative framework staked out by the novel's epilogue, and hence by rejecting the ideological narrative contained with in that framework, that students may finally get a word in edgeways in Briony's cunning and manipulative tale, whose implications – when unearthed by a conscious close reading of the text – move from the personal to the political and connect past and present.

## *Notes*

1 A good example in the case of *Bridget Jones* are the 'instants' to which the protagonist is periodically addicted. The reference could open up an

extensive cultural investigation of the theme of addiction in Fielding's novel – if readers understand what instants are. However, I am aware of a few colleagues in Germany who were puzzled by the term.

2 My emphasis on resistance reaccentuates James Harold's observation that the novel is open to multiple interpretations. By contrast, I suggest that McEwan urges the reader to actively reject the novel's overt story line to explore its more unsettling implications. *Atonement* eschews the idea that ' anything goes' in literary analysis and instead urges its readers to distinguish between fact and fiction.

3 All references in the text are to the 2002 Vintage paperback edition.

4 On seventeenth-century country house discourse see Boyd McBride, on its continuing ideological function in today's popular culture see Wayne.

5 The role of World War II in Britains's collective memory has been treated extensively by historians and writers of historical literature concerned with the question of Englishness (see also Ruth McElroy's contribution to this collection). For seminal historical studies that explore the mythical dimension of the Second World War see Angus Calder's *The Myth of the Blitz* and Sonya O. Rose's *Which People's War*. Amongst the literary texts which deal critically with the function of World War II in the British imagination are the plays *Hitler Dances* (1972) by Howard Brenton and *Plenty* by David Hare (1978), as well as novels such as *The Remains of the Day* by Kazuo Ishiguro (1990), *Spies* by Michael Frayn (2002) or *The Rules of Perspective* by Adam Thorpe (2005).

6 On point of view in *Atonement* see Frank Kermode's review of the novel.

## *Bibliography*

Calder, Angus: *The Myth of the Blitz*. 1991, London, 2004.

Finney, Brian: "Briony's Stand Against Oblivion: Ian McEwan's *Atonement.*" [http://www.csulb.edu/~hfinney/McEwan.html] (22 March 2004).

Harold, James: "Narrative Engagement with *Atonement* and *The Blind Assassin*", *Philosophy and Literature* 29, no. 1, 2005, 130-145.

Kermode, Frank: "Point of View" (Review of *Atonement*), *London Review of Books* 23, no. 19 (2001).

McBride, Kari Boyd: *Country-House Discourse in Early Modern England: A Cultural Study of Landscape and Legitimacy*, Aldershot, 2001.

McEwan, Ian: *Atonement*, London, 2002.

Rose, Sonya O.: *Which People's War? National Identity and Citizenship in Wartime Britain, 1939-1945*, Oxford, 2003.

Wayne, Don E.: Penshurst: The Semiotics of Place and the Poetics of History, Madison, WI, 1984.

*Mitchell R. Lewis (Elmira)*

# The Gothic Gaze: The Politics of Gender in Patrick McGrath's *Asylum*

Patrick McGrath's *Asylum* (1997) is a contemporary gothic novel that explores the objectification of women in gothic literature and psychoanalysis. In the classroom teachers can use McGrath's novel to raise important issues about gender, first-person narration, the relationship between power and knowledge, and especially the gaze. It is written after the manner of a Freudian case history about an extraordinary female patient named Stella Raphael, but it calls into question the motives of the male narrator, Peter Cleave, a criminal psychologist who is attempting to heal his patient and to account for her behaviour. In doing so the novel critiques the narrator's perceptions, his narrative protocols, his professional knowledge, and his relationship to the asylum, suggesting that Stella is a victim of a patriarchal institution. What becomes clear by the end of the novel is that McGrath is trying to expose the gender politics that informs so much of the gothic and psychoanalytic traditions.

Thus, pedagogically speaking, *Asylum* is particularly suitable for courses on gothic literature, gender studies, and psychoanalytic theory. I routinely assign the novel in such courses, and the way in which I teach it has developed in response to my students' tendencies to identify with Peter, to assume that his narrative is accurate and authoritative. Typically, I encourage students to question the narrator by guiding them through a close reading of the novel that focuses on the similarities between Peter and one of his psychotic patients, Edgar Stark, a major character who becomes involved with Stella. I then proceed to discuss the novel in a series of illuminating contexts, including McGrath's other work, the gothic genre, Freud's case histories, and literary theory. In this way students may begin not only to critique Peter, but also to consider the larger issues of gender and representation that are central to my courses and to literary and cultural studies.

Before elaborating on my pedagogic practice, let me briefly summarise the novel. In the summer of 1959 Forensic psychiatrist Max Raphael takes up a job as deputy superintendent at an asylum for the criminally insane. Soon his wife Stella secretly falls in love with a patient, Edgar Stark, a talented but psychotic sculptor prone to "morbid jealousy", the pathological delusion that whoever he is involved with is cheating on him.[1] Edgar's condition eventually will prompt him to kill his lover, and he is presently in the asylum for having killed his first wife, Ruth, who was also his model. Apparently Edgar had decapitated his wife, stuck the head on his sculpture stand, and "worked it with his tools as though it were a lump of clay" (241). Edgar eventually manages to escape from the asylum, hiding out in the underworld of London, and Stella soon joins him, leaving her husband and child behind. Edgar's delusions begin to emerge, as he attempts to sculpt a bust of Stella's head, but the police intervene before Edgar can kill Stella, although Edgar apparently escapes. Avoiding the fate of Ruth, Stella is then reunited with her husband, whose career is now in ruins because of his wife's infidelity and some bad decisions he has made.

Stella's psychological condition, however, begins to deteriorate. Still in love with Edgar, she becomes increasingly unhappy with her marriage, growing "hysterical" and then clinically depressed (189). Tragically, while on a school field trip with her son Charlie, she sits idly by and watches him drown, as "black waves" of depression wash over her consciousness and distort her sense of reality (200). The public outrage at her apparent indifference to her child's death only speeds up her admission to the asylum, where she comes under the care of Edgar's doctor, Peter Cleave, the narrator of the novel who apparently falls in love with Stella and, after getting permission from Max, offers to marry her. An art collector as well as a psychologist, Peter is taken with Stella's beauty and thinks of her as a "fine *objet*" that he might add to his personal art collection (222). Stella, however, is still in love with Edgar. Although she accepts Peter's proposal, she appears to be manipulating him in order to see Edgar, whom she believes to be back in the asylum. When Peter eventually lies to Stella, telling her that Edgar is not in the asylum, Stella commits suicide. The novel ends with Peter thinking that he still has his Stella after all, in the form of Edgar's sculpture, now cast in black bronze, "a thin, beautiful, tiny, anguished head" that Peter keeps in his desk to remind himself of Stella (254).

The conclusion of the novel literally ends with the objectification of Stella, the reduction of her to an art object. To make matters worse, the sculpture is a reflection of the psychotic gaze of Edgar. In fact, Stella refers to it as "pathology in clay" and as "an account of [Edgar's] fraught and increasingly tortured relationship with her" (130). Stella's descriptions are apt since the bust is scarred and mutilated by the carvings of a psychotic. In this context, Peter's concluding thought that he still possesses his deceased fiancé calls into question his reliability as a narrator, in spite of his pose as a disinterested psychologist narrating a case history about Stella. The conclusion, in effect, completes the novel's developing parallel between Peter and Edgar, suggesting that they are doubles, both misreading Stella, seeing in her what they want to see, not what she is. McGrath establishes this connection by equating Edgar's sculpture with Peter's first person narrative of Stella, conflating the psychotic perceptions of these two characters. It is this equation that I bring to my students' attention for close analysis.

The parallel between Peter and Edgar begins early in the novel when Peter says, "I have always been fascinated by the artistic personality, I think because the creative impulse is so vital a quality in psychiatry; certainly it is in my own clinical work" (5). Here Peter begins to break down the distinction between art and psychiatry, and what we later learn is that Peter does indeed rely on his often-overheated imagination to construct his narrative of Stella. On one occasion, for instance, when Stella refuses to betray the details of her sex life with Edgar, Peter notes,

> I imagine it was urgent and primitive, a thing of hunger and instinct. I imagine he took her at once, without finesse, and that she wanted this, she was as avid as he was, no coyness now, no hesitation at all. And I imagine it was over rather quickly. (25)

Peter's narrative is frequently punctuated with such moments, where his imagination takes over. In fact, when Stella runs off with Edgar to London, where a significant part of the novel takes place, Peter has to admit that "I lose sight of Stella at this point, and have only her own account, offered to me in conversation tentatively and disjointedly, and sometimes emotionally, of the days that followed" (103). The result is a narrative grounded more in imagination than in observation, reflecting the needs and biases of the narrator, saying more about the perception of the narrator than his subject.

The parallel between Peter's psychoanalytic attempt to comprehend Stella and Edgar's artistic attempt to do the same becomes clearer when Peter explains, "The problem was that the further [Stella] moved away from the hospital the harder I found it to reconstruct her experience, to mold it into something with a shape and a meaning I could recognise" (115). Here in this metafictional moment Peter not only admits to the difficulty of telling his story, but also draws an implicit analogy between writing and sculpting in his use of the word "mold", a term connoting work with clay. Underscoring this analogy all the more is the very next sentence, which starts a new paragraph: "Edgar had started working in clay and it wasn't going well" (115). The project in which Edgar is engaged is his bust of Stella, so in these passages we see both Peter and Edgar attempting to understand Stella, to deal with the difficulties involved, and we see their two efforts as analogous, as relying on imagination. McGrath, in effect, is equating the characters of Peter and Edgar, suggesting that Peter's perception is as distorted as Edgar's, each amounting to a kind of gothic gaze.

The result is the objectification of Stella. Indeed, both Peter and Edgar treat Stella merely as an art object. Before the affair between Edgar and Stella develops, Edgar attempts to sketch her head and, as Peter notes, "in a few minutes had produced a strange sketch, all smudged lines, not at all naturalistic, with none of the roundedness and monumentality I saw in Stella, but a curious likeness all the same" (15). Here the emphasis is on Stella as an abstract art object. Later Edgar tells a friend that he can identify Stella because she looks like a "Rubens" (83). Finally, after Peter proposes to Stella, he thinks, "I had more than once imagined her in my house, as she once so frequently had been, among my furniture, my books, my art. Oh, she had a place there, among my fine *objets*" (222). Whether we look at Edgar or Peter, in each case Stella is regarded as an art object, and the implication throughout the novel is that Stella's being viewed as a piece of art is a metaphor for the distorted perceptions that the male characters have of her.

Repeatedly, in fact, the novel emphasises the gaze of the male characters, which is linked to misreading and misinterpretation. The most striking instance is when Edgar begins his sculpture of Stella in his secret London flat. Here Peter explains that Edgar wanted "to do her head" so that he could "translate his relationship with Stella, the complex of strong emotion she had aroused in him, into some form of expression" (104). Here the word "translation" brings in the note of interpretation. Moreover, as Stella observes Edgar, she "watch[es] his gaze on her, his impersonal gaze, and hear[s] the darting pencil scratching at the pad" (105). Stella also hears "the grunts and sighs that [suggest] he was performing a delicate surgical operation rather than making a drawing. She had never seen him properly at work before. She felt she didn't know him" (105). In these passages there is not only an emphasis on Edgar's eyes, but also a link to the medical profession in the phrase "performing a delicate surgical operation", another clue in the novel that works to break down the distinction between art and psychiatry. The passage also recalls Stella's remark that the doctors at the asylum have "terrible psychiatric gazes" (49). Also interesting in this passage is that Stella feels like Edgar is misrepresenting her. In response to his work she says to Edgar, "It's as if you don't know who I am" (105), and he responds that he doesn’t want "to see you" (105). Edgar says he doesn't want "certainty" just a "likeness" (105). Edgar's goal, apparently, is to produce a pure representation of Stella divorced of any psychological factors, what Edgar's friend Nick calls "the truth" (106). The final results, however, are baffling to Stella, who when Edgar finished "would sit by herself in the kitchen with her compact mirror, tying to see what he saw" (106), but being unable to do so.

The implication, of course, is that Edgar is repeating the same psychological process with Stella that he went through with Ruth, his growing delusions eventually blocking out all perception of his wife. As with Stella, Edgar attempted to sculpt Ruth before he killed her, eventually decapitating her. Near the end, he claims, "I couldn't see her at all" (127). This carries over into the portrayal of Peter, who also fails to see Stella not only because his account of her is not grounded in observation, but also because he apparently develops a romantic attachment for her that loses sight of Stella herself, ignoring her problems with mental health, family, and Edgar. At the end of the novel Peter discloses that in his love for

Stella he had been "blind" (250) and that he had suffered from "classic countertransference" (251), the Freudian notion about a doctor losing his objectivity by projecting his own thoughts and feelings about another person onto a patient. So like Edgar, Peter cannot really see Stella, even though he claims at the end of the novel to have pieced everything together. There are other interesting references to Peter's distorted vision. Frequently Stella observes that Peter watches her in a "rather dreamy way" (79). Moreover, when she becomes Peter's patient, Peter notes, "My eyes, she said later, seem to bore into her soul like a pair of skewers" (212). As was the case with Edgar, Stella feels scrutinised by a cold clinical gaze. In fact, she says, "You make me feel like a specimen! God knows I don't bear scrutiny these days" (213). The characterization of Peter's eyes recalls the description of Edgar's, again driving home the parallel between the two.

The upshot of all this is that in relation to the men in her life Stella feels herself to be "the invisible woman" (90), and this is indeed the impression that the reader feels by the end of the novel, when Peter claims that he still has Stella, as he gazes at the bronze head of his fiancé, whose function as a fetish is finally clear. The reader's perception of Stella is shaped by Peter, who narrates the entire novel, and the reader gradually realises that Peter's point of view is as unreliable as Edgar's and that Edgar is in fact a double of Peter, "doubling" being a typical convention of gothic novels. It is striking how little is really known about Stella even though she is the central character of the novel. She remains a mystery to the reader, who can see her only through the psychotic eyes of Peter, whose gothic gaze transforms Stella into a symptomatic fantasy saying more about Peter than Stella. *Asylum* is thus a textbook example of the objectification of women, made all the more horrifying in the context of a contemporary gothic novel about madness. The reader comes away with the sense that Stella is a victim in relationship to all three men in her life, Edgar, Peter, and Max, among whom she is passed back and forth like a commodity, without whom she has no money, home, means of support, friends or family. It is a chilling tale, indeed, but McGrath exposes the distorted perspectives of the men in Stella's life, pointing to larger issues about gender politics in gothic literature and Western culture in general. In fact, Peter himself might be taken as a symbol of patriarchy, his power and knowledge combined in a controlling institutionalised gaze. In Peter's gothic gaze we can see McGrath critiquing patriarchal authority, which the author shows as intersecting with culture, social institutions, and politics, weaving a web for victims like Stella.

Teaching *Asylum* can focus on the type of close reading I gave above, but it can also place the novel in a number of other revealing contexts that can enhance student appreciation of the novel and its critique of patriarchy. First, one can link *Asylum* to McGrath's other fiction. The theme of the self-absorbed artist, for instance, is a frequent one in McGrath's work, and it is often linked to the themes of repression, psychopathology, and crime. Two stories from McGrath's *Blood and Water and Other Stories* (1988) are relevant here. In "Lush Triumphant" the painter Jack Fin, recently separated from his wife Erica, becomes obsessed with his work on a painting entitled *Wharf*, the subject of which evolves into a bull with blazing eyes, apparently galloping out of the mouth of hell. By the end of the story, it is also apparent that the imagery in the painting reflects the sexuality of Jack, being charged with displaced homosexual desire for a young boy he sees on the Wharf, but it's a sexuality of violence, anger, and alienation stemming from incipient madness. In "The Arnold Crombeck Story" a woman reporter interviews the infamous "death gardener", Arnold Crombeck, who views murder as a fine art.[2] Crombeck poisons women and then dresses them up as nymphs, sylphs, and goddesses, posing and arranging them for aesthetic effect, to produce what he calls "tableaux morts".[3] As in "Lush Triumphant", the story emphasises the connection between madness and art, portraying characters whose imaginations are shaped by madness. In *Port Mungo* (2004), finally, bohemian artist Jack Rathbone believes "art to be primarily a vehicle for the externalization of psychic injury".[4] His paintings thus become self-portraits, all of which are variations on the myth of Narcissus, as in the case of his piece "Narcissus in the Jungle". Tormented by the loss of his daughter, he becomes a self-absorbed artist whose relationships are characterised as "knots of tedious solipsism" (207).

As in the two stories from *Blood and Water*, we see in *Port Mungo* another example of a theme explicitly stated in McGrath's first novel, *The Grotesque* (1989). Here the narrator Sir Hugo claims, "in the absence of sensory information, *the imagination always tends to the grotesque*".[5] This idea is certainly affirmed in *Asylum*, as seen in the cases of Peter and Edgar. Whether artists or not, McGrath's characters weave a world of imagination shaped by their unconscious needs and frustrations, to such an extent that objective observation is called into question. In *The Grotesque* Sir Hugo is a scientist, but even he questions objectivity, noting,

> pure empiricism is extremely hard to achieve, so hard in fact, that one begins to doubt the possibility of constructing any version of reality that is not skewed in advance by the projections, denials, and impostures of the mind [...]. Out of such accidents does "truth" emerge; I begin to think it a chimera. (61)

This idea of truth being a chimera is linked to the notion of a diseased imagination running wild, creating a little world of madness as convincing as reality, and both are recurring themes in McGrath's work.

The themes are also linked to a recurring device in McGrath's fiction, the unreliable narrator. In *The Grotesque* the unreliable narrator observes that he is "trapped in a false world of shadows and phantoms" where "the borders and boundaries of the real and the fantastic have become blurred, unreliable, faulty" (80). He also notes his tendency to "cast nets of my own thought outward onto those close to me, and see them not as separate and distinct from myself but rather as extensions or manifestations of elements of my own mind" (151). In *Port Mungo* the narrator notes of her brother Jack,

> I knew his account of his own experience was not rigorously objective, but what account is? Any version of as dense a weave of events and feelings and intentions and effects as <u>life</u> will inevitably be flawed, its stresses and emphases reflecting not the truth – as if there were such a thing – but shapes of bias and denial, rather, crafted by memory in the service of the ego. (227, emphasis in the text)

In *Martha Peake* (2000) McGrath links the themes of unreliable narrators and diseased imaginations to history, equating the historian and the poet. At one point the narrator Ambrose Tree, who is writing his family history as told by his uncle, explains, "I could not be sure that what I remembered had actually been told me by my uncle, or was, rather, mere tissue I had manufactured to flesh the bare bones of his own spare narrative."[6] The fever that the narrator undergoes, which troubles his sense of what is real and what is fantasy, recalls the quote from Lord Byron that is the epigram for the third chapter of the novel: "Of its own beauty is the mind diseased, and fevers into false creation." Similar examples of unreliable narration – or "false creation" – can be found in *Dr. Haggard's Disease* (1993) and especially *Spider* (1990), the latter being the first person narrative of a schizophrenic.[7] Thus, with McGrath's other fiction teachers can foreground the aspects of *Asylum* dealing with art, imagination, point of view, and unreliable narration, allowing students to speculate about the author's preoccupation with distorted perception.

Teachers can also place *Asylum* in the context of his non-fiction. Those interested in autobiographical or historical approaches to McGrath's novel might look at his essay "A Childhood in Broadmoor Hospital" (1989), McGrath's personal account of growing up on the grounds of an asylum run by his father, who was the superintendent.[8] The essay presents an overview of some interesting patients, while also chronicling the end of the superintendent and the rise of a network of administrators, departments, and specialists. Also important are McGrath's essays on the gothic genre, the history and characteristics of which provide an interesting context for his fiction. Key essays in this regard are the Introduction to *The New Gothic* (1991), coauthored by Bradford Morrow, "Poe's Dank Vaults" (1991); and "Transgression and Decay" (1997). The essays reveal two major reference points for McGrath. The first is Edgar Allan Poe because in McGrath's opinion Poe's work marks a fundamental transition for the gothic genre as it turns from exterior objects of horror to the interiority of the mind, particularly the pathological mind. As McGrath explains in the Introduction:

> With this shift a fresh vein of gothic ore is opened, and in Poe's work we encounter minds and souls haunted by the urge to transgress and do evil, crippled with distortions of perception and moral sense, and obsessed with death and morbidity. With Poe the gothic turns inward, and starts rigorously to explore extreme states of psychological disturbance.[9]

What's striking about this quote is not only its emphasis on "psychological disturbance", a key subject of *Asylum* relating it to the Poe tradition, but also its mention of "distortions of perception". For McGrath a key characteristic of the gothic genre is its emphasis on distorted perception and particularly unreliable narration. In "Poe's Dank Vaults" McGrath notes that Poe is a master of the unreliable narrator. He cites "The Cask of Amontillado" as an example, explaining, "In Poe's tale no direct access to the real or the implicit meaning of Montresor's words can be given, because it is Montresor who narrates. The reader has no way of verifying his suspicions. "[10] As a result, "it's the reader who's walled up by Poe in this hermetic tale, immured in Montresor's insanity".[11] This "breakdown of logical and ontological categories" in Poe's story is very much a characteristic of *Asylum* and much of McGrath's other work.[12]

The second major reference point for McGrath is Sigmund Freud. As he explains in "Transgression and Decay", McGrath sees Freud as essentially expanding and exploring the ground already staked out for the gothic genre, the pathological mind. For McGrath Freud's great contributions to literature are his case studies, which "stand alongside the best of Poe".[13] These case studies, as he explains in his Introduction to *The New Gothic*, are "some of the most inspired tales in the [gothic] genre" (xiv). The relevance of the case histories to *Asylum* includes not only the question of the gothic genre, but also the fact that the novel itself is cast in the form of a case study. The novel, in other words, is narrated by a criminal psychologist about his patient and draws on the jargon and conventions of the case history. The opening sentences of the novel alone suggest its relationship to the case study:

> The catastrophic love affair characterised by sexual obsession has been a professional interest of mine for many years now. Such relationships vary widely in duration and intensity but tend to pass through the same stages. Recognition. Identification. Assignation. Structure. Complication. And so on. Stella Raphael's story is one of the saddest I know. (3)

Here the narrator presents the events of the story in hindsight, while using the professional language of psychology to classify and explain his patient (and while also making a faint allusion to the famous first sentence of Ford Madox Ford's *The Good Soldier*, another novel with an unreliable narrator, who claims the story he is about to tell is the "saddest story I have ever heard"). Later Peter will talk of such things as transference, countertransference, and "morbid jealously" (45), in the last instance alluding to Freud's theory of the delusion of infidelity in his famous case study on Dr. Schreber.[14]

McGrath's essays suggest that teachers might supplement the reading of *Asylum* with Freud's case studies. One way to use the case studies is not only to note similarities of form, but also to note the similar conflicts between doctor and patient. As *Asylum* demonstrates, McGrath's intention is to explore the tension between the male psychologist and his female patient, and the presence of this tension resembles similar and well-known ones in Freud's case histories on his female patients. The famous Dora case, published as "Fragment of an Analysis of a Case of Hysteria" (1905) is a notable instance that points out Freud's problems with intelligent female patients who resist his interpretations. Josef Breuer's equally famous case study "Anna O" (1895) is also relevant here, not only because it inspired Freud, but also because a similar problematic dynamic between doctor and patient can be seen. In each case study there is a problematising of the male psychiatric perspective in relationship to women, with hints of unacknowledged sexual issues and tensions, along with the usual transferences and countertransferences. Reading these case histories along with some notable feminist critiques as well as some biographical background on Freud can help to foreground the form, language, and conflicts of the novel, and it can lead to productive questions about point of view, narrative, gender, sexuality, power, knowledge, and the gaze.[15]

Another relevant case study is Freud's "Delusions and Dreams in Jensen's *Gradiva*" (1906). In this work Freud psychoanalyzes characters in a fictional story that in some ways replays the Pygmalion myth. The story focuses on an archaeologist named Norbert Hanold who falls in love with a woman depicted in a classical bas-relief from Pompeii, whom he names Gradiva. Hanold later finds a living Gradiva, who turns out to be a childhood friend named Zoe Bertgang whom he had loved before he become absorbed in his work. The story concludes with the two resuming their forgotten childhood love affair. Details of plot aside, Freud reads the story as evidence for his theory of dreams, repression, and treatment, but it can also be read as a male cultural fantasy involving fetishism, sublimation, art, wish-fulfillment, and the objectification of women. In fact, the story focuses on the aesthetics of women, as filtered through the masculine traditions of western art, and it raises the disturbing issue that men not only relate to women as aesthetic objects, but also require them to play the roles and rituals that men establish. In *Asylum*, as we have seen, the narrator is an art collector, frequently musing on the aesthetics of Stella's beauty, and Stella's lover, Edgar, is a sculptor who attempts not only to sculpt Stella, but also to come to know her through the sculpture itself. In each case we see a gothic gaze that fetishises Stella, transforming her into an aesthetic object. All that remains of Stella, at the end of the novel, is the distorted perceptions of her, the symptomatic fantasies which the bronze represent, and reading Freud's case history on *Gradiva* can bring out this dimension of the story as it too deals with the fetishising of women.

In addition to using Freud's work, teachers might also use examples from the gothic genre as a means of providing a context for *Asylum*. Poe, of course, would be useful here. The example McGrath cites is "The Cask of Amontillado", but another relevant Poe story is "The Oval Portrait" (1842), in which a beautiful maiden marries a painter whose work becomes her rival. Eventually the painter paints his wife, momentarily making her happy with his attention, but the process of transferring her image to canvas saps her health – a fact visible for all to see except the self-absorbed painter – and eventually, when the painting is completed, she dies. The death of the woman at the completion of the painting can be read as an allegory of the gaze, pointing out how the objectification of a woman leads to her metaphorical death in that the image of her becomes the reality for the bearer of the look. Other relevant Poe stories are the so-called "women tales" – "Berenicë" (1835), "Morella" (1835), "Ligeia" (1838), and "Eleonora" (1841). In each story a neurotic or psychotic male narrator transforms a female character into an object of obsession, fantasy and fetishism. In accordance with Poe's aesthetic dictum about the death of a beautiful woman, the female character eventually dies, as fantasy gradually consumes the narrator's sense of reality. Art also figures prominently in each case, raising the issue of the relationships between art, fantasy, and reality. As these characteristics suggest, the women tales have a lot in common with *Asylum* – disturbed unreliable narrators, obsession with women and their objectification and death, fetishism, and a blurring of the distinctions between art, fantasy, and reality. Reading *Asylum* in the context of Poe's stories will bring out these features, allowing for a discussion not only of the gothic genre, but also of the gender politics that the genre often entails.

Other relevant works from the gothic tradition include E.T.A. Hoffmann's "The Sandman" (1817), in which the main character Nathaniel falls in love with an automaton named Olympia, whom he believes to be human. The story questions the sanity of Nathaniel, whose point of view is constantly questioned in the novel, but it also questions his ability to love, Olympia symbolically standing for his own projection of an idealised woman, which is contrasted with his childhood love Clara. Freud famously analyzed the story in his essay "The Uncanny" (1919), where he noted the recurrent imagery associated with blindness. Freud associates such imagery with castration and the Oedipal complex, but it also fits in well with the theme of distorted perception common to the gothic tradition and McGrath's novel. Indeed, both stories exploit a wide range of imagery related to vision and blindness, and the contrast between Clara and Olympia is similar to that between Stella and the bronze (and to the contrast between Zoe and Gradiva). Just as Nathanial is fixated on Olympia to the exclusion of Clara, so is Peter and Edgar really fixated on the bronze to the exclusion of Stella.

Several other works of literature might also be read in conjunction with *Asylum*. One such work is Honoré de Balzac's *Sarrasine* (1830), which foregrounds the problem of perception and point-of-view in its central narrative about a sculptor who falls in love with his ideal woman, La Zambinella, who in the end turns out to be a castrato. The sculptor believes that he has found his perfect model of a woman and thus produces an idealised sculpture of her that becomes the basis for subsequent statues and paintings, but what the story really points out is that his preconceived conceptions about women derived from the history of Western art distort his perception of La Zambinella. These conceptions prompt him to draw unwarranted conclusions about the relationship between gender and sexuality. Another relevant work is Christina Rossetti's "In an Artist's Studio" (1856) which points out the contrast between what the painter sees in his subject and the subject herself, noting the he paints her "Not as she is, but as she fills his dream". Sarah Grand's new woman story "The Undefinable: A Story of an Artist's Model" (1894) goes well with the Rossetti poem because it features a female model – a new woman – who preempts the fantasising of her male painter by leaving him before he can complete his painting of her, declaring that she will not return until a new age has dawned for relationships between men and women. The theme of the quest for beauty leading to the eventual death of a woman can also be found in Nathaniel Hawthorne's "The Birthmark" (1854), a story that recalls Poe's women tales.

Lastly, teachers might also use theory in the study of *Asylum*. Particularly relevant is the discussion of fetishism, voyeurism, scopophilia, and the gaze in Laura Mulvey's classic feminist piece, "Visual Pleasure and Narrative Cinema" (1975), which draws from semiotics and psychoanalysis.[16] In this essay Mulvey discusses the ways in which images of women in film are constructed from a male perspective and according to male codes of perception, and this discussion can be directly related to an examination of *Asylum*, in which male characters, particularly the narrator, are constructing similar kinds of images of Stella, fetishising her, as seen in the novel's dominant aesthetic imagery and Stella's final reduction to a bizarre sculpture. To this classic feminist piece might also be added the critique of the clinical gaze in Michel Foucault's *The Birth of the Clinic* (1973) or the critique of the Freudian gaze in Luce Irigaray's *Speculum of the Other Woman* (1985).[17] Another relevant theoretical text is Roland Barthes' *S/Z* (1970). Significant here is not only Barthes' discussion of the various codes structuring and undermining representation, but also and perhaps more importantly his close reading of Balzac's *Sarrasine*. Barthes' attention to the ways in which the sculptor's perception and his final sculpture of the castrato are determined by the cultural connotations or codes of femininity provides another excellent context for a discussion of *Asylum*, where similar codes and connotations come into play not only in Edgar's sculpture of Stella, but also in the point of view of Peter's overall narrative. In fact, Barthes' idea that "*Sarrasine* represents the very confusion of representation" might well be said of *Asylum* itself.[18]

In questioning representation McGrath is ultimately questioning the gothic gaze that objectifies and fetishes women. McGrath thus provides teachers with an excellent novel for exploring the politics of gender in literature. In the classroom this fundamental topic of contemporary literary studies can be explored, as I have suggested, through ever widening contexts. First one can begin with a close reading of *Asylum*. Next one can proceed to McGrath's other fiction and essays, then to related works of gothic or mainstream literature (including Freud's case studies), and finally to literary theory, especially feminist, poststructuralist, and cultural theory. The progression also involves increasing abstraction until one arrives at theoretical issues about gender and representation that inform the study of literature and culture in general.

*Notes*

1 McGrath (1997b: 45). Further references to this edition will be included in the text.
2 McGrath (1988: 70).
3 *Ibid.* 80.
4 McGrath (2004: 14). Further references to this edition will be included in the text.
5 McGrath (1989b: 61, emphasis in the text). Further references to this edition will be included in the text.
6 McGrath (2000: 140).
7 For more on *Spider*, *Dr. Haggard's Disease*, and McGrath's 'diseased narrators', see Ferguson (1999).
8 See McGrath (1989a: 155-162).
9 Morrow & McGrath (1992: xi). Further references to this edition will be included in the text.
10 McGrath (1991: 239).
11 *Ibid.*
12 *Ibid.*
13 McGrath (1997a: 156).
14 See Freud (2003: 53-55).
15 For feminist critiques of Dora, see Bernheimer & Kahane (1990), a notable collection of essays including work by Jacqueline Rose, Toril Moi, Jane Gallop, and Hélène Cixous. For useful background on Anna O. and Dora, see Gay (1988: 63-69, 246-255).
16 See Mulvey (1989: 14-27).
17 See Foucault (1973: ix-xix, 107-124, 195-199) and Irigaray (1985: 47-48, 133-146, 147-151).
18 Barthes (1974: 216).

## Bibliography

Barthes, Roland: *S/Z: An Essay*. Trans. Richard Miller, New York, 1974 [1970].

Bernheimer, Charles & Claire Kahane (Eds.): *In Dora's Case: Freud-Hysteria-Feminism*, second edition, New York, 1990.

Ferguson, Christine: "Dr. McGrath's Disease: Radical Pathology in Patrick McGrath's Neo-Gothicism". – In Glennis Byron & David Punter (Eds.): *Spectral Readings: Towards a Gothic Geography*, New York, 1999. pp. 233-243.

Foucault, Michel: *The Birth of the Clinic: An Archaeology of Medical Perception*. Trans. A.M. Sheridan Smith, New York, 1973 [1963].

Freud, Sigmund: *The Schreber Case*. Trans. Andrew Webber, New York, 2003 [1911].

Gay, Peter: *Freud: A Life for Our Time*, New York, 1988.

Irigaray, Luce: *Speculum of the Other Woman*. Trans. Gillian C. Gill, Ithaca, 1985 [1974].

McGrath, Patrick: *Blood and Water and Other Stories*, London, 1988.

---: "A Childhood in Broadmoor Hospital", *Granta* 29, 1989a, 155-162.

---: *The Grotesque*, New York, 1989b.

---: *Spider*, New York, 1990.

---: "Poe's Dank Vaults". – In Philomena Marian (Ed.): *Critical Fictions: The Politics of Imaginative Writing*, Seattle, 1991, pp. 239-241.

---: *Dr. Haggard's Disease*, New York, 1993.

---: "Transgression and Decay". – In Christoph Grunenberg (Ed.): *Gothic Transmutations of Horror in Late Twentieth Century Art*, Boston, 1997a, pp. 153-158.

---: *Asylum*, New York, 1997b.

---: *Martha Peake: A Novel of the American Revolution*, New York, 2000.

---: *Port Mungo*, New York, 2004.

Morrow, Bradford & Patrick McGrath: "Introduction". – In Bradford Morrow and Patrick McGrath (Eds.): *The New Gothic*, New York, 1992, pp. xi-xiv.

Mulvey, Laura: *Visual and Other Pleasures*, Bloomington, 1989.

*Sara Crangle (Cambridge)*

# Silence and Noise: Understanding Christine Brooke-Rose's *Such*

## *1. Introduction*

Asked to give close readings of passages from Christine Brooke-Rose's *Such* and *Amalgamemnon*, students traverse a wide range of reaction, from cynicism of the hasn't-this-all-been-done-before variety, to near outrage about her insistent self-reflexivity and tendency to "show off" intellectually, to admiration for her rapid transitions, cinematic technique, and fruitfully odd juxtapositions. Scepticism quietly enters the room, and presides over an impromptu debate about the value of narrative continuity. Everyone suddenly wants to discuss the role of personal preference in the critical act; faced with Brooke-Rose, no one assumes Barthes' intertwining of pleasure and text. Class runs overtime in a bid to determine the success or failure of Brooke-Rose's artistry. What does she accomplish? Interspersed with all the musings are plausible responses to these questions: her writing is characterised as slippery, ambiguous, irreverent, annoying, playful, and subversive. Brooke-Rose, says one student, "pushes language as far as it will go so that you, the reader, are always striving to find the meaning". Murmurs of disapproval greet this assertion.

These sorts of noisy, unresolved debates are at the heart of Brooke-Rose's authorial agenda. A novelist and critic since the fifties, Brooke-Rose claims to feel "dead scared" at the possibility that at the end of the twentieth century, art continues to be perceived as a form of intellectual authority. Instead, she prefers to think of art as a "true system of mutation", one involving

> the paradox of the liar who says he is a liar, the paradox of using words to say meaninglessness, the paradox of letting everyone *prendre la parole*[1]

> when everyone knows that real power, whether political, economic, social, psychological or even mystical, functions silently and has no need of the semblance of speech, even though it never ceases to use that semblance to persuade that we participate. If art can cope with that kind of terror and humour, it has a long future yet.[2]

If power is unspoken, fiction writing forms an inaudible but babbling counter – yet another paradox in Brooke-Rose's compilation. But in Susan Sontag's "The Aesthetics of Silence" – an essay Brooke-Rose is fond of citing – silence stands for more than this: it is a tool by which artists generate opacity, confuse audiences, and ultimately, refuse art itself. Art resistant to interpretation Sontag considers silent, and Brooke-Rose's own strenuous novels meet Sontag's criteria. Critic William Paulson also uses sound as a measure of aesthetic comprehension, claiming readers of difficult fiction encounter the unknown or obscure as a kind of noise. In Brooke-Rose's *Such*, audibility prefigures and aligns with the debates Sontag and Paulson elucidate. In *Such*, sound signifies approaches to knowledge and determines narrative events, in turn guiding readers through the difficulties of Brooke-Rose's writing. In other words, *Such* reinforces the etymological connection between 'audible' – that which can be heard – and 'audience' – an individual or group engaged in listening, paying attention, or reading.

In *Stories, Theories, and Things* Christine Brooke-Rose observes that her work has been labelled science fiction, British, postmodernist, and occasionally, feminist. In Sarah Birch's *Christine Brooke-Rose and Contemporary Fiction*, the only book-length study of Brooke-Rose's work to date, she is also defined, somewhat breathtakingly, as a writer of "cybernetic interface fiction" and "surfiction" – the latter refers to writing that exposes the fictional constructs embedded in our daily existence.[3] There are plausible explanations as to why Brooke-Rose receives some of these labels. Certain tics and interests place her fairly firmly in the postmodern camp; most obviously, her refusal of authority: she argues "[t]he notion of mastery is no longer tenable", noting that aporias are the order of current theory and fiction, a relationship she considers symbiotic.[4] Her novels are not science fiction in the sense of portraying extended futuristic scenarios, but do make prevalent use of scientific or theoretical discourses – in *Such* this includes frequent, extended reference to concepts central to astrophysics and psychoanalysis. And although it is difficult to envision a novel that doesn't address gender issues to some degree, Brooke-Rose often goes out of her authorial way to point out disparities between the sexes. Most of these categories amuse Brooke-Rose, but she takes issue with the term "experimentalist", believing a "prejudice against the unfamiliar effects all who experiment".[5] Bucking the suggestion that experimental writers merely tinker with reality, she contends "true realists [may be] those who look so hard at reality that they see it in a new way" – a way as legitimate as so-called realist fiction (*STT* 260-261). New, unstable realities interest Brooke-Rose immensely, fuelling the contemporary freshness of even her earliest works. Shifting identities and plot lines are her narrative trademarks, while her critical work frequently contradicts its own assertions, preferring recognised uncertainties and loose categories over absolutes and labels.

Modernism and postmodernism are two such labels; in *Rhetoric of the Unreal*, Brooke-Rose derides each of these terms as "peculiarly unimaginative" for a criticism "purport[ing] to deal with phenomena of which the most striking feature is imagination .[…] For one thing, they are purely historical, period words" (344). Additionally they are imprecise; Brooke-Rose suggests most aspects of literature characteristic of modernity are still prevalent today. "Only the simplest fairy-tale or the most elementary narrative forms are wholly continuous, and the novel has been playing with […] discontinuous moments for a long time.[…] Postmodernism […]simply take[s] the process to its logical conclusion" (*RU* 357). "Logical conclusion" is an odd and contentious phrase for Brooke-Rose to use; elsewhere in the same volume she declares, "of course there can be no 'last word'" (*RU* 50). Champion of the open-ended, her work does not complete, but certainly extends many of the modernist tendencies she lists, including an interest in urban settings, technological themes, frank eroticism, randomness, and self-reflexivity. And yet, an identifiably postmodern interrogation concerns Brooke-Rose in *Stories, Theories, and Things*, where she observes, "there is nothing new under the sun, not only because all is undecidable (or is it undecidable?), but because, as well, we already know what each will say". In a world both resoundingly known and resolutely undetermined, we experience an "acceptance of non-interpretability, nevertheless interpreted *ad nauseam* by each and everyone, be it through instruction, constructivism, or deconstruction". Our "paralysing over-consciousness" may only be surmounted, asserts Brooke-Rose in one of her many paraphrases of Sontag, by self-indulgence or silence (*STT* 165-166).

If, as Sontag suggests, silence can be equated with obscure artwork, then silence is Brooke-Rose's way around contemporary over-consciousness. Of all of her modernist tendencies, Brooke-Rose's attempt to disorient her readers is probably her most pronounced. In Birch's words, Brooke-Rose's novels "are generally thought of as difficult"; in 1964, a reviewer described her work as "resplendently unreadable".[6] In *The Difficulties of Modernism*, Leonard Diepeveen asserts that since modernism, good art and difficultly are inextricably associated; Brooke-Rose is clearly prepared to cast her work into this arena, striving to have her readers see anew in a fashion very reminiscent of Ezra Pound – who, like Samuel Beckett, she considers an influence. Birch contends that Brooke-Rose's writing is difficult in part because of the odd, continual juxtapositions within her narrative sequences. While perhaps not popular, this style is arguably canonical, as anyone who has encountered *Tristram Shandy* or *The Waves* can attest. But Brooke-Rose's second mode of difficulty is somewhat more distinct: that of incorporating highly specialised knowledge into her writing.[7] Brooke-Rose claims, "the novel's first task […] is to stretch our intellectual, spiritual and imaginative horizons to the breaking point". She brings theoretical, philosophical, and scientific discourses into her novels both to stretch her reader's horizons further, and because she perceives fiction as a legitimate means of knowing and understanding the world. But additionally, she uses intellectual concepts to call into question the prevalent twentieth-century belief that the primary task of fiction is the relaying of personal experience (*STT* 188-189). Unlike so many of her peers, Brooke-Rose is not primarily interested in the machinations of the human ego.

She is, however, fascinated by her reader:

> The English novel has been dying for a very long time, enclosed in its parochial and personal little narrated lives, and if American postmodernism has seemed at times to bring new vigour and a breath of fresh air, it is often still too concerned with the narcissistic relation of the author to his writing,

> which interests no one but himself. The reader, although frequently addressed, is only taken into account with reference to this narcissistic concern in a 'look-what-I'm-doing' relationship. (*STT* 183)

Brooke-Rose returns to this idea, noting that postmodern authorship, though declared dead by Roland Barthes, nevertheless maintains an omniscience, hangs resolutely on to the "topos of author as God vs. his creature and flogged it to death". She attests that most postmodern writing includes the reader overtly, as in the Victorian "dear reader", or, as Barthes himself argues, tacitly, "in the many demands that are made upon him to decipher, fill in, co-write" (*STT* 216). Brooke-Rose does not escape the latter half of these accusations; readers of her own work have a lot of filling in to do. Birch counters dissent on this front, championing Brooke-Rose's attempts "to break people's reading habits", and pointing out that the author claims to write "the way she does 'to teach people to read'".[8] But there is an inescapable level of control at work here; Brooke-Rose imposes her own version of language even as her disjointed narratives undermine authorial autonomy, and may well, by extension, undo what she considers the problematic way "[o]ur very institutions of learning encourage 'mastery' of the arts" (*STT* 44). Writing as she does, Brooke-Rose takes part in what Allon White, in *The Uses of Obscurity*, describes as difficult writing's greatest asset: its propensity to generate a closeness between ourselves and a text that evades familiarity, a knowledge, like intimacy, defined by risk. The content of Brooke-Rose's early works extends this relationship between bewildered reader and difficult artwork; in books like *Out*, *Such*, and *Between*, her protagonists experience identity crises and metaphoric "rebirths", "striv[ing] to construct some form of coherent identity out of [...] scraps of other people's languages".[9] In these novels, the protagonist's experience helpfully replicates the reader's, providing insight as to how the work itself might be read.

## *2. On Silence and Noise*

Around the same time that Brooke-Rose began writing her experimentalist fiction, Susan Sontag wrote "Against Interpretation" (1964), "On Style" (1965), and "The Aesthetics of

Silence" (1967)—essays largely preoccupied with postmodern aesthetics. "Against Interpretation" opens with Sontag's insistence that before Greek philosophy, art didn't have to justify itself: its role was "incantatory, magical; art was an instrument of ritual".[10] Come the Greeks, art was newly perceived as mimesis, and as representation of the world around us, underwent value judgement. For Sontag, Western societies have struggled ever since to rationalise art and individual artworks, which we believe should "*sa[y]* something"; in turn, we feel compelled to defend, quarrel, and redefine art.[11] Interpretation is the word used to describe this process of listening to, then discussing, art. Sontag takes issue with interpretation on a number of fronts: she believes the interpretative act assumes that an audience cannot or will not understand a work of art, then resolves this issue far too authoritatively, often by promoting use-value or generating limited and limiting aesthetic categories. Taken to excess, Sontag claims interpretation is "the revenge of the intellect upon art", an overlooking of emotion and the visceral:

> Interpretation takes the sensory experience of the work of art for granted, and proceeds from there. This cannot be taken for granted, now [...]. Ours is a culture based on excess, on overproduction; the result is a steady loss of sharpness in our sensory experience. All the conditions of modern life—its material plenitude, its sheer crowdedness—conjoin to dull our sensory faculties. And it is in the light of the conditions of our senses, our capacities (rather than those of another age), that the task of the critic must be assessed.[12]

Sontag does not want criticism to indicate how a work of art means but rather, what it is; she wants critics to teach themselves "to *see* more, to *hear* more, to *feel* more".[13] Art, Sontag argues, can often mean nothing at all, and the critic must be prepared to acquiesce to its ineffability, as sensation always, to some degree, escapes description. Furthermore, the critic must remember, "The most potent elements in a work of art are, often, its silences."[14]

Nostalgia for art as self-evident, fundamental spiritual instrument permeates these essays, and resurfaces in "The Aesthetics of Silence". Art, Sontag suggests, has been promoted to the groundskeeper of postmodern spirituality:

> As the activity of the mystic must end in a *via negativa*, a theology of God's absence, a craving for a cloud of unknowing beyond knowledge and for the silence beyond speech, so art must tend toward anti-art, the elimination of the 'subject' (the ' object,' the 'image'), the substitution of chance for intention, and the pursuit of silence.[15]

Silence is artistic transcendentalism: Sontag cites as examples Rimbaud's disappearance to Abyssinia to make a fortune in the slave trade and Duchamp's obsession with chess following his artistic success. The abolition of artistry, Sontag suggests, has become the greatest artistic statement of all: "So far as he is serious, the artist is continually tempted to sever the dialogue he has with an audience."[16] But just as silence is a gesture that relies on verbal communication, so too does the vast majority of silence entail noise: "More typically, [the artist] continues speaking, but in a manner that his audience can't hear" – displeasing, provoking, and frustrating one's audience are all measures on Sontag's inaudible scale.[17] Speech and emphasis depend on silence, which can shut down meaning – a silent individual is opaque – even as it opens up an array of possibilities and explanations. "The art of our time is noisy with appeals for silence [...]. Discovering that one has nothing to say, one seeks a way to say *that*."[18] Sontag thus divides silence into two categories: the soft – ironic, classical, decorum-driven, and the loud – frenetic, near apocalyptic. The tendency to babble Sontag labels an "ontological stammer", observable in the work of Stein, Burroughs, and Beckett, writers who believe "it might be possible to out-talk language".[19] Sontag maintains contemporary artistic silence has a violent aspect, one she hopes will ultimately prove beneficial: "Through its advocacy of silence and reduction, art commits an act of violence upon itself, turning art into a species of auto-manipulation, of conjuring – trying to bring these new ways of thinking to birth."[20]

Sontag's silence is a powerful, punishing, excluding artistic medium; she asserts unequivocally that audiences confronted with silence are compelled to respond. William R. Paulson's *The Noise of Culture: Literature in the Information Age* might be considered an attempt to delineate that response. Paulson suggests readers of difficult texts encounter elements that cannot initially be decoded or integrated and "thus appear as noise". He observes, "rather than dismissing them as noise [...] the reader makes a particular kind of assumption about them, namely that they indicate the presence of as yet unknown codes or levels of meaning at work within the text".[21] This assumption Paulson considers false; at the heart of his writing – as for Sontag – is the claim that art should not be treated as an object of knowledge; Paulson applies this supposition to the entire discipline of English literature, from criticism to instruction. For Paulson, literature occupies a marginal place in post-modern society, and this is a beneficial locale. The written word cannot be seen "as a message nor as an object but rather as a source of differences" – a minor but significant forum to reconsider the way we use language.[22] Literary complexity necessitates a never-ending understanding of language and human relationships, and differs from the scientific discourse so widely venerated in contemporary society because it can never provide fixed meaning. Paulson contends:

> Literature is not and will not ever again be at the center of culture, if indeed it ever was. There is no use in proclaiming or debunking its central position. Literature is the noise of culture, the rich and indeterminate margin into which messages are sent off, never to return the same, in which signals are received not quite like anything emitted.[23]

'Noise', then, is Paulson's term for reader bewilderment and the place literature occupies more generally in the world. His work extends Sontag's, placing literary reception in a cacophonous, distinctly celebratory byway adjacent to, and dependent upon, her hermitage of silent artists. But both Sontag and Paulson use sound as an indicator of human creativity and understanding. Their decision to do so appears tied – implicitly in Sontag's case, explicitly in Paulson's – to the incessant audible barrage proffered by contemporary culture: the voices of mass media, the hum of an increasingly urban world. For both, literature is meant to resonate in the midst of this inundating tide, either as silent, powerful point of production or as chorus of difference – a sound or soundlessness somehow distinct from the static of the information age.

Comparatively speaking, Brooke-Rose's authorial voice goes largely unheard: as a writer of difficult fiction, she occupies the very margins of Paulson's literary margin. But like Sontag and Paulson's critical writings, Brooke-Rose's *Such* self-consciously intertwines audibility and comprehension, providing a fictive, sound-fuelled account of confusion and understanding that reads as an excellent example of the relationship between art, intellectuality, and sensation. *Such* details the certainties and uncertainties of Brooke-Rose's palpably bewildered protagonist, Larry. Pronounced medically dead, Larry miraculously returns to life; the novel opens with his entry into his cosmic and somewhat comic afterlife, where Larry is dubbed Someone by a very feminine figure content to go by the moniker Something. Together they have five children named after blues songs to whom Larry occasionally gives 'rebirth' with the assistance of a large, elderly, flatulent midwife. Between babies, Larry travels constantly with his family, taking journeys in a plane-like "vehicle of communication" as well as more readily identifiable modes of transportation such as cars and trucks, eventually travelling back to the land of the living. Larry's return to his former life dominates the second part of the novel, where it emerges that he has been psychiatrist to a laboratory of astrophysicists, husband to an adulterous wife, and father to two nearly grown children. Many of the names from his afterlife resurface at this juncture; it becomes increasingly clear that events from the past have been conflated with, or influenced, his expectations and perceptions during his brief death. Throughout, rapid-fire, disorienting changes and events preclude Larry's understanding of even the most basic information, including the status of his mortality. At the novel's end Larry is not yet fully adjusted to terrestrial existence, but his perception of the world has clearly shifted: he has abandoned his former absolutism. The narrative portrayal of sound signals much of this transition.

A great deal of the dialogue between Larry-as-Someone and Something centres on their differing approaches to knowledge; they exchange a protracted battle over the terms by which Larry comes to understand what is happening to him. Larry's knowledge is distinctly scientific; he repeatedly asserts his knowledge of the five geometries and the language of orbits; he likes collecting evidence and examining appearances. Larry's dogmatism is signalled on many occasions, perhaps none more tellingly than when he and his celestial family lose their way whilst driving down a darkened bumpy road; encouraged by all to back up, Larry announces: "No, I won't. I never go into reverse."[24] By contrast, Something's knowledge is much more intuitive; she claims to follow instructions Larry cannot hear, and regularly describes his thinking as dense and opaque. Deeply offended by Something's accusations, Larry jeers:

"You know everything, don't you girl-spy?" But Something won't take his bait, "Not everything. But I came prepared." Asked what she came prepared for, Something replies, "Not necessarily" (20) – her evasiveness annoys Larry still further. This debate – fundamentally a traditionally gendered split between intuitive and reasoned knowledge, just as 'Someone' is a masculine subject, while 'Something' remains feminine object – frequently guides events in the cosmic afterlife. In an instance aboard a boat, the argument resumes; Something derides Larry for his belief in clarity – "that each moment has its own separateness" – to which Larry responds, "Oh dear, here we go again with your mystifications" (43). Something tells him he "enmesh[es] the mathematical process with verbal pedantry and tangential arguments" and at the same moment, the boat proves unable to move forward, clogged with weeds and verbiage. Directed by Something to "[d]ive into his reflections", Larry uses a combination of his clarity and Something's intuition to disentangle and free their vessel, and androgynous knowledge wins the day (44-46).

The water journey, however, is a rare triumphal moment. For much of the novel, Larry struggles to assert the familiar and rational, only to have Something indicate that his knowledge is useless: "You think too much, Someone. Just listen" (11). "Just keep [...] your eyes and ears open" she tells him as they sit at a travel agent's, ordering a journey beyond language. And again: "Listen before speaking" (13). But a great deal of what Larry hears is akin to what Paulson describes as noise: oscillating from his afterlife to his before-life, he is increasingly perplexed by what he hears. Listening to a colleague, he thinks to himself: "I have heard this conversation in waves that run backwards through time, I even seem to supply the words and their internal combustion pushes them along though I don't do the steering" (103). At this juncture, Larry recognises that he pursues a meaning beyond his control. A longing to grasp the sounds around him emerges more poignantly in his cosmic life, where his newly chatty daughter, Potato Head, proves incomprehensible, emitting only noises that sound like "[g]ug-gug-grr". Larry is both embarrassed by his daughter's strange language and envious of Something's ability to comprehend her meaning (110-111). Confusion gives way to acceptance; in a macabre scene wherein the top of Larry's head is removed and Something ladles his brains out to his eager, salivating family, the narration reads: "One for mommy she says in silence or perhaps in her glug language which I now hardly notice" (119). Here silence and noise are almost interchangeable, and Larry finds alternate ways – gesture – to glean what goes on around him. Throughout, noisiness generally indicates a sense of being overwhelmed; Larry tells his son he didn't suffer his children gladly because he "couldn't bear the noise", and struggles to remember when, if ever, he liked noise – "Perhaps the thunder of ambition?" (132, 168). And Larry describes his reluctant transition from death back to life as a falling sensation accompanied by a "loud ticking inside the district of my time" (136).

Within the cacophonous present, Larry strives to assert the value of silence: "I collect silences" is a favoured statement. His love of silence predates and is exacerbated by his near-permanent death; equally afraid of dying and living again, he asks, "Why me, I fear those fumbling, healing hands, why couldn't you let me lie in silent decay and darkness? I have acquired a painful sensitivity to noise" (95). Sontag describes silence as transcendence of daily existence; in *Such*, silence and death are ecstatic absolutes. After dying, Larry feels "unreal"; believing he can no longer talk to people; he wants to go away and find "Silence perhaps, merely" (146). As the qualifiers 'perhaps' and 'merely' suggest, Larry both seeks out silence and comes to realise that it will not and cannot save him from bewildering noise. These limitations are intimated at the outset of the book, which reads: "Silence says the notice on the stairs and the stairs creak. Or something creaks in the absolute dark [...]. Someone creaks, levelling out nails perhaps with the pronged side of a hammer" (7). Even in the absoluteness of silence and death, noise prevails. Again, Sontag: "A genuine emptiness, a pure silence is not feasible – either conceptually or in fact .[...] Silence remains, inescapably, a form of speech [...] and an element in a dialogue."[25] Because no two silences are the same – as we might well expect from total and totalising quiet – we witness Larry reading silences, deciphering their individual sounds. He observes how entire marital quarrels can occur within silence: "My silence says I have proved my point, her silence says don't mention it, my silence says smile, Something, hers says you smile first" (18). Larry also notes how silences contain "sheer pressure", and can indicate that an individual feels trapped (18, 74). Furthermore, people are often unwillingly silenced: a surgeon instructs Larry not to talk; one of

Larry's ex-patients believes therapy consists of listening dumbly to their psychiatrist (57, 100). As *Such* progresses, silence is increasingly exposed as an unsustainable authoritative ploy, as when Dr. Dekko, an astrophysicist, asserts his ability to "tap the silent phones of outer space" (75). Certainty belongs to whoever believes silence is in their control, but the slightest creak undermines this tenuous authority.

Brooke-Rose associates silence, certainty, and death, then negates the absoluteness she has engendered by having Larry – also known as Lazarus – rise from the dead. Hospital staff, journalists, friends, and family are fond of telling Larry, "You died you know" – a refrain equating certainty and death, but anxiously, because repeated, and because Larry is dead no longer. If death is not certain, what is? Overawed by the complexity of his lives, Larry constantly tries "to avoid the issue of [his] death and amazing recovery"; he distracts himself with scientific trivia – minor but certain knowledge – and by closing his eyes when he sees himself in the mirror (51, 139). But even with his eyes closed, he cannot avoid the sound of his own heartbeat, his blood pumping anew through his body. And so he is haunted by the fact that he has emerged out the other side of a supposedly irreversible experience. He tells his former wife, "Sometimes I feel that during my death I became everyone I know and I left myself behind. Or else, if that means nothing nowadays, as if I had acquired something of creation, but nothing of humanity" (123-124). For Larry, there was something totalising about death: he became omniscient, knew everyone around him completely. While this may have been incredible, it was also inhuman; although he "understood more inside the coffin", in the end, he can "remember nothing but opaqueness" (11, 107). 'Opaque' is the adjective Something applies to Larry's rational, scientific, complete knowledge; here Larry transfers Something's valuation of certainty to the absoluteness of death. "You died, you know" – in *Such*, neither death nor knowledge is as consummate as it sounds. As a result, Larry increasingly calls his own assurances into question; faced with Something's impenetrability, he loses his equations; returned to his former life, he misplaces his five geometries (33, 83). Larry no longer admires the scientific perspective, but recognises "the labyrinthine knowledge of alternate proofs and truths within [t]his strange profession built on the failures of men" (145). Absolutely nothing is certain or dead-ended: even the telling of Larry's own story is, as the last lines of *Such* read, "unfinished unfinishable" (193).

*2. Strains of Uncertainty*

Brooke-Rose's authorial career began with a more traditional narrative style. In 1962, just prior to her transition to more avant-garde writing, Brooke-Rose suffered a near-terminal illness, during which she believes she attained "a different level of consciousness".[26] The appeal of this biographical connection to *Such* is unavoidable, if weak. Personal near-death experience aside, Brooke-Rose's depiction of mortality in this novel is remarkably in line with other postmodern refusals of finality, particularly with that of avant-garde poets writing in the United Kingdom in the 1970s and beyond. As Helen Regueiro Elam writes: "[D]eath is a theme in contemporary criticism and poetry because it stands for what is unthematizable, unrepresentable, unnameable, unteachable – [in short] for an insoluble difficulty synonymous with thought itself."[27] We recall that having known, the inhabitants of Eden became aware of their own mortality; so too do many postmodern poets suggest the information age is stultifying, death-like, even as expert rendering necessarily continues. For Peter Riley, writers try to grasp life whole and cast it into the poem at each juncture; each line represents an attempt at a complete mortality, and as such, "[t]he poet dies constantly into the poem".[28] Fortunately, as John Wilkinson argues, total articulation is impossible:

> Lyric won't come to the point [...] The point is a net result which [...] actually courts sudden death; whereas the enduring poem endures through its continuous dying, lives through productive decay like the sun [...]. Purity of diction is the deadly idea of a culture so *fearful of death it stops dead in its tracks.*[29]

To believe in and aim for total certainty is to shut the creative process down; for Riley and Wilkinson, writing and communication depend upon constant regeneration of dead matter. In *Proud Flesh*, Wilkinson derides the tenuous certainty creativity requires, and its end result: "We who are husbands of death / slip through light with our acid tensity, we connoisseurs / who anchor the torso in an image, oracle of its own silence."[30] Writing is oracular, akin to the delivery of ambiguous, inarguable messages from the gods; like Sontag, Wilkinson equates obscurity with silence. So too does Denise Riley's poem "noise levels" reinforce Sontag's perception of silence as a violence art does to itself, one giving way to a regeneration of artistry. Riley writes: "to speak / is to pit the self in a series of transformations across space, space / that is always all ready moulded by time which is / powerless."[31] Language occurs across a mortal backdrop; to assert oneself – linguistically, creatively – is to remind that time is finite. So too to receive art; as Harold Bloom contends, "One of the uses of reading is to prepare ourselves for change, and the final change, alas, is universal" – we all read against the clock. For Bloom, "the strongest, most authentic motive for deep reading [...] is the search for a difficult pleasure [...]. There is a reader's Sublime, and it seems the only secular transcendence we can ever attain."[32] The creation of this sort of infinite, difficult pleasure arguably motivates Brooke-Rose and her poetic contemporaries.

This is not to suggest that Brooke-Rose values the constant regeneration of all things literary. Describing literary critics as an intergenerational, near-incestuous, "self-perpetuating and confraternal industry" Brooke-Rose wonders "whether anyone else reads these texts, critical and fictional", a problem that will surely only worsen:

> for the next generation will soon be or already are wholly televisual. The eternal and instinctive desire to be told a story is already satisfied otherwise than through writing, and after all why not? The fabula had already migrated from the Greek epic to tragedy and then to romance, then again from the medieval epic to the metrical romance in the twelfth century, which turned into the prose romance until the fifteenth then 'story' migrated to the theatre in the sixteenth, then back to a sort of epic, before being reborn in the prose novel that seems to us so classical, permanent, and eternal. (*STT* 163)

Brooke-Rose is partially calling her own bluff here; she does not fully believe, as she goes on to state, that story can find a perfectly happy home in soap operas and comics.[33] If the media were to bring the novel to its "logical conclusion", why spend so much time reconsidering and disrupting its form? Brooke-Rose's writing evinces implicit hope for the televisual generation and their ability to understand the noise her own narrative opacity generates. As Larry says of his estranged son, he "astonishes me with his polite charm and his love of noise" (125). Buried within these fictional statements may well be a bid for the possibilities represented by literate, teachable generations to come.

Fundamentally, Brooke-Rose is very concerned about the creaks, groans, and occasional silences with which difficult literature is received: "Over and over again, in a freshman class, I have been discouraged by the silence, or at very best the vaguest one-word paraphrase, that greets my request for reactions to a text, until I give them some clue as to how to read it" (*STT* 11). Knowledge is central to her novels, both as theme and via her integration of specific intellectual discourses – but also because she is a critic and instructor fascinated by the meaning of literature in her own time. In one of her earliest monographs – *A ZBC of Ezra Pound* – Brooke-Rose reassures in very personal terms how Pound "can be explicated" even as she argues that readers should "let it just roll over you, with perhaps only a gloss or two".[34] And she continues to take the anxious reader by the hand:

> I realise that I am here plunging you in at the deep end. But I really can't do it any other way and isn't that how one is supposed to learn to swim? Rather as when one comes up to Chaucer from behind (or rather, from before), after several centuries of Anglo-Saxon, and then twelfth, thirteenth and early fourteenth century English, as I did, then he seems so delightfully easy and above all modern, not "quaint" or "difficult" at all [...] the analogy is meant to go no further than to show how easy everything can be if you do the difficult first.[35]

For all her postmodern eschewal of systematic formulations and endless rivers of criticism, Brooke-Rose does not deny the value of the odd gloss. She understands that we live in an intensely complicated era where "meaning is an illusion, absolutely necessary to us but an illusion" (*RU* 46). Fundamentally, she doubts only the longevity of any given meaning, even as she extols the value of the search: "statements of position" and narrative thematics alike she considers "protean, capturable for brief moments in language, but already changed even into their opposites another brief moment later" (*STT* Preface).

What then, might the reader – student, instructor, layperson – take away from Brooke-Rose's work? Books like *Such* are presumptuously full of postmodern and psychoanalytic theory, not to mention astrophysical terminology. This narrative hammering does not disappear; as my students discovered with varying degrees of dismay and pleasure, later works by Brooke-Rose, like *Amalgamemnon* (1984), are increasingly convoluted, even more dogmatic and opaque in their insistent references to canonical works and postmodern theory. The reader's struggle is real. But Brooke-Rose is interesting precisely because of her insistence that literary prose is knowledge and ought to be treated as such; her attempts to dismantle popular novelistic renderings of individual egos may be overwhelming, but do force readers to reflect on what makes fiction. She makes inevitable Paulson's ideal:

> What literature solicits of the reader is not simply reception but the active, independent, autonomous construction of meaning [...]. This construction of meaning is surely a form of knowledge, but a form that is not identical with knowledge of the text. It exists in the irreversible time of reading and of the reader, not in the abolished time of convergence towards a text's unchanging truth. Constructed meaning is not a representation of what has already occurred but an elaboration of newly significant material that participates in the unforseeability of what is coming into being.[36]

For Paulson, students should be offered rhetorical and historical training, while at the same time "encouraged to respond in original ways to texts", and recognise that in literature "we find an inextricable mixture of the unknown to be investigated and the intelligible to be decoded".[37] This is not a process devoid of emotionalism or the visceral; it is not, in other words, purely intellectual. Brooke-Rose recognises that her readers will be excluded by her specialist knowledge – "the intelligible to be decoded" – even as in works like *Such* she incorporates audible clues as to how to proceed. The sounds of Larry's confusion guide and reassure. For Sontag, as for Brooke-Rose, the exploration of "new 'sensory mixes'" may well regenerate contemporary art, and provide a viable means of fusing knowledge and creativity. Sontag writes: "Such art is, in principle, experimental – not out of an elitist disdain for what is accessible to the majority, but precisely in the sense that science is experimental."[38] *Such* is art that may well pave the way to sense-oriented, rather than censorious, interpretation.

*Notes*

1 Meaning: to speak.
2 Brooke-Rose (1981: 389). Further references to this edition will be included in the text, demarcated by *RU*.
3 Birch (1994: 289).
4 Brooke-Rose (1991: 25). Further references to this edition will be included in the text, demarcated by *STT*.
5 A more bitter example: her novels, she writes, are considered plotless, "usually by those who [...] betray lack of reading intention" (*STT* 15).
6 Birch (1994: 162).
7 *Ibid.* 164.
8 *Ibid.* 163.
9 *Ibid.* 53.
10 Sontag (1994: 3).
11 *Ibid.* 4-5.
12 *Ibid.* 7; 13-14.
13 *Ibid.* 14.
14 Sontag (1966: 29, 36).
15 *Ibid.* 4-5.
16 *Ibid.* 6.
17 *Ibid.* 7.
18 *Ibid.* 12.
19 *Ibid.* 27.
20 *Ibid.* 18.
21 Paulson (1988: 134-135).
22 *Ibid.* viii.
23 *Ibid.* 180.
24 Brooke-Rose (1966: 67). Further references to this edition will be included in the text.
25 Sontag (1966: 11).
26 Birch (1994: 2).
27 Elam (1991: 81).
28 Riley (1992: 102).
29 Wilkinson (1992: 160-161).
30 Wilkinson (1986: 53).
31 Riley and Mulford (1979).
32 Bloom (2000: 21, 29).
33 As Larry asserts in *Such*, "I can't let what I know be appropriated into a television programme" (186).
34 Brooke-Rose (1971: 3).
35 *Ibid.* 16-17.
36 Paulson (1988: 139).

37 *Ibid.* 185.
38 Sontag (1966: 300).

## *Bibliography*


Birch, Sarah: *Christine Brooke-Rose and Contemporary Fiction*, Oxford, 1994.

Bloom, Harold: *How to Read and Why*, London, 2000.

Brooke-Rose, Christine: *Such*, London, 1966.

---: *A ZBC of Ezra Pound*, London, 1971.

---: *A Rhetoric of the Unreal*, Cambridge, 1981.

---: *Stories, Theories and Things*, Cambridge, 1991.

Diepeveen, Leonard: *The Difficulties of Modernism*, New York, 2003.

Elam, Helen Regueiro: "The Difficulty of Reading". – In Alan C. Purves (Ed.): *The Idea of Difficulty in Literature*, New York, 1991, 73-89.

Paulson, William R: *The Noise of Culture: Literary Texts in a World of Information*, Ithaca, 1988.

Riley, Denise and Wendy Mulford: *No Fee*, Cambridge, 1979.

Riley, Peter: "The Creative Moment of the Poem". – In Denise Riley (Ed.): *Poets on Writing: Britain, 1970-1991*, Houndmills, 1992, 92-113.

Sontag, Susan: "Aesthetics of Silence". – In S.S. *Styles of Radical Will*, London, 1994.

---: "Against Interpretation", *Against Interpretation and Other Essays*, New York, 1966, 3-14.

--- "On Style", *Against Interpretation and Other Essays*, New York, 1966, 15-36.

--- "One Culture and the New Sensibility", *Against Interpretation and Other Essays*, New York, 293-304.

Wilkinson, John: *Proud Flesh*, Lodz, 1986.

---. "Imperfect Pitch". — In Denise Riley (Ed.): *Poets on Writing: Britain, 1970-1991*, Houndmills, 1992, 154-172.

White, Allon: *The Uses of Obscurity: the Fiction of Early Modernism*, London, 1981.

*Richard Hudson (Southampton)*

# The Writer as Scholar: Education by Stealth

> Well-motivated students have always succeeded in Higher Education and will continue to do so: the challenge has always been to stimulate, engender and enhance the motivation of those students whose enthusiasm for learning cannot be taken for granted. In mass systems, where large amorphous groups are taught by over-stretched staff in resource poor environments, ways in which to encourage all students to give their best to their studies are eagerly sought by those whose business is to teach them.[1]

This paper is as much a product of my work as a writer as an academic; as such it takes the form of a narrative rather than an academic paper. This paper concerns itself with a specific issue encountered while teaching Creative Writing as an academic discipline: i.e. how does one motivate students to read novels out of their own volition, rather than out of a sense of duty, or as a strategic task to enable them to pass an assignment?

It is perhaps useful for me to detail my background; although now a Senior Lecturer in Writing, prior to entering Higher Education, I worked for fifteen years as a commercial writer in industry and produced commercial fiction in various genres (specifically science fiction, horror and fantasy), for a number of magazines and anthologies. I am a firm believer that one can only teach writing skills to a point; once that has been attained a student can only improve their writing by a process of continual study of good and varied practice, a process which is followed by assimilation of styles and methods: i.e. students must read *literature* analytically. This stems from my own personal history; having become a commercial writer after leaving school at 18, my own writing developed out of a love of literature rather than receiving any formal training in how to write. It has become more and more apparent to me that writers who are successful in either literary or commercial writing are those with the passion to study writing critically – whether it be within a formal educational framework, or informally out of personal enthusiasm. I do not know, or know of, any writer in any field who has become successful purely by 'learning the rules' of how to write. Professional writers in industry are able to produce effective copy because they understand how, for example, Shakespeare, Wordsworth and Ted Hughes use words; *not* because they have undertaken any courses on how to promote consumer durables and financial services, or any psychological training on how to sell products and tailor their writing to the marketplace. However, within the context of teaching writing, I have experienced an increasing tendency in students to expect a 'recipe' for writing success.

Many of us who are engaged in the teaching or writing are often stunned and amazed when students, who we assume would have an intrinsic interest in literature, fail to demonstrate an enthusiasm for any reading at all. We are often engaged in a mutually frustrating exercise; the lecturer expecting a degree of enthusiasm for literature from the students, the students expecting to be delivered with a series of bullet-pointed instructions on how to write effectively. In such situations, the lecturer is often confronted with hostility from many students, who often fall into one of the following types:

1. Students who do not read, but just want to write 'their stuff'
2. Students who read, but who do so from a limited repertoire of authors and/or genres
3. Students who do not want to work in prose; for example fledgling scriptwriters and copywriters, who are not convinced that studying literature will enhance their general writing skills

Having to explain to students that if they want to improve their musical ability they would listen enthusiastically to varied types of music, and if they wanted to become footballers they would passionately follow football, to illustrate the flaw in their thinking countless times – to no avail – I realised that an alternative strategy to teaching literature was essential. Having taught many 'hands-on' units I have found it productive to engage student interest by implementing projects that are constructed to be as near to the working environment as possible. I was particularly impressed by a colleague who used work-based projects with Advertising students. In these assignments, the students worked as a creative team – developing a campaign and then delivering this as a pitch to a client (the lecturer) rather than produce a regular group presentation. These role-play exercises work particularly well with students who demonstrate ability, but are alienated by standard academic practice. The question then arises, how can one incorporate this approach into the study of literature?

I had always taken my lead in teaching from colleagues working within disciplines such as Literature and other Humanities subjects; particularly Media and Cultural Studies, i.e. *academic* disciplines. It occurred to me that useful insights might be gained from investigating how theoretical and historical materials were included within *creative* subjects. Looking at the work of educationalists specifically within the field of Visual Art, I considered how they viewed the inter-relationship between studio practice and art history. The central problem identified by many academics working in this field was that they believed that the inclusion of art history in their teaching programmes was often motivated by a cynical agenda, rather than a will to enhance the students' learning experience. Marcia Pointon (1980) claims that "art history is still introduced into college curricula as a way of satisfying the authorities that students are capable of thinking as well as working with their hands".[2] This point is taken up by Rosalind Billingham (1989), who argues that although this may well be the case, the situation can be exploited to the advantage of the students: "The case for art history cannot be based on intellectual stiffening [....] It must, instead, be based on an awareness of its importance to the creative development of the young artist and to the understanding of the world he or she inhabits."[3] She maintains that the role of art history in the study of art practice is essential if a student is to have a comprehensive understanding of their own work and its position within 'art' as a whole: "[...] many day-to-day attempts to engage young artists' interests could be described as relating their work to a suitable tradition with its corresponding canon [....] What is quite certain is that it is very difficult for them to recognise originality from a position of ignorance."[4]

Rod Taylor (1989) elaborates on Billingham's position further, claiming that such study goes beyond "making students aware of their cultural heritage"[5] to become a "bridging link between the study of other people's art and one's own practice [thus enabling a student to] become aware of possibilities relevant to their own art making".[6] Taylor supports his claims by citing a number of his students, one of whom states that, after art history was studied "you look at things differently now. Things that you wouldn't have found interesting before, now you do. It's changed the way I look at things."[7] Tony Collins (1989) suggests that although creative students may display hostility to critical study, it is not necessarily the analytical nature of the material that prompts this hostility, but the form in which the material is presented:

> In my experience, most students of art and design are not endemically resistant to the disciplines of theoretical analysis and historical exegesis; only to the genre of academic commentary which assiduously avoids all reference to the contemporary world. Any model of art history which seeks to *justify* the past will hold little interest for those who are immersed in the present. Instead, I am proposing a model for reorientation which embraces both the existential present of making art and the co-existent presence of works form the past as the route and roots of contemporary practice.[8]

If such a 'reorientation' of study can be achieved, Collins claims, students will not perceive theoretical analysis as an isolated facet of their study, but an integrated component that informs their practice: "[…] all works of art propose solutions […] to problems of material representation and realisation. Each work of art represents one among many possible solutions to a particular problem surfacing from a frame of problematic reasoning",[9] and continues: "In this way, art history will offer the art student a framework against which he/she can measure personal practice. In this way art history may come alive."[10] The manner in which art history can act as a "catalyst"[11] is also interrogated by Andrew Mortimer (1989). Mortimer proposes that the study of art history can develop students' work so that it will be "both original and of high quality because of their extended perceptions of the potential functions and processes of art".[12]

These considerations of the conjunction of theory and practice illustrate a great enthusiasm for the principle, but do little to indicate how it may be achieved. This issue is explored by Michael Buchanan (1995) in his article "Marking Art and Critical Literacy: A Reciprocal Relationship". Here, Buchanan makes the claim that:

> The task of teachers of art and design is to maximise opportunities for creative thought and action: developing art-making activities which represent more than simply the acquisition of practical skills; and

> encouraging forms of critical study which foster understanding and creative reasoning and avoid sterile knowledge gathering [....] It is unreasonable to expect [students] to develop "insight, awareness and understanding" by osmosis, by mere confrontation with practical experience. It is necessary to establish the means by which experience is captured and considered: particularly the establishment of structured, guided yet open-ended activities and versatile teaching.[13]

To develop this, he states that environments must be created in which "the expression of personal feelings, points of view, tentative judgements and emotional responses is socially acceptable and safe".[14] From such a position, Buchanan maintains, "critical skills develop over time, with practice and support. Progression in learning involves systematically gaining access to an increasingly wide range of sources, of complexity."[15] However, although Buchanan identifies the central issues here, he does not provide specific examples of actual practice that can be transferred directly to the teaching of writing and literature.

For inspiration here, and to explore how this could be achieved, I turned to writing on educational theory, so as to ascertain whether any research in this area had been produced. Michael Prosser and Keith Trigwell (1999)[16] identify the importance of recognising the difference between 'deep' and 'surface' learning. For them, 'deep' learning is used to describe the learning that takes place within a student who not only has an *intrinsic* desire to learn, but gains enjoyment from doing so, and sees the relevance and connections between diverse elements of the subject area and 'lived experience'. 'Surface' learning is the learning undertaken by a student responding to *extrinsic* motivations: to pass assignments, to get a job, etc., who *strategically* learns what they perceive to be required essentials. This distinction between 'deep' and 'surface' learning is important, not because it describes a condition that is preferable to academics and educationalists on an abstract level – but because research has demonstrated that there is a distinct higher success rate in 'deep' learners than 'surface' learners at degree level.[17] Research has also indicated that deeper learning is "associated with perceptions of high-quality teaching, some independence in choosing what is to be learned, and clear awareness of the goals and standards required in the subject".[18]

I decided that these principles would be utilised in the construction of my work-based teaching sessions. To promote 'deeper' learning in the student body, a task would have to be devised that would enable the students to assert a level of independence and choice, while at the same time giving the students clear guidelines to what was required of them. Furthermore, if students' understanding was to be maximised, in the role-play tasks I would have to function as an active, responsive participant in the learning situation, as Prosser and Trigwell point out: "[…] university teachers who focus on their students and their students' learning tend to have students who focus on meaning and understanding in their studies, while university teachers who focus on themselves and what they are doing tend to have students who focus on reproduction."[19]

At this point I turned to educational theories of problem-based learning (or PBL), which had their origins in American medical schools in the 1960s.[20] To summarise briefly, PBL reverses the logic of traditional Higher Education teaching strategies in which students are delivered a series of lectures that provide them with a thorough theoretical grounding in a subject area prior to being given practical tasks to solve. Rather, PBL initially confronts students with 'real-life' situations for which they have to find solutions. As such, the PBL method prompts students to research and discover answers in the manner of a professional work-like environment rather than draw upon knowledge learnt in a passive educational environment. As John Biggs explains:

> PBL reflects the way people learn in real life; they simply get on with solving the problems life puts before them with whatever resources are at hand. They do not stop to wonder at the relevance of what they are doing, or at the motivation for doing it. Formal schooling, on the contrary, operates on a fill-up-the-tanks model of knowledge acquisition. Young people are taught the sorts of things they are likely to need to know one day, and some skills for finding out more, before they are let loose on the world.[21]

He continues:

> Education for the professions for years followed this proactive model, and much of it still does. The disciplines are taught first, independently of each other, and armed with all that declarative knowledge, and with some skills, the student is accredited as ready to practice as a professional. Professional practice, however, requires functioning knowledge that can be put to work immediately, not just declarative knowledge. If the objectives nominate

professional competency on graduation, but declarative knowledge is the output, something has been missed.[22]

Biggs outlines the goals of problem-based learning as follows:

1. Structuring knowledge for use in working contexts
2. Developing effective reasoning processes
3. Developing self-directed learning skills [and]
4. Increased motivation for learning.[23]

Problem-based learning, he maintains, develops a high level of student engagement and active participation as the learning process "*requires* students to question, to speculate, to generalise solutions".[24] In so doing, the method enables less academic students to function on higher cognitive levels. Traditional lecturing methods, according to Biggs, teach *declarative knowledge* (facts, formulas and models) and *procedural knowledge* (procedures, methods) and students are expected to gain *functional knowledge* on their own.[25] However, problem-based learning reverses this process by recreating *in field* experiences:

> In sum, if the target is functioning knowledge, the theoretical (declarative) knowledge needs to be developed to relational/extended abstract levels in order to provide both the knowledge of the specific context, and the conditional knowledge that enable the skills to be performed adequately. It is a matter of addressing and integrating several domains of knowledge. In designing our objectives, we should be ensuring that by the exit level at graduation, students' knowledge is alive and functioning.[26]

Biggs is adamant that problem-based learning not only facilitates more affective learning – but it also develops a more *intrinsic* motivation to learn, rather than purely *strategic* motivation in students:

> Students need to find academic activities meaningful and worthwhile. Nowhere is this clearer than in problem based learning, where real-life problems become the context in which students learn academic content and preferential skills. When faced with a patient with suspected broken leg whom they have to help, learning all the necessary knowledge leading to the diagnosis and treatment of the patient is manifestly a worthwhile activity for a medical student, and learning is usually very enthusiastic.[27]

Therefore, I deduced, my task was to devise situations that were not just an exercise in theoretical knowledge *per se* – but also a demonstration of *how* theoretical knowledge is used in practical experience. Consequently, whatever this role-play exercise was to be it should:

1. Facilitate deep learning and *intrinsic* motivation in the students
2. Engage both the students and myself in active participation
3. Re-create activities in which the students exercised a degree of independence
4. Re-create activities which engaged the students in 'real-life' situations
5. Use *functional knowledge* and practical tasks as a means of attaining *theoretical understanding*

Drawing on both the educational discussions of problem-based learning and the principle of introducing the commercial environment, I decided to 'cast' students in the roles of a magazine's editorial team. Rather then 'set' the students readings on which they were to produce an essay, the students were given a brief: they were writing for a magazine aimed at 21-35 year olds interested in music, sport and culture. They were initially set the task of reviewing a book for this magazine, and informed that their grade would be affected by the chosen book's suitability for the intended market: i.e. they would be writing for a readership like themselves, only older (and consequently, in their minds, more sophisticated). This task masqueraded an academic exercise as a pragmatic task; it motivated students into taking an active interest in contemporary literature. This, in itself, was enough to overcome hostility towards the principle of 'reading for study' as the seeming pragmatic nature of the task gave the reading a 'relevance' in the eyes of the students. As the students were (to a degree) determining their own reading and independently choosing their own texts (albeit within guidelines) the students did not display any of the hostility familiar to students' approaches to 'set texts'. In fact, as the students felt they were discovering books for themselves, the exercise generated a surprising degree of enthusiasm in the students. Students who would have balked at reading *Black Dogs* or *Lanark* were overcome with evangelical zeal for writers such as Ian McEwan and Alisdair Gray who they believed they had found themselves. This simple exercise of guiding, rather than setting, student reading was enough to awaken an active interest in literature in many of the students. In numerous specific cases, students approached me excitedly with their discoveries, urging me to read writers, who to them were new exciting names. Once started, this interest became a desire that had to be actively fed – and often I found myself exhausting my list of suggested reading and struggling for new suitable writers.

As this 'work-based' approach appeared to be successful, it was developed further. I extended the magazine scenario, instructing students to imagine that they were going to interview a specific writer for the same magazine and the same readership. Each student had to produce a list of questions they would ask the author – keeping in mind that the theoretical readership was slightly more mature and sophisticated than the students themselves. In other words, they would have to ask the author questions regarding style, theme, imagery, etc. (dreaded 'literature stuff'). Once these questions were formulated, the students were then instructed to take the role of the novelist themselves and answer their own interview questions. This they did, not only effectively, but with active engagement and enthusiasm. In the majority of cases the students had produced what amounted to an outline of a relatively sophisticated analytical essay, which could then be fully developed more in keeping with academic protocols. This, I confess, I find rather frustrating. As a lecturer I feel that strategies such as the one detailed above run the risk of 'dumbing down' Higher Education, and place me in the role of schoolteacher rather than lecturer. However, this strategy has proved to be a very effective method for transforming begrudging students into active, self-motivated readers of contemporary literature. As such, it is perhaps for me to question whether my own hostility is a result of me being overly precious over my 'intellectual' status and I should pay more heed to my role as an educator. As Paul Ramsden (1992) states:

> The aim of teaching is simple: it is to make student learning possible. Teaching always involves attempts to alter students' understanding, so that they begin to conceptualise phenomena and ideas in the way scientists, mathematicians, historians, physicians, or other subject experts conceptualise them – in the way, that is to say, that we want them to understand them.[28]

Therefore, if we want students to think as writers, or as literary critics, our duty as educators is to implement strategies that will produce the desired method of thinking *not* to necessarily adhere to a prescribed formula that has the approval and authorisation of the academy. Habit, fear and inertia should not prevent us from applying imaginative solutions to problems, as A.N. Whiteherd claimed in 1929, the university is a site of "the imaginative acquisition of knowledge".[29] A danger we all face as academics is compliance to accepted techniques and practices – the methods we are familiar with rather than producing imaginative and effective solutions to problems. Barbara Duch, Susan Groh and Deborah Allen (2001) in their article "Why Problem-Based Learning?" argue:

> […] we teach as we were taught. For most of us, that experience revolved around lectures. In a traditional undergraduate classroom, lectures are usually content-driven, emphasising abstract concepts over concrete examples and applications. Assessment techniques focus on recall of information and facts, and rarely challenge students to perform at higher cognitive levels of understanding. This didactic instruction reinforces in students a naïve view of learning in which the teacher is responsible for delivering content and the students are the passive receivers of knowledge […] Lecturing is *still* efficient and has persisted as the traditional teaching method largely because it is familiar, easy and how *we* learned. It does little, however, to foster the development of process skills to complement content knowledge.[30]

Ironically, in Higher Education, a situation where students themselves are encouraged to be independent and creative thinkers – as E. Ashby put it in 1973, transformed "from the uncritical acceptance of orthodoxy to creative dissent [in an environment where…] there must be opportunities for the intellect to be stretched to its capacity, the critical capacity sharpened to the point at which it can change ideas"[31] – lecturers themselves are often unwilling, or unable due to institutional policies and pressures, to be as unbound by orthodoxy as they would want their students to be. I do not propose that these strategies should in any way be utilised to 'trivialise' the intellectual content of any learning situation; rather they are to be used to stimulate the intellectual engagement of previous low achievers so that they can participate fully with the complex issues involved in the study of writing/literature. These strategies are not 'games', or if they are, their aim is to stimulate learning not act as a lightweight diversion for students. Indeed, many of the methods and strategies discussed have been shown to have a positive effect on student learning, as Kurt Burch (1992) observes:

> Educational research demonstrates that active learning is the most effective technique for students to learn, apply, integrate and retain information. Also, people prefer active, problem-orientated learning because it arranges information in students'' preferred sequence from concrete to abstract.[32]

Active learning, he argues, is particularly engaged by problem-based learning in which activities promote learning by enabling students to learn through experimentation, exploration and discovery. Problem-based learning, shifts focus of the learning environment from the lecturer to the students and the process not only engages greater student interest, but results in students being able to "retain information longer and recall it more quickly and accurately".[33] Furthermore, Burch argues that problem-based learning does not *exclude* the gaining of theoretical knowledge – rather it allows students to attain it in practical situations: "The foremost role of instruction should not be to convey information, but to assist students to develop the necessary skills to direct their own learning and to 'construct' knowledge in ways that are effective for them. This conclusion reinforces my goal to teach substance *and* skills."[34]

Other pragmatic benefits of problem-based learning are noted by Elizabeth Lieux (2001),[35] such as a dramatic increase in attendance amongst the students as a whole. However, she also observes that problem-based learning does encounter hostility from students who expect and want their lecturers to act as authority figures as the perceived authority comforts the students; they feel secure in their role of student *receiving* knowledge. Indeed, some students are disconcerted by being expected to take an active learning role, expecting and *wanting* to be *delivered* with information: "Many students would still prefer that I revert to previous teaching methods and tell them everything they need to know. I continue, however, to believe that using active learning methods is key to helping students become lifetime learners."[36] Harry Shipman and Barbara Duch (2001)[37] also discuss student hostility to problem-based learning, and resentment towards taking an active role in lectures/seminars, preferring the anonymity of the formal lecture theatre environment.

Despite these concerns, there is considerable documented evidence to support the claim that more active learning strategies have a significant positive effect on student learning, principally due to the methods engaging student motivation. Increased motivation to study in the student body is not merely satisfying for the academic staff, but has demonstrable improving effects on student performance; and this improved performance itself leads to increased motivation. Noel Entwistle (1998) challenges the preconception that many lecturers hold; that motivation is a character trait that some students have and others don't. He suggests that the reasons behind a student's degree of motivation are complex and manifold,[38] and students can have their motivation 'awoken' by intellectual challenges that directly engage the student and the student's direct experience rather than traditional information tradition.[39] The case for active learning strategies grounded in 'the swamp' of experience is supported further by David Beckett and Paul Hager, in their book *Life, Work and Learning: Practice in Postmodernity* (2002), in which they argue that the assumption of a dualistic opposition between 'high theory' and 'low practice' that is inherent in Higher Education must be ungrounded and replaced with more *holistic* and *organic* learning methodologies which enable learning through strategies that embed practice in theory and theory in practice. Such approaches, they claim, will stimulate a more engaged, enthusiastic and effective understanding in students.

In the current academic climate, with increased class sizes and greater variation of ability within the student body, traditional methods of teaching are being challenged more than at any other time. Lecturers find themselves in situations where new methods of teaching need to be found to satisfy the requirements of new circumstances – without eroding the level of quality and sophistication of the content. The method/strategy I have proposed is not intended as a magic formula, or a catchall solution; it is merely an example of an alternative that has proved to work in my experience. The 'work-based' model of learning is one I am sure has been implemented by many lecturers in one form or another, and has been used across disciplines. The method has its own limitations and causes its own frustrations. It is a method I am still experimenting with and developing. However, when used appropriately it has demonstrated to have benefits that far outweigh its disadvantages.

At this point it is perhaps useful to consider comments from some of the students themselves. In both informal and formal feedback, students demonstrated an enthusiasm for these teaching techniques; one student responding that they "could see how the literature fitted in with my work, because it showed how the critical side of things connected with actual writing". While another stated that they found that they could engage with literature and literary theory when it was introduced to them in a less daunting situation, rather than a strict 'academic' framework: "I didn't get the theory at all, and found the way it was discussed very intimidating – which put me off. But when we did the practical exercises it all made sense and I could get my head round it." Students also responded well, as they had previously felt hostile towards the critical study of literature as they believed *their* opinions and responses to texts were disregarded in favour of orthodox and monolithic critical systems. The new exercises enabled students to air their own views on literature verbally, in seminars, and in written form in the preliminary assignments. As a consequence, the students no longer felt abandoned and isolated with a series of texts that had to be studied under duress and an intractable corpus of critical theory; rather they believed that they were engaged in a dynamic interrogation of their own work and its location within a larger literary context. The students also benefited from this approach as the journalistic tasks allowed them to get their emotive and personal responses 'out of their system'. Thus, they could be slowly and methodically steered towards a more analytical exploration of literature without the students realising that this was, in fact, what was happening.

I should clarify that it is my intention, in employing these methods, *not* to reduce or breakdown the critical approaches to literature into easily digestible chunks that can be delivered to less able students, rather it is my aim to enable these students to 'up their game' so that they are able to consider literature with a level of sophistication required by degree level study. What employers require from degree level graduates is not a particular skills-set in isolation, but an ability to understand and explore complex issues within complex frameworks. As such, graduates need to demonstrate a solid theoretical understanding of their subject area and an advanced analytical ability. Despite what students may believe, an exclusively pragmatic approach to their chosen discipline is not sufficient to qualify either as a degree level student, or gain employment in a graduate level position.

My own background in commercial writing, and statements from professionals within the publishing and media industries, has demonstrated to me that the competition for jobs that writing graduates face is not from Journalism or Advertising students; but graduates in traditional Humanities subjects such as English Literature and History. Students, therefore, do need an ability to engage with the history and analysis of literature as well as an ability to produce effective copy. Experimental teaching techniques, therefore, should be encouraged if they enable more students to acquire these skills, but not be utilised as a method of 'dumbing down' the intellectual content of a degree to expedite the processing of more students at the expense of quality and sophistication.

*Notes*

1 Brown, Armstrong & Thompson (1998: 1).
2 Pointon (1980: xi).
3 Billingham (1989: 154).
4 *Ibid.* 151.
5 Taylor (1989: 27).
6 *Ibid.* 30.
7 *Ibid.*
8 Collins (1989: 136).
9 *Ibid.* 139.
10 *Ibid.* 141.
11 Mortimer (1989: 69).
12 *Ibid.*
13 Buchanan (1995: 47).
14 *Ibid.* 42.
15 *Ibid.*
16 Prosser and Trigwell (1999: 3, 4, 90-92).
17 *Ibid.* 3-4.
18 *Ibid.* 4.
19 *Ibid.* 142.
20 Biggs (2003: 231).
21 *Ibid.* 232.

22 *Ibid.*
23 *Ibid.* 233-234.
24 *Ibid.* 4 (emphasis in the text).
25 *Ibid.* 42.
26 *Ibid.* 43.
27 *Ibid.* 63.
28 Ramsden (1992: 5).
29 *Ibid.* 19.
30 Duch, Groh & Allen (2001: 4-5).
31 Ramsden (1992: 19).
32 Burch (2001: 194).
33 *Ibid.* 203.
34 *Ibid.* 204.
35 Lieux (2001: 228-229).
36 *Ibid.* 234.
37 Shipman and Duch (2001: 150).
38 Entwistle (1998: 16).
39 *Ibid.* 22.

## *Bibliography*


Beckett, David & Paul Hager: *Life, Work and Learning: Practice in Postmodernity*, London & New York, 2002.

Biggs, John: *Teaching and Quality Learning at University*, second edition, Buckingham, 2003.

Billingham, Rosalind: "Art History and Art Students". – In David Thistlewood (Ed.): *Critical Studies in Art and Design Education*, London, 1989, pp. 149-157.

Brown, Sally *et al.*.: "The Art of Motivating Students in Higher Education?". – In Sally Brown, Steve Armstrong & Gail Thompson (Eds.): *Motivating Students*, London, 1998, pp. 1-6.

Buchanan, Michael: "Making Art and Critical Literacy: A Reciprocal Relationship". – In Roy Prentice (Ed.): *Teaching Art and Design: Addressing Issues and Identifying Directions*, London, 1995, pp. 29-49.

Burch, Kurt: "PBL, Politics and Democracy". – In Barbara Duch, Susan Groh & Deborah Allen (Eds.): *The Power of Problem-Based Learning*, Stirling VA, 2001, pp. 193-206.

Collins, Tony: "Before the Vanishing Point: Some Perspectives on Teaching Art History to Studio Practioners". – In David Thistlewood (Ed.): *Critical Studies in Art and Design Education*, London, 1989, pp. 133-148.

Duch, Barbara, Susan Groh & Deborah Allen: "Why Problem-Based Learning? A Case Study of Institutional change in Undergraduate Education". – In Barbara Duch, Susan Groh & Deborah Allen (Eds.): *The Power of Problem-Based Learning*, Stirling VA, 2001, pp. 3-12.

Entwistle, Noel: "Motivation and Approaches to Learning: Motivating and Conceptions of Teaching". – In Sally Brown, Steve Armstrong & Gail Thompson (Eds.): *Motivating Students*, London, 1998, pp. 15-24.

Lieux, Elizabeth: "A Sceptics Look at PBL". – In Barbara Duch, Susan Groh & Deborah Allen (Eds.): *The Power of Problem-Based Learning*, Stirling VA, 2001, pp. 223-236.

Mortimer, Andrew: "Approaches to the Teaching of Critical Studies". – In David Thistlewood (Ed.): *Critical Studies in Art and Design Education*, London, 1989, pp. 57-70.

Pointon, Marcia: *History of Art: A Student's Handbook*, London, 1980.

Prosser, Michael & Keith Trigwell: *Understanding Learning and Teaching: The Experience of Higher Education*, Buckingham, 1999.

Ramsden, Paul: *Learning to Teach in Higher Education*, London & New York, 1992.

Shipman, Harry & Barbara Duch: "Problem-Based Learning in Large and Very Large Classes". – In Barbara Duch, Susan Groh & Deborah Allen (Eds): *The Power of Problem-Based Learning*, Stirling VA, 2001, pp. 149-164.

Taylor, Rod: "Critical Studies in Art and Design Education: Passing Fashion or the Missing Element?". – In David Thistlewood (Ed.): *Critical Studies in Art and Design Education*, London, 1989, pp. 27-41.

White III, Harold: "A PBL Course that Uses Research Articles as Problems". – In Barbara Duch, Susan Groh & Deborah Allen (Eds.): *The Power of Problem-Based Learning*, Stirling VA, 2001, pp. 131-140.

Dr. Steve Barfield, Senior Lecturer, University of Westminster, Department of English and Linguistics, 32-38 Wells Street, London W1T 3UW, United Kingdom.

Dr. Robert Bond, Lecturer, University of Westminster, Department of English and Linguistics, 32-38 Wells Street, London W1T 3UW, United Kingdom.

Dr. Nick Bentley, Lecturer, Keele University, English Department, Keele ST5 5BG, United Kingdom.

Dr. Doryjane Birrer, Assistant Professor, College of Charleston, Charleston, SC29424, USA.

Dr. Katharine Cockin, Senior Lecturer, University of Hull, English Department, Cottingham Road, HU6 7RX, United Kingdom.

Dr. Sara Crangle, Research Fellow, Queens' College, University of Cambridge, Cambridge CB39ET, United Kingdom.

Dr. Mike Doherty, Research Fellow, London Consortium, Birkbeck College, University of London, Malet Street, London WC1E 7HX, United Kingdom.

Dr. Richard Hudson, Lecturer, Southampton Solent University, East Park Terrace, Southampton, Hampshire SO14 OYN, United Kingdom

Dr. Mitchell Lewis, Assistant Professor, Elmira College, One Park Place, Elmira, NY 14901, USA.

Dr. Ruth McElroy, Senior Lecturer, School of Media Critical and Creative Arts, Dean Walters Building, St James Road, Liverpool John Moores University, Liverpool L19EB, United Kingdom.

Prof. Dr. Anja Müller-Wood, Department of English and Linguistics, Johannes Gutenberg-Universität Mainz, D-55099 Mainz.

Prof. Philip Tew, Brunel University, School of Arts, Uxbridge, Middlesex UB8 3PH, United Kingdom.

Dr. Leigh Wilson, Senior Lecturer, University of Westminster, Department of English and Linguistics, 32-38 Wells Street, London W1T 3UW, United Kingdom.